# Web
# Photoshop 6
## Primer

ISBN 0-13-027008-3

90000

9 780130 270085

Prentice Hall PTR
# The Primer Series

# Web Photoshop 6 Primer

### JASON I. MILETSKY

Prentice Hall PTR
Upper Saddle River, NJ 07458
www.phptr.com

**CIP data available**

*Production Editor:* Wil Mara
*Acquisitions Editor:* Tim Moore
*Technical Reviewer:* Craig Little
*Editorial Assistant:* Allyson Kloss
*Marketing Manager:* Debby van Dijk
*Manufacturing Manager:* Alexis R. Heydt
*Buyer:* Maura Zaldivar
*Cover Designer:* Anthony Gemmellaro
*Cover Design Direction:* Jerry Votta
*Art Director:* Gail Cocker-Bogusz
*Composition:* Ronnie Bucci

© 2001 Prentice Hall PTR
Prentice-Hall, Inc.
Upper Saddle River, NJ 07458

The publisher offers discounts on this book when ordered in bulk quantities. For more information contact: Corporate Sales Department, Prentice Hall PTR, One Lake Street, Upper Saddle River, NJ 07458. Phone: 800-382-3419; Fax: 201-236-7141; E-mail: corpsales@prenhall.com

Printed in the United States of America

10  9  8  7  6  5  4  3  2  1

ISBN 0-13-027008-3

Prentice-Hall International (UK) Limited, *London*
Prentice-Hall of Australia Pty. Limited, *Sydney*
Prentice-Hall Canada Inc., *Toronto*
Prentice-Hall Hispanoamericana, S.A., *Mexico*
Prentice-Hall of India Private Limited, *New Delhi*
Prentice-Hall of Japan, Inc., *Tokyo*
Pearson Education Asia Pte. Ltd.
Editora Prentice-Hall do Brasil, Ltda., *Rio de Janeiro*

*To my Mom and Dad,*

*Two years after the first dedication, you're still great parents,*

*and still my best friends*

# CONTENTS

# CHAPTER 2

# CHAPTER 5

# CHAPTER 6

## NAVIGATION, BUTTONS, AND BULLETS . . . . . . . . 135

### The Importance of Navigation . . . . . . . . . . . .136

### Creating Beveled Buttons . . . . . . . . . . . . . .137

### Creating Circular Bevels . . . . . . . . . . . . . .142

### Creating Buttons with Texture Added . . . . . . . .150

# CHAPTER 7

## INLINE GRAPHICS: IMAGE IS EVERYTHING . . . . . . 159

# CHAPTER 8

# CHAPTER 9

# CHAPTER 10

# ACKNOWLEDGEMENTS

There are always a lot of people to thank when it comes to writing one of these things...

First all the gang at Prentice Hall—Tim, Jim, Craig, Wil, Allyson, the copy editors (I don't know them, but they were still a part of it!), and everyone else who was in the mix.

My parents, of course, and my family that have always supported me while I was writing.

I want to thank the friends that have never abandoned me while I was writing, like Jackie (the best DJ ever!), Chris and Ida (even though you moved off to Geneva, I don't consider that abandonment), Chris Senft (who should have given up on me considering how often I cancel plans), Jason Violetti, Lydia, Tara, Vineeth and Shireen.

I'd like to thank the academy...

Everyone at my office deserves a huge amount of thanks, especially Dennis and Deirdre, who have been awesome partners, and have made the struggle that much more fun!

I'd also like to thank everyone who has ever seen one of my books, and said, "I was thinking that I'd write a book someday..." without having any clue how time consuming it is. You inspired me to write harder.

Lastly, I want to thank the people of a small village called Lalanduce, in southwestern France, just for building the nicest small village I've ever been to.

And, as I do in every book, thank you to Lisa. I know that you still watch over me, and I still miss you.

# INTRODUCTION

## SO HERE WE ARE AGAIN...

A lot of things have changed since I wrote the predecessor to this book, *Web Photoshop 5 To Go*. The name of the series, for one, has switched from "*To Go*" to "*Primer*" and sports a much, much cooler cover. I've gotten two years older, have become a much better typist (by the way—thanks to the 187 of you who wrote me all those e-mails about the spelling errors in that first book. Made my day. Really.) And of course, Photoshop has seen two versions since that original text. First it was 5.5, which came out almost solely for Web designers and was, in my opinion, the best version of the program that Adobe ever shipped. A year later, with a lot of media attention, Photoshop 6 was released with its own set of interesting changes.

And then there is the Web itself, and how sites are developed. In the first book, a lot of time was taken to explain things like color palettes, download time, and wallpapered backgrounds. Today, though, the obstacles that designers deal with rarely involve color management, acceptable trends almost never allow for wallpapered backgrounds, and vastly improved connectivity has given more breathing room for the size of graphics.

On the flip side, some things haven't changed at all. The Web is still one of the fastest-growing mediums ever (even considering the dot-com crash) and continues to be a major part of people's lives. Careers and opportunities are still strong in the Web market, and designers need to be far more professional, sophisticated, and knowledgeable than they had to be when the earlier edition of this book first came out. And for all the changes that Photoshop has gone through, it remains the same in one very important aspect: it is still the king when it comes to graphic design for print or the Web. No other application even comes close. The additions that were made, in version 5.5 especially, have solidified Photoshop as one of the key ingredients in Web design.

So where does that leave this book in relation to the original *Web Photoshop 5 To Go*? Well, like everything else, it has changed in some ways, but in others it hasn't. Much of this book is directly reprinted from the original (hey, there may be some readers who never read the 5.0 book). But a good portion has changed to reflect the times, as the current state of Web development is not nearly what it used to be. It has also changed or included portions that deal with the additions and upgrades seen in the last couple of versions of Photoshop. And, of course, it has the same sarcastic wit that helped rank *Web Photoshop 5 To Go* alongside literary classics such as *Moby Dick* and *A Tale of Two Cities*. Well, at least, I've placed my own copy of *Web Photoshop 5 To Go* next to those other works on my bookshelf. I think that's just about the same thing.

# WHO SHOULD READ THIS BOOK

Because talent is a tough quality to measure, it's nearly impossible to write a book like this for "everybody." Have you won awards for your amazing Photoshop abilities or regularly give seminars on the secret design tips of Photoshop experts? If so, this book may not be for you, Is your copy of Photoshop still in its box and your dedication to learning how to use it dwindling faster than your weekly trips to the gym? If so, this book may move a bit too fast for you.

Basically. this book was written for the following people—

◆   Your Photoshop ability falls somewhere between "basic working knowledge of" and "strong control over" the program, and/or

◆   You've been using Photoshop for print or other media and now either need or want to get involved with Web design, and/or

◆   You've been working with Photoshop 5.5 or an even older version, and want a practical resource through which to understand the improvements in version 6.0, and/or

◆   You're a relative of the author and are willing to buy at least a dozen copies to keep sales up.

If you fall into one or more of these categories, this book is for you. It's not important to have any real knowledge of HTML to understand this book, and the few pages that do reference HTML tags will explain how they are used.

# HOW THIS BOOK HAS BEEN WRITTEN

For everything that this book is, it is certainly not the "everything you never really wanted to know about Photoshop" book that you might expect. Instead, it's a clear, to-the-point text that that doesn't bother with the boring stuff that you don't really need to know. For example, the section about file types gives you what you need to choose a proper file type for your images, but stops short of explaining how a JPEG image is built or how color palettes are indexed. I know you want to get into the creation process as quickly as possible, so aside from my witty interjections, most of the fluff, or "fat" if you will, has been trimmed out.

It is not necessary for you to read this book in a linear fashion—in fact, I'd recommend jumping around from section to section. If possible, try to read this book at your computer. There are a lot of follow-along examples for each topic, and practicing while you read is the best way to learn.

Throughout each chapter, you'll be confronted with a few symbols to help you better understand what you're reading. The symbols are—

**Note icon gives a more detailed explanation of the topic.**

**The Warning icon tells you when there is a potential for a problem. You'll see very few of these—in my opinion, as long as you end up in your bed at the end of the day, there are a few problems worth stressing about.**

**The Tip icon provides additional information of the topic.**

Another thing that you may notice as you read is that most all references, including screen shots, are taken off the Macintosh version of Photoshop. When I give an example and include a keyboard command, the command configuration will be for Macintosh, and the equivalent Windows command will follow in parentheses.

# WHAT YOU WILL NEED

In *Web Photoshop 5 To Go*, I recommended having at least 32 megs of RAM in your computer. Good luck with that.

Photoshop 6 has pushed the term "RAM hog" to new heights. Because of some of the additions and changes, you'll need far more than 32 megs to get anywhere with this program. On my Mac, I allocate 80 megs just to Photoshop alone, and sometimes *that* wasn't enough.

I recommend you have at least 128 megs installed and either a G3 or Pentium II system at the very least. I'm not going to tell you whether to use a Mac or a PC—I'm not that suicidal, and I've written this book for fans of both.

Of course, you should also have a copy of Photoshop 6 lying around, but it's not crucial. You can read this book on a plane or in a waiting room and still get a lot out of it. But, because of some of the radical changes that were made in version 6.0, you probably won't do too well if you are still working on version 5.5, so go and get the upgrade.

You also need a browser. I'd recommend IE 4.0 or higher, but for the purposes of this book any browser will be fine.

# STAYING IN TOUCH

Figuring it was my one chance in a lifetime, I made a certain plea in *Web Photoshop 5 To Go* for one person in particular to get in touch with me. This is what I wrote:

"If you are Katie Couric from the *Today* show (who I have an enormous crush on), you can contact me…."

Well, believe it or not, she responded! Through a long chain of people, one of my clients got the book to her, and then got the book back to me with a note from her. Referring to my "enormous crush," she wrote, "Get in line."

Of course, she also wished me luck with the book, blah, blah. But I'm not defeated. So, Katie, if you are still single when you read this, I still am, too. And if I'm not, I'll make myself single again!

As for anybody else that wants to get in touch with me, my e-mail address is jmiletsky@pfsmarketwyse.com. If you have any questions or comments on this book, or you want to show me something you created using some of the techniques that you read about, please write to me. I'm more than happy to help where I can…

*However*—and I say this from experience—while I am more than happy to help out, I'm also a hard-working guy and can't be a free Photoshop tech support line (so, to the guy in Canada who calls me once or twice per week for help, you can stop now). Also, please assume that I already know and feel very badly about the missed comma on page 97 or the run-on sentence on page 125.

But seriously, I might play around a lot and can sometimes be sarcastic, but I really do welcome e-mail and letters. And if anybody is looking to join the Jason Miletsky fan club, let me know–I'm the president, and there's a newsletter…

# PHOTOSHOP

# REVIEW

As design quickly made the transformation from traditional rubyliths and hand-drawn sketches to computer-based art, Adobe Photoshop rose to the forefront and has become a staple in the graphic design industry. It's almost impossible to look at a billboard, flip through a magazine, or browse through a CD-ROM without seeing at least a few images that have passed through Photoshop for one reason or another. With the popularization of the Web, Photoshop has become even further entrenched as a must-know tool for designers.

But you undoubtedly know all of this already. Chances are, you've been working with Photoshop 5, 5.5, or 6 for awhile now. But there is a difference between knowing Photoshop and *knowing* Photoshop. Over the years, my agency has had a constant need for quality graphic designers. And over those same years, the help-wanted ads that we place have stayed pretty much the same: Qualified applicant must have expert knowledge of Photoshop.

I've probably interviewed hundreds of potential designers, and over and over again, the same thing has happened: A designer will come in and claim to know Photoshop. In most cases, I think they actually believe that they really do know it. But that's like saying you know how large the iceberg is just by seeing what lies above the water's surface. The real bulk is what lies beneath the surface—the part that you can't see on first glance.

So with each successive portfolio that I review, I see more and more color correction. To most people, that's what Photoshop is—a color correction tool. But it really is so much more than that. There are whole worlds of design to be discovered by looking just a little deeper into this program.

At the same time, the Internet has changed remarkably over the last couple of years. We've lived through the early times when the web was an open canvas, and large companies were hiring the president's 15-year-old nephew to build the corporate web site. Sites then were basic in layout, and typically atrocious in design. Wild backgrounds, large text, no uniformity within a site. But having any site at all was a mere novelty, anyway. Then, suddenly, Wall Street found the Internet, and every college grad with a new idea (regardless of how silly it was) was getting venture capital money, and becoming an overnight billionaire. Sites popped up all over the place, with an avalanche of advertising to prove it. They were more sophisticated and more structured. The crazy backgrounds and large, disjointed text were replaced with more sleek designs. HTML, the primary language that drove the web, became just a function, as Java, CGI, and other languages started to invade. Photoshop unleashed version 5.5, staking its claim as the predominant king of designing for the web.

And then came autumn in the year 2000. Wall Street got tired of waiting for sites to become profitable, and stock prices fell off a cliff. "Out of business" signs were posted on home pages, and a lot of those instant billionaires were back to asking "would you like fries with that?" The large, brick and mortar marketers like K-Mart, Wal-Mart, Toys R Us, and others were starting to take the reins and seize control over the web.

Designers, meanwhile, had to learn to temper their graphics for wide range use over multiple platforms, a huge bandwidth gap between home and office, as well as numerous other programs and languages. XML, DHTML, ASP, and other languages have made HTML almost as relevant as hieroglyphics, and design applications such as Macromedia's Flash have risen dramatically in use and popularity.

So where does that leave the Photoshop designers, in terms of the web? Photoshop is still one of the centerpieces of Internet design. Regardless of whether the project is a small site for a local retailer or even just for personal use, or a massive site for a Fortune 500 company, nearly all graphic and layout design begins with Photoshop.

So the idea, then, is to understand the Internet in its modern form as well as gain a more relevant knowledge of Photoshop beyond simple color correction. And that's where *Web Photoshop 6 Primer* comes in. But before you get to the really fun stuff—the special effects, the collages, and other exciting areas—use this chapter as a quick refresher for the Photoshop basics: how palettes work, what each tool does, what's new in Photoshop 6 that didn't exist in previous versions.

So rev up the mouse, launch the application, place your seat back and tray table in their upright and locked positions, and get ready to take full advantage of Photoshop 6 on the Web.

# WHAT'S NEW IN THIS VERSION?

Basically, there are three types of people about to read this book: those who are completely new to Photoshop, those who are upgrading from version 5, and those who are coming from version 5.5. It's an important distinction to make, because each version focuses on a different audience. The upgrade from version 5 to 5.5 was clearly a gift to web designers, and it secured Photoshop's place as the predominant tool for web designers moving into a growing cyber age. Version 6, however, is aimed at ... well, I'm not really sure what market version 6 is trying to reach. There are a few upgrades for web designers, a few for print designers, some general changes for everyone, but mostly it seems to be created just to give the Photoshop developers something to keep them occupied. While there are a few clear improvements to the program in this latest version, the plain truth is that there is little here to generate any real emotion (except the frustration of needing more RAM to run the thing than CompUSA will likely have in stock).

**Note** ▸ **Next year, if I am late in writing the update to version 7, assume that that little editorial just cost me my spot on the Beta list ...**

Because 5.5 is geared so heavily toward web designers, I am providing a list of updates for that version as well as for version 6. The rest of the book, however, will deal strictly with 6 screen shots and descriptions.

## The Upgrade From 5 to 5.5

If your only reason for using Photoshop is to create images for print, then very few of the changes in the 5.5 upgrade will interest you. But if that's the case, what are you doing reading this book? Put it down, and ask your friendly salesperson to direct you toward my other brilliantly written work, *Photoshop 6 To Go*. Please, though—there is a surprise ending in that one, so don't tell your friends ...

Nearly all of the changes in this version are web-related, as Adobe aptly responded to webmaster requests that Photoshop become a more web-friendly program. However, while the web improvements are abundant and super-exciting, there are few features non-web users will appreciate as well. The following list reviews all of the major improvements and additions.

### The ImageReady Addition

Adobe's ImageReady, a specifically web-based program, now comes bundled with the Photoshop software. The nearly identical (to Photoshop) interface and crowd of great features make ImageReady an easy-to-use "no brainer" for web professionals. Plus, the new Jump button at the bottom of the Photoshop toolbar makes working between the two programs a seamless process. Chapter 8 discusses ImageReady in a bit more detail.

## Easier Optimization

Not only does Photoshop 5.5 make optimizing your JPEG and GIF files more convenient but, with true brilliance, it now uses an incredible new dialog box. The Save for Web dialog box lets you compare and contrast the image quality, file sizes, and download times of your original image against up to three previews of that image with customized settings. This should be a huge time saver, but it's so much fun to play with that you might end up spending more hours than you planned!

## New Masking Tools

Photoshop designers always get giddy about new masking tools, but there are some new tools especially worth the hype. The two new Eraser tools and the Extract function make creating transparencies so easy that the GIF 89a format has become obsolete.

## Enhanced Color Picker

Finally, getting both a hexadecimal value and a web-safe color are convenient and easy in the new Color Picker.

## Better Text Features

Nothing earth-shattering here, but the text feature improvements are good enough to make text easier to manipulate. (Although it doesn't really matter, as text is a whole new ballgame in version 6.)

## History ... Monet Style

I'm not too excited about this, but if you're into watercolor paintings, you might like this feature.

## Picture Package

Photographers and grandparents will appreciate this one. With just a click on a few buttons, Photoshop will lay out one image in various configurations on an 8.5" x 11" page. If you have a quality color printer, go nuts printing endless pages of you, your family, and the goldfish in 5" x 7", 4" x 6", and wallet size.

# The Upgrade From 5.5 to 6

On first glance, Photoshop 6 looks and acts differently than it ever has before. In a way, Adobe's star product is beginning to integrate certain qualities from Illustrator and ImageReady, making me wonder how much longer before it just becomes one, really large, all-encompassing program? When you start using it for a while, you realize that some of the changes are pretty cool but, except for a few distinct areas, not terribly dramatic.

Because I have already stirred the ire of the folks at Adobe with those first few paragraphs in this section, I may as well go all out. I have a growing concern that the saturation point is being reached, and we'll soon be in the area of overkill. The Liquify dialog box, for example, is cute and a lot of fun, and may by itself be worth the upgrade purchase price just to tool around with, but I'm not too sure it has real, practical value.

Looking at this new version is almost like watching a great TV show, that after years of success, feels the need to add that adorable 4-year-old to the cast—a sure indication that a downward spiral is inevitable. This new version is a RAM hog, and it forces even the hobbyists to go out and purchase state-of-the-art computers, or at least increase their current stock of RAM to get any use out of the program. Plus, it doesn't work for any Macintosh version below 8.5, or with any version of Windows older than Windows 98. While I believe that there is always room for improvement, there is also the train of thought that says, "If it ain't broke, don't fix it." I don't really mind this upgrade for what it is, but I am frightened by what might come: Based on what I see here, future upgrades might actually begin to seriously detract from what is still a great program.

The following are just some of the major changes, or at least the more interesting ones, made to Photoshop in the new 6 version. Other new features will be more prevalent throughout the rest of the book.

## The Options Palette

The first upgrade that you'll notice when you launch the program will be the new Options palette. No longer a small floating palette like all the others, the Options palette is now a virtual command center, stretching the length of your monitor.

## The Layers Palette

The Layers palette has made some dramatic changes—mostly for the better. Some of the changes are fairly modest; Layer effects are now where they belong—conveniently at the bottom of the Layers palette, along with the Adjustment layers. Both also have far more options than they ever did. More significantly, you can now lock layers from being edited or moved, and you can preserve the image as well as the transparent portions of a layer. Probably best of all, you can easily organize layers in sets, making the lives of designers (who use an inordinate number of layers in practically any image) far, far easier.

## The Text Editor

Just when Adobe had finally gotten it right, Photoshop 6 introduces the worst upgrade of them all. Now, you apply text directly onto the canvas rather than use the Text Editor—a good idea in theory, but it ends up being a huge pain. I'll save my frustrations for the editorial in Chapter 5.

## Liquify

OK, this is definitely not really one of the most important new features, but it's surely the most fun! A rip-off of Kai's Power Goo, Liquify makes your image a little less solid, allowing you full control of contortions, distortions, and just all out craziness. This addition will, at first glance, likely get you all tingly and excited, causing you to spend hours playing with it unwittingly. Don't be surprised, though, when you look at it again a week later, and say to yourself, "I'm going to actually need to use this *when*?"

## The Slice and Slice Selection Tools

An addition to Photoshop that could be predicted since day one of version 5.5, the Slice and Slice Selection tools have migrated over to Photoshop. Slicing has been a great help to web designers since ImageReady was bundled with Photoshop in version 5.5, but there is no real reason to slice an image in Photoshop rather than in ImageReady. ImageReady has more options for slices and makes them easier to manipulate.

## Other New Tools

Other tools make their debuts in version 6, including (finally) ways to make polygons, to fill in shapes with color upon creation, and to leave notes in certain places either for yourself or as instructions for someone else who may be working on the same piece at another time.

### Saving Files

The Save a Copy command is gone as a stand-alone option in the File menu. It's now incorporated into the Save As dialog box, along with some other fairly annoying changes.

### Easier Color Management

Color management is about as easy at it ever has been, as setting color profiles within Photoshop now practically holds your hand in deciding how to set up your profile and when to include the profile with a saved file. The problem here is reality: Even though everybody should worry about color management and profiles, the only people who really do are the fanatics who actually fly to Photoshop conventions (and enjoy a good long conversation about whether Kirk or Picard was the better Star Trek captain). Those people didn't have a problem setting profiles before it was easier.

### Increased User Friendliness

Photoshop seems to have recognized how difficult the program can be, and that too many "designers" never actually move beyond the program's color correction functions. Although it's not "in your face," the program has provided small descriptions here and there for tools, dialog boxes, and select other things that designers typically have trouble understanding, to make life just a little bit easier.

There are other upgrades, which we'll review in more detail at the appropriate time.

# THE TOOLBAR

Figure 1–1 shows the Photoshop 6 Toolbar. The tools are sectioned off into various groups, dividing them conveniently into their respective functions. Each of the tools, and most of the other commands, has its own keyboard shortcut. To get the most use out of Photoshop, I recommend using the keyboard shortcuts instead of the mouse whenever possible. Keyboard shortcuts are provided in Figure 1–1, or can be obtained by leaving your mouse on a tool for a couple of seconds. Other shortcuts are provided in Chapter 10.

Some tools have small arrows next to them. Holding the mouse button down on these tools for a couple of seconds reveals alternative tool choices.

The contents of the toolbar follows.

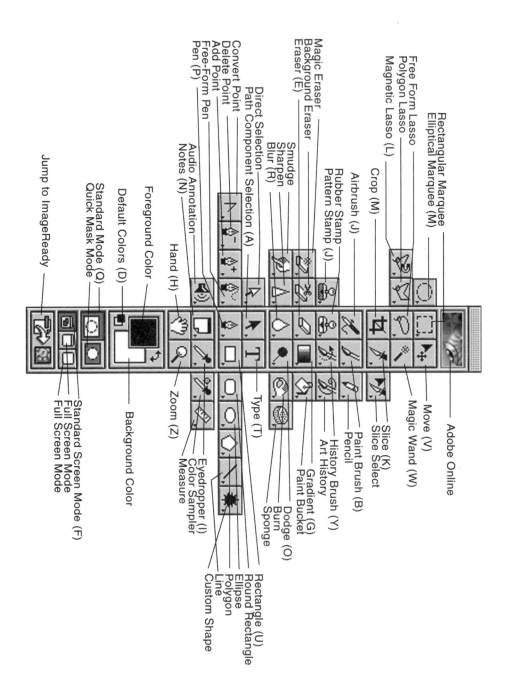

Figure 1–1: The Toolbar. The letters pointing to each tool are the keyboard shortcuts for simplified activation. Shift + letter will scroll through underlying tools.

# Selection Tools

### Elliptical and Rectangular Marquees

These tools allow you to make selections in circles (or ovals), or squares (or rectangles), respectively.

### Row and Column Marquees

These tools allow you to select an entire row or column of pixels. Although I personally have never found a use for them, there are rumors that they are somehow helpful in certain instances.

### Crop

Selecting part of an image and pushing "Return" ("Enter" for Windows) will cut away and eliminate everything outside your selection, as will double-clicking inside your image. Handles on all corners and sides allow you to manipulate the selection, and pushing "Esc" will escape from the crop feature. This will be a vital tool in removing edges that will otherwise just increase file size and make your images download more slowly.

### Magic Wand

The Magic Wand is one of the coolest tools (besides the Rubber Stamp); you can use it to select a specific color in your image. All adjacent colors will also be selected, within a certain hue range (established in the Magic Wand's Option palette).

### Free-Form and Polygon Lassos

The Free-Form lasso allows you to make free-form selections, while the Polygon lasso makes selections using straight lines and corners.

### Magnetic Lasso

A new selection tool, the Magnetic lasso creates a selection by finding the edges between two colors or color tones.

### Move

The Move tool lets you move the part of the image you've selected to another area of your canvas. Actual selections do not need to be made for the Move tool to be functional—even without selections, it will move everything on the active layer.

### Airbrush

The Airbrush allows you to airbrush over your image. See Figure 1–2 for an example.

### Paintbrush

The Paintbrush allows you to paint over your image. See Figure 1–3 for an example.

*Figure 1–2: The Airbrush at work.*

*Figure 1–3: The Paintbrush at work.*

### Rubber Stamp: Clone and Pattern

One of the truly awesome tools, the Rubber Stamp tool lets you clone one part of your image onto another. Figure 1–4 shows an example of the Clone Stamp. The Pattern Stamp allows you to select a portion of your image and use that selection as a pattern.

### History Brush

The History brush works in conjunction with the History palette. It allows you to erase back to an earlier version of your image. With this new addition, you can feel free to experiment more, and not be afraid to lose your work if you make a mistake.

### Art History Brush

Not a really outstanding new tool, the Art History brush was introduced in version 5.5, and it functions the same as the regular History brush with a small twist. As you revert back to previous states, the reversion happens in a watercolor. I haven't been able to figure out, though, why this has to be a History brush, and not just a Watercolor brush, to make your current image into a watercolor picture; either way, it's not my favorite new tool.

### Note Tool    NEW TOOL!

Another silly new addition, the Note tool, lets you leave notes to yourself or associates who may work on your project at a later date. I never knew that leaving a simple yellow Post-It Note on someone's desk was such a

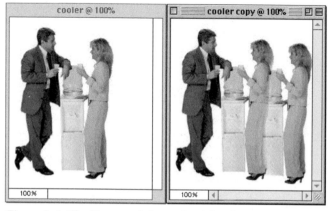

*Figure 1–4: The Stamp tool clones the girl at the water cooler.*

hassle. Regardless, there are two ways to leave notes: You can leave a text note, or, if you have a microphone handy, leave yourself an audio note.

### Shape Tool   NEW TOOL!

This was a good addition to version 6. Lifted from ImageReady, the Shape tool lets you quickly make triangles, stars, pentagons, octagons, and any other shape you can imagine. It even lets you make your own custom shape.

### Slice Tool   NEW TOOL!

Once again, Photoshop has wisely stolen a tool from ImageReady. The Slice and Slice Select tools help you to cut up your image quickly and reassemble it in an HTML table (which Photoshop will write for you).

### Eraser

The Eraser tool allows you to erase part or all of your image or layer.

### Line

The Line tool allows you to draw lines on your canvas.

### Pencil

This tool allows you to draw as you would with a pencil.

### Smudge

Use this tool to "fingerpaint" over your image. Figure 1–5 shows an example.

*Figure 1–5: The Smudge tool at work.*

**Blur**

Blur portions of your image with this tool. See Chapter 7 for other ways you can blur an image.

**Sharpen**

Sharpen portions of your image with the Sharpen tool (honestly, I don't think this is a really great tool). Better techniques for sharpening a blurry image can be found in Chapter 7.

**Burn**

Use this tool to burn, or darken, portions of your image, as you might in a darkroom.

**Dodge**

Use this tool to lighten portions of your image, also as you would in a darkroom.

**Sponge**

Kind of a neat tool, the Sponge lets you saturate or desaturate colors in your image.

**Pen**

A somewhat intimidating tool, the Pen occurs in a number of other programs as well. Utilizing Bézier Curves, this Pen tool is the most powerful yet for making selections, outlines, or paths for export. The Pen establishes points to determine where and when your path will change direction.

**Magnetic Pen**

The Magnetic Pen tool creates a path between tonal differences in color, placing editable points.

**Free Form Pen**   NEW TOOL!

The Free-Form Pen creates a path and places anchor points as you draw freehand around your image.

### Plus and Minus Pens

The Plus and Minus Pens add or subtract points from your path.

### Arrow Tool

The Arrow tool allows you to select, move, and adjust a path or path segment.

### Convert-Anchor-Point Tool

The Convert-Anchor-Point tool allows you to, well, convert an anchor point between a smooth point and a corner point, or vice versa.

### Type    NEW TOOL! (some)

The Type tool is probably the biggest revision in 6. Use this tool to place type directly on your canvas. Three separate palettes allow you to change font size, color, style, attributes, and so forth.

### Ruler    NEW TOOL!

For use with the Info palette, the Ruler tool helps you measure lengths and angles.

### Gradient    NEW TOOL! (some)

This tool lets you set a multiple color gradation across part or all of your image in various configurations. More detail about the Gradient tool is given in Chapter 4.

### Paintbucket

The Paintbucket lets you fill an area or selection with a chosen color.

### Eyedropper and Color Sampler    NEW TOOL! (some)

Think of the Eyedropper as "absorbing" a color from a particular point. The Color Sampler tool is pretty useful, allowing you to anchor a number of points around your image for color comparison in the Info palette. The Color Sampler is a new feature.

### Hand

When your image is too large to fit in a given window, you can use the hand tool to move it around. Access the Hand tool instantly by pressing the space bar, no matter what tool is active.

### Magnifying Glass

Not super important, the Magnifying Glass allows you to zoom in and zoom out of your picture. Keyboard commands are a better alternative to this.

### Colors

Photoshop allows you instant access to two colors at once, provided as your foreground and background colors.

Clicking on either color will access Photoshop's Color Picker (explored in detail in the "Photoshop Color" section of this chapter).

The curved arrow in the top right corner switches your background and foreground color, while clicking the black and white boxes in the bottom left turns your colors to black and white.

### Edit Modes

Standard mode, accessible with the left-hand button, is the default and usual mode of working on your image. Quick Mask mode creates a temporary mask, which can be used to edit active selections, or make new selections. A more advanced way of working with selections than with the typical selection tools, masking is more fully explored in my other book, *Photoshop 6 To Go*.

### View Modes

Each selection will affect how you view your image, as well as to which menu items you have access.

Standard Screen mode, the default option, displays your canvas in a window with a titlebar and scroll bars on the side and bottom. It allows you complete access to the menu bar, as well as the ability to view multiple open images at once, including the images on your desktop. Figure 1–6 shows an example.

Full-Screen mode (gray) hides other open images and your desktop. The titlebar and scroll bars disappear, and your image is placed on a full-screen, gray background, as shown in Figure 1–7. You still have access to all menu options.

Full-Screen mode (black) is similar to the gray version, except that the background your image is placed on is black instead of gray, and you will not have access to the menu bar (shown in Figure 1–8).

*Figure 1–6: Standard Screen mode. The underlying desktop behind Photoshop is visible, while the image appears in an adjustable window. The menu options are available.*

*Figure 1–7: Full-Screen mode (gray). A neutral gray acts as the background. Menu options are still available.*

*Figure 1–8: Full-Screen mode (black). The background is completely black. The menu and its underlying options are hidden and inaccessible.*

# PALETTES

"Floating" palettes are a primary resource for functionality in Photoshop. They are the control center for organizing many Photoshop capabilities, giving you easy access to tools and their options, as well as a place to enter essential information. Much of what happens on your canvas will be a direct result of what type of information appears in your palettes. Some palettes, such as the Layers and Channels palettes, will rely on your input. Other palettes, such as the Info and History palettes, are geared more toward providing you with information based on what's going on in your image. Still others act more like toolboxes, holding items and information until you need them, such as the Brushes, Action, and Swatches palettes.

Palettes can be opened or closed directly through the Windows menu in the menu bar. You can also customize them by literally dragging one palette into another palette window (called a "pane"). Personally, I keep my Layers, Channels, and Paths palettes in one window and open all the time, and my Options, Info, and Brushes palettes in another window and open all the time. Over the years I have found that this configuration works best with my particular style. I keep all the other palettes closed until I need them. You can also "dock" your favorite palettes in the new Palette Dock at the right end of the Options Palette.

**As each Adobe program goes through various upgrades, they have (with the exception of PageMaker) started to incorporate the same palette structure that exists in Photoshop. This is extremely convenient, although they're all starting to look so alike that at first glance it's sometimes hard to tell one apart from the other!**

The following sections describe the various palettes Photoshop provides.

## The Navigator Palette

Particularly useful for large images, this palette offers the most specific options for navigating through portions of your image (Figure 1–9). Use the slider to make your image larger or smaller within its current window, or type in a zoom in/out percentage for more precise control. If your image falls outside the boundaries of the window or your monitor, move the red square in the Navigation palette preview window to find the exact spot in your image that you wish to use.

## Info Palette

This palette (Figure 1–10) provides information on relative color values for CMYK and RGB images, the location of your mouse pointer, the width and height of any selection, and the angle and distance of measurements being made. More can be learned about the Info palette in Chapter 4.

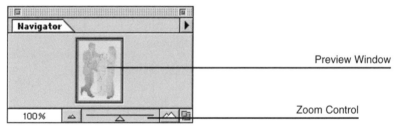

Preview Window

Zoom Control

*Figure 1–9: The Navigator palette.*

RGB Color Info

CMYK Color Info

Coordinates

Selection Measure

*Figure 1–10: The Info palette.*

# The Options Palette

Each of the tools that you'll be using has its own Options palette. In previous versions of Photoshop, there wasn't a tremendous difference between most of the Options palettes. But with Photoshop 6, the Options palette has turned into a virtual command center, with new functions and options provided for nearly every tool.

If you're familiar with older versions of Photoshop, the new Options palette will be the first change that you see upon launching version 6. Instead of being confined in a small box-style area like all the other palettes, version 6 offers it as a horizontal bar across the top of your monitor, directly under the menu choices. It's convenient, I guess, but it takes up more room than it did in previous versions.

**By default, the Options palette will be lodged in place and won't move. To make it a free-floating palette, click the mouse button on the far left of the palette and hold it while dragging it from its position. The palette can now be placed wherever you'd like it (although having a long, free-floating horizontal bar in the middle of your screen is even more annoying than having a long, free-floating horizontal bar**

at the top of your screen). To lodge the palette at the bottom of your screen instead of at the top, drag it to the bottom left corner of your monitor. The palette will snap into place.

As we'll see throughout this book, certain tools will have multiple palettes associated with them, and the functions provided in their Options palette will change depending upon how you are using the tool. The Shape tool, for example, offers one set of options if you are using the tool simply to place the shape on an existing layer, and another set of options if you are creating a Shape layer. It can be confusing, but you'll get used to it. When it's important to mention it, I'll review certain cases like this in various chapters.

**One of the few, very cool new features about the Options palette goes largely unnoticed by a lot of users. If you have your monitor resolution set to 800 x 600 pixels or higher, the far right of the Options palette sports a funky, dark gray box that looks more like just a design than anything else. But this "design" is actually the Palette Well. To save space, just drag the tab of any open palette into the Palette Well, and it'll hold the palettes there until you need them. They'll even open from the Palette Well, until you decide, for some reason, to drag them out and let them be free-floating palettes again. It's a good idea, but could have been better if the Palette Well were a free-floating palette itself, rather than part of an oversized Options palette.**

Figure 1–11 shows the Options palette for the Paintbrush tool.

## Color Palette

The Color palette is one of several ways that Photoshop gives you to choose a specific foreground or background color. Use the sliders or enter a numeric value (Figure 1–12). Many Photoshop users find it to be a convenient means of accessing and mixing colors, although I'm personally not a huge fan—after sitting in front of a monitor day in and day out, the last thing I want to do is try to discern color shades in that tiny preview box. I find the Color Picker much better for choosing the color and shade that I want.

options change for each tool          Palette Well saves space by holding other palettes

*Figure 1–11: The Options palette for the Paintbrush tool.*

# Swatches Palette

Kind of a neat tool, this palette (Figure 1–13) acts as a storage center for colors, allowing you to save specific shades that you like for later use. This palette will also help you reduce the file size of your image, as well as assist in solving problems associated with transparent portions of your images. Find out more about this in Chapter 2, "Preparing Images for the Web" and Chapter 3, "Transparency."

# Brushes Palette

In version 5.5, the Brushes palette was always accessible—even if you were using a tool that doesn't need brushes. Version 6, however, put the Brushes palette only within the Options palette of a tool that would require you to use a brush (such as one of the painting tools).

To access the Brushes palette in version 6, select the tool that you wish to paint with, and open the Brushes pull-down menu (click on the small, downward-pointing arrow). The palette, shown in Figure 1–14, allows you to select a size and shape for the brush you'll be using. As you can see, a number of standard circular brushes are already loaded into the palette. The hard-edged circles indicate brush strokes will be hard edged, whereas the circles that fade out indicate strokes will have softer edges. The numbers underneath some of the circles indicate their diameter in pixels (the numbers only appear if the brush is too big to fit in the iconic display of the Brushes palette).

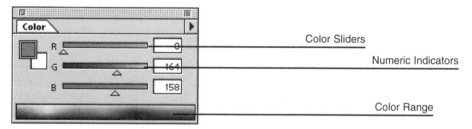

*Figure 1–12: The Color palette.*

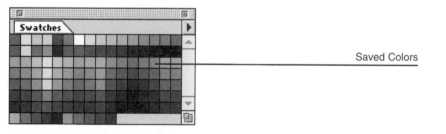

*Figure 1–13: The Swatches palette.*

# Layers Palette

One of the main features that really separates Photoshop from the crowd, the Layers palette (Figure 1–15) is your window into how your image is being built. Acting like a stack of acetates, this palette allows you to add to your image on one layer without affecting portions of your image on other layers. A full description of the Layers palette can be found later in this chapter.

# Channels Palette

This palette (Figure 1–16) acts as a storage area for image color and saved selections, as well as allowing you to create cool effects with masks. It is a treasure chest of color-mixing capabilities, and version 5 includes a new feature for creating spot colors to really excite print designers. While Channels are briefly touched upon in a few examples in this book, a full explanation is provided in my other book, *Photoshop 6 Primer*.

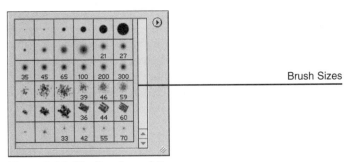

Brush Sizes

*Figure 1–14: The Brushes palette.*

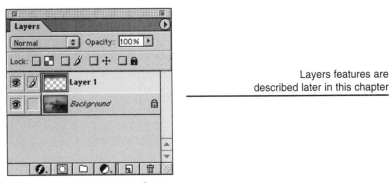

Layers features are
described later in this chapter

*Figure 1–15: The Layers palette.*

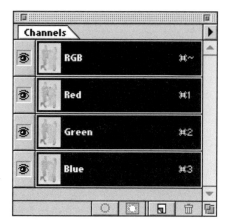

*Figure 1–16: The Channels palette.*

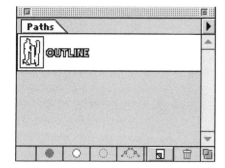

*Figure 1–17: The Paths palette.*

# Paths Palette

For use with the Pen tool, the Paths palette (Figure 1–17) retains path information and allows for path adjustments. Use this palette to turn paths into selections, fill them with color, or stroke your path with varying widths of color outlines. For print designers, save paths to isolate images for use in page layout programs (Web designers can make use of this feature as well, by laying out a page in Quark or PageMaker to be turned into a PDF, as explained in Chapter 10).

# History Palette

This palette (Figure 1–18) saves a preset number of moves and changes to your image. Use it in conjunction with the History brush for recapturing portions of your image at earlier stages. Because it allows for multiple undos, you can experiment on your image with little fear of mistakes becoming permanent. This feature is explored in greater detail in "Freedom of Expression: The History Palette" later in this chapter.

# Actions Palette

A useful tool, this palette (Figure 1–19) creates and remembers sequences of actions as macros so you can expedite otherwise mundane Photoshop functions. A great time saver, it is especially helpful for Web designers, who often repeatedly have to perform a tedious chain of events. It is explained in more detail in "Saving Time with Actions" later in this chapter.

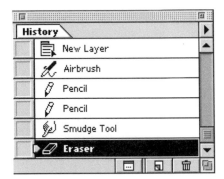

*Figure 1–18: The History palette.*

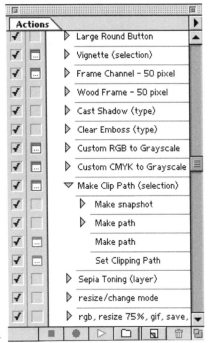

*Figure 1–19: The Actions palette.*

# WORKING WITH LAYERS

Unlike earlier versions of Photoshop, versions 4 and 5 literally force you to use layers. Any time you place text, paste a new item into your image, or drag an image from one canvas to another, a new layer will be created. In addition, certain functions will be unavailable to you until you create a new layer, including color blend modes and the new Layer effects.

In a nutshell, you can use layers to alter, add, subtract, or otherwise experiment on your image without having to disturb other aspects of your work. Each layer acts as a transparency, so that its contents remain independent from the rest of the image and allow all other layers to be viewed at the same time if needed.

## Layer Palette Changes in Version 6

The Layers palette is one of the areas that got a lot of attention in the upgrade, and I'm happy to say that even if all of the changes weren't necessary, at least most of them were pretty good. I'll go into some of the more prominent changes later in the book, where applicable, but a few of the improvements you should be aware of include the following:

◆ The addition of Layer sets, which allow designers like me, who work with an inordinate number of layers for each project, to organize certain layers into groups that make items and graphic elements more easy to locate.

◆ While earlier versions allowed you to preserve the transparency of any layer, version 6 allows you to preserve the image, or simply lock the layer altogether, so that no changes can be made. This update may be a bit trivial because the introduction of the History palette minimized the chance of permanent mistakes, but it can still be useful.

◆ Adjustment layers and Layer effects (now called Layer attributes) options are more conveniently found as a button at the the bottom of the palette. Even better, each layer effect appears as its own separate sublayer that you can make invisible or throw out without changing the other effects.

## Creating and Deleting Layers

Figure 1–20 shows and describes the Layers palette, while Figure 1–21 graphically illustrates layers.

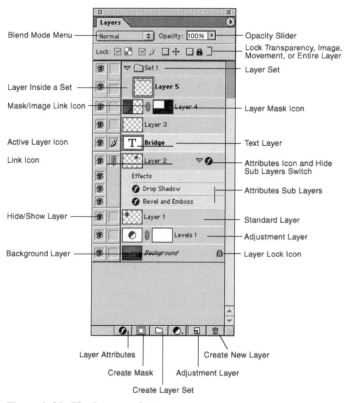

*Figure 1–20: The Layers palette.*

*Figure 1–21: Graphical depiction of layers.*

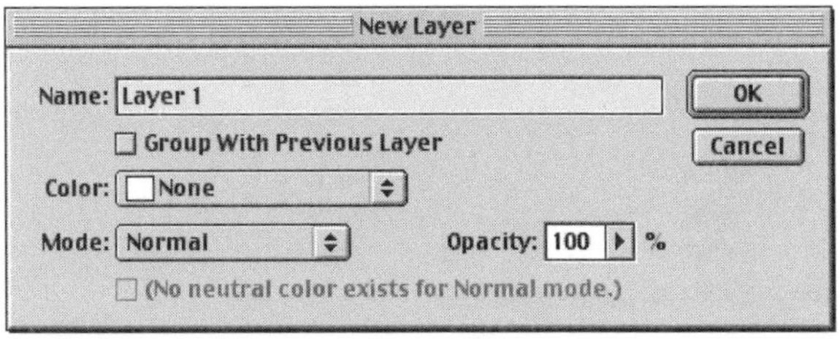

*Figure 1–22: New Layer dialog box.*

When you open a new file, you automatically begin work on the background layer. This is the only layer that remains unchangeably opaque (although you can remove the layer if necessary—see "Renaming Layers" later in this chapter. As you draw on or change the canvas in your layer, you will notice that the icon in the Layers palette changes also (Figure 1–20).

To add a new layer to your image, you have a number of choices, including:

◆ Place text on your canvas, or paste something from the clipboard into your image. (Don't worry that the image you paste will no longer retain its selection.) To select the items in a particular layer at any time, press Command (Control in Windows) then click on the desired layer.

◆ Push the Create New Layer icon at the bottom of the palette.

◆ In the Layers palette menu (accessed by clicking on the arrow on the upper right), choose New Layer.

◆ From the menu bar, choose Layers -> New -> Layer (kind of an out-of-the-way method, but it's there, and I'm just the messenger ...).

If you choose either of the latter two methods, you will be presented with the dialog box shown in Figure 1–22. Among other things, you can use this dialog box to give your layer a unique name. This could help later, when your image has 30, 50, or more layers and you need to find something in particular. If you choose not to name your palette, it will be given the name Layer 1 (or Layer 2 or whatever is the next number). (You can always rename any layer whenever you like—see section "Renaming Layers.")

Layers stack upward, so that each new layer that you create is directly above the active layer (the layer that is currently being worked on—highlighted in the Layers palette).

To delete a layer, you do one of the following three things:

◆ Simply drag the layer to the garbage can in the lower right corner of the Layers palette

◆ From the Layers palette menu, choose Delete Layer

◆ From the menu bar, choose Layer -> Delete Layer

## *Renaming Layers*

After you put part of an image in a layer, you may want to name it so the object can be easily found again. For example, if your image has multiple shadows, each with its own layer, you may want to give names like "shadow under car," so that you can quickly identify it.

To rename an existing layer, right-click on it in Windows, or press Control then click on it, in Mac. A pop-up menu will appear. Choose Rename Layer to access a dialog box, within which you can create a new name for your layer.

 **In older versions, you accessed this dialog box by double-clicking on the layer that you wanted to rename.**

If you rename the Background layer, it'll take on the same properties of the other layers—you can change its opacity, move it, and so forth.

## Managing Multiple Layers

As you've probably experienced, it's easy for a simple image to turn into a monster, and have 50, 60, even 100 layers of text, images, shadows, and the like. So how do you manage all of these without spending all of your time trying to figure out where things are? Well, naming each layer as described previously is a start, but another good way is to use the keyboard. If you can see the layers that you want to work on, hold down the Command (Control in Windows) key and click on the image in your canvas. The layer that image is located on will become active.

For better or for worse, most of my designs tend to use an inordinate number of layers. Because I am not alone in this practice, Photoshop 6 now provides the ability to create Layer sets. Creating a set, which you can do by clicking the Layer set icon at the bottom of your Layers palette, is like creating a folder or directory in your Layers palette.

Within each folder that you create, you can organize the layers for any given area of design. This is helpful in two ways:

1. By placing all of these graphics into one folder, they're very easy to find again.

2. When I'm not working on this portion of the overall design, I can keep the folder closed, making working with the Layers palette more manageable.

To place existing layers into a folder, simply click on the layer and drag it as you would if you were moving it to a new location. Place it right on top of the Set layer, until the Set layer is highlighted. Release the mouse button, and your layer will be placed within the set.

To create a name for your set, simply double-click the Set layer to access the dialog box.

**When you throw out a set, you are throwing out every layer within that set, too. So make sure that you really want to discard all of those layers before trashing an entire set.**

Unfortunately, you can't have a folder inside another folder. A minor technicality, but regardless, Layer sets are among the more exciting new features.

# Moving, Linking, and Merging Layers

At any given time, it may become necessary to bring layers forward or send them farther into the background. To move a layer, simply drag it from its original position in the Layers palette to wherever you want it.

A feature new to Photoshop 5 is the ability to send your layer one level backward or forward, or directly to the front or back, by choosing, from the menu bar, Layer -> Arrange -> (your preference).

If you want the contents of two or more layers to move in conjunction with one another, simply "link" them together. Figure 1–20, illustrates the chain-link icon that links your active layer to other layers. When you use the Move tool to move the contents of one layer, the contents of all linked layers move as well.

Another feature of Photoshop 5 is the option of aligning your linked layers either flush left, right, top, bottom, vertical center, or horizontal center. You can do this by choosing Layer -> Align -> (your preference). If you have three or more layers linked, you will also have the option of choosing Layer -> Align -> Distribute Linked, which will distribute the items on linked layers evenly.

To merge the contents of two or more layers into a single layer, the following options are offered to you:

◆  If your layers are linked, choose Merge Linked from either the Layers palette menu or the menu bar Layer menu.

◆  To merge your layer with the layer below the active layer, choose Merge Down from either the Layers palette menu or the menu bar Layer menu.

◆  If any of your layers are turned off (see below), choose Merge Visible from either the Layers palette menu or the menu bar Layer menu.

## Viewing Layers: Turning Them On or Off

As shown in Figure 1–20 you can turn a layer on or off by clicking on the Eye icon on the left-side column. Turning it off means that it will be invisible in your canvas, although you will still be able to see the contents in the Layers palette. You will not be able to manipulate or add elements that reside on invisible layers.

## Flattening Layers

When you save an image that has multiple layers, Photoshop will be the only format option available to you. To save your image in any other format, so that you can use it when putting together your Web site, you have to first "flatten" your image, which means that all visible layers will be merged into the Background layer. To do this, choose Flatten Image from either the Layers palette menu or the menu bar Layer menu.

**Many other Adobe programs, such as ImageReady (bundled with Photoshop) and Illustrator, not only use the same layering system that Photoshop uses, but the layers are transferrable between programs without having to flatten them first.**

The Layers palette's features don't end there, however. There are many more exciting features that the Layers function has to offer, which unfortunately fall out of the scope of this book. Look for *Photoshop 6 Primer* for a more detailed discussion of how Layers works.

# SAVING TIME WITH ACTIONS

The hi-tech version of creating macros, the Actions palette helps to streamline your work and saves you loads of valuable time. By recording actions, you can perform a complex set of functions that can replay repeatedly through any number of images. The

Actions palette is shown and described in Figure 1–23. Fortunately, this is one resource that Adobe has pretty much left alone for the new version, and really hasn't changed too much about it.

As an example of a simple Action, let's say that you are going to be building a series of buttons for your Web site. All of the buttons are going to look the same, although each is going to say something different, such as "Home," "Products," "Contact," and so on. As Figure 1–24 shows, the buttons have already been built, and they are made up of three layers each, in RGB color, and are obviously too big to be useful on a web site. You want them to be 50% smaller, and flattened. To make this sequence of commands into an Action, follow these steps:

1. In the Action menu options (accessed through the arrow in the upper right of the palette) choose New Action. The dialog box in Figure 1–25 appears. I recommend giving new actions a name. (For this example, I've named my action "Flat, 50%sm" to later remember what this action does. I have also allocated a keyboard command for the action by selecting the function key F1 + Shift, which I knew was available.) Hit OK.

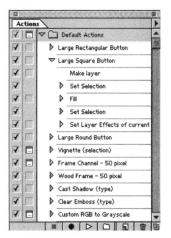

*Figure 1–23: The Actions palette.*

*Figure 1–24: Predesigned buttons for my site.*

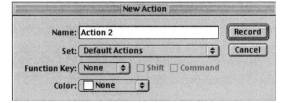

*Figure 1–25: New Action dialog box.*

2. Notice on the Actions palette that the Record icon (the classic red circle) is highlighted to show that it is recording.

3. Choose Flatten Image from the Layers palette.

4. Choose Image -> Image Size and reduce the Print Size width to 50%. As long as the Constrain Proportions box is checked, the height will also reduce by 50%. Hit OK.

5. Push the Stop icon (the universal square) at the bottom of the Actions palette to stop recording. You have just finished making your first action.

6. Make a different button your active canvas. Play your action by either pushing the Play icon (the universal triangle) at the bottom of the Actions palette, or by using the keyboard command (which I had set as F1 + Shift).

The Action "plays" without you having to go through each tedious step. Figure 1–26 shows the process.

## Batching Actions

What's even easier than having an action do all the work for you on open images? Having an action do all the work for you on closed images, of course! (Who knows, by Photoshop 7 or 8, maybe our images will just design themselves.) Use the batch option to perform your action on a folder full of images.

1. Simply select your desired action and choose File -> Automate -> Batch to access the dialog box shown in Figure 1–27.

2. Select the folder where all the images on which you want to run this action are located.

3. Sit back and relax.

**If your images are not located in the same folder, either batch the process multiple times—once for each folder—or move all the images into one directory before you begin this process.**

## Viewing an Action Before Completion

If you create a particularly long and involved action (or even a short one, for that matter), you can program it to stop in midstream so you can judge for yourself the progress of the action and decide if you wish the action to continue. To do this, choose Insert Stop from the Actions palette menu. Enter any message you wish in the text field and check the box Allow Continue. When an action is played and the stop is reached, your message will be displayed, and you're given the choice of stopping or continuing. You won't be able to make any changes, but you'll at least be able to judge whether you want the action to complete.

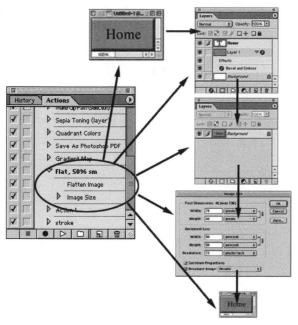

*Figure 1–26: The Actions palette at work.*

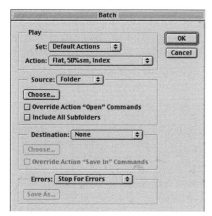

*Figure 1–27: The Batch palette.*

# Forcing Menu Items to Work

There may be instances when you try to record a command but are prevented from doing so because it's grayed out. You can force the Actions palette to recognize it by choosing Insert Menu Option from the Actions palette pull-down menu. Type in the name of the command and click the Find button. You'll be able to insert functions into your actions that would otherwise be unavailable to you.

## Changing the Look of the Palette

Due to the specific nature of the commands placed in each action, the palette can get somewhat jumbled. One way that you can alleviate this problem is obvious: Close any of the triangles on the left side that are open, hiding the action contents.

The more efficient way to clean up the palette is the convenient ability to turn each action into a button. To do this, make sure you are not currently recording an action and choose Button Mode from the pull-down menu. The benefit of this is in its simplicity: If you've named your actions well, or applied a specific color to them (in the New Action dialog box), each will be easy to find. You also won't need to click on the Play button anymore—just push the button that applies to the action you want to run.

The downside is that you cannot edit or move an action while in Button mode. You also cannot create new actions. If you need to do any of these things, simply choose Button Mode again from the palette pull-down menu.

## Creating and Saving Sets

Although this is a relatively simple process, you'll find it useful as you work on images for your Web pages, especially for aspects like buttons that often assume the same properties and dimensions. To begin a set, choose New Set from the Actions palette pull-down menu. You can create new actions within this set, or you can move already existing actions into it by dragging them into the Set folder.

To save a set, click on the set name and choose Save Actions from the palette pull-down menu. Place the set in your desired directory.

The next time you want to use that particular set, simply choose Load Actions from the palette pull-down menu.

## Some Useful Actions—My Personal List

There are any number of combinations of commands you can put together to create an action. The following constitutes a short list of the actions that I have found useful in creating content for the Web. I have also tried to assign keyboard commands to as many as possible, also in the name of saving time and creating convenience (isn't it amazing that I have to resort to an actual *key* to run an action, instead of using the mouse to push the Play button? A hundred years ago, people still churned their own butter...).

◆ Duplicate                    ◆ Add Drop Shadow 50%

◆ Duplicate 2x                 ◆ Add Drop Shadow 75%

◆ Duplicate 4x                 ◆ Copy & Paste

◆ Add Emboss                   ◆ Change Hue + 10

◆ Cut & Paste                  ◆ Change Hue + 30

◆ Create New Layer             ◆ Save & Close

◆ Duplicate Layer              ◆ Save Selection

# PHOTOSHOP COLOR

Understanding color can be a vital part of utilizing Photoshop well. It can also be a major factor in causing you to send your computer hurtling through an open window 20 floors above street level. For those of you who, like myself, have a print background, you know how frustrating it can be trying to match the color off a press to the color you see on your monitor.

Color on the Web used to be a similar headache, as different operating systems and various monitor resolutions posed tough color challenges. But as Chapter 2 will explore in more depth, color on the web isn't really that much of an issue or a challenge anymore. All the same, however, it always helps to have at least a basic working knowledge of color issues you may face as you work with Photoshop and the Internet.

## Color Modes

By selecting Image -> Mode from the menu bar, you'll see a list of various "color modes" in which you can choose to work. Although each has its own separate set of properties, the modes you'll be concentrating on for Web design are RGB and grayscale.

◆ RGB is the mode in which you will usually create and manipulate your images. In this mode, images are comprised of red, green, and blue pixels that mix to create other colors. RGB is used when creating electronic material, as monitors can accurately display the color ranges. This is different from CMYK (Cyan, Magenta, Yellow, and Black), the mode used for printed material, which is generally comprised of fewer colors.

◆ Grayscale is, as you may guess, the mode that allows you to work only in shades of gray. It is not used often on the Web, except for aesthetic purposes or to reduce file sizes.

In most cases, you will work in RGB color and then switch to index color for the preparation of GIFs.

## The Color Picker

Clicking on either the foreground or background color in the toolbar gives you access to the Color Picker shown and described in Figure 1–28. Although there are many different ways to view the color options, my personal favorite, and probably the most popular, is the one that allows you to work in the default hue (select one of the other radio buttons to see how the color wheels change).

You can choose which color or color family you want by using the slider to the right of the main color field. Once you have chosen your color, the field will offer you all the available shades for the color you have chosen.

1. Move your cursor throughout the field until you're happy with the color and shade you have selected. The before and after color boxes to the right of the slider show you the new color (top box) and your original color (bottom box).

2. If you need to know the hexadecimal value of any color (we'll review hexadecimal values briefly in Chapter 4), a small box at the bottom of the Color Picker provides the code for any color within the color field. This feature was introduced in Photoshop 5.5, along with another feature—the checkbox Only Web Colors. But again, as we'll see in Chapter 2, time and technology have made this a pretty useless feature.

3. When you have chosen your desired color, click OK and that color will be in either your foreground or background color in the toolbar, depending on which you used to access the Color Picker.

If you or your client needs to match a PMS (Pantone Matching System) color for the web site, you can select it by hitting the Custom button on the Color Picker. The Custom Color dialog box, shown in Figure 1–29, lets you choose from a number of different color matching systems often used in printing logos or corporate identification. If you know the exact number of the color you want to use, simply type it in to find it quickly.

**If a client gives you a PMS color to use in their Web site, don't be surprised when they ask why it looks different on screen than it does in print. RGB Web graphics will display slightly differently than CMYK print colors.**

# FREEDOM OF EXPRESSION: THE HISTORY PALETTE

Designers who've been around for awhile might remember (though not very fondly) the days before the History palette was introduced in Photoshop 5. They were frustrating design days in which only one Undo was allowed. Make two mistakes in a row, and you were done. The History palette has since become as much a part of the Photoshop tradition as the Layers palette, and as impossible to live without.

The main function of the History palette is to provide for multiple undos—make 18, 19, even 20 mistakes in a row, and you can still go back to fix what you've done. Maybe even more importantly, the History palette allows you to experiment in ways you never could before. In earlier versions of Photoshop, you would apply a color correction, filter, or other effect, and then have to undo that before trying something else or accept your original experiment as permanent. With Photoshop 5's History function, you can apply an effect, then apply an effect to that effect, and continue for up to 20 new manipulations with the option of undoing any one of them.

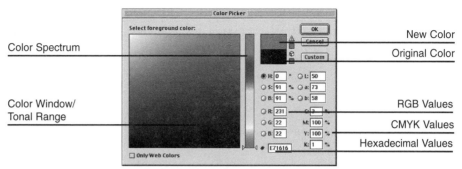

*Figure 1–28: The Color Picker.*

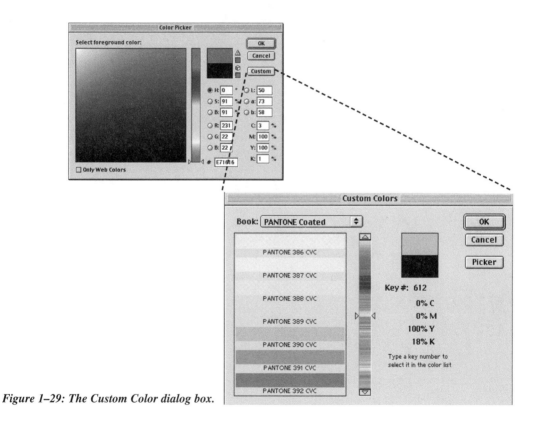

*Figure 1–29: The Custom Color dialog box.*

# The History Palette

Figure 1–30 (also Color Figure 1) shows and describes the History palette. Above the solid black line is a picture of the original image, as it was before any manipulations. When you double-click on it, the picture will revert back to its original state.

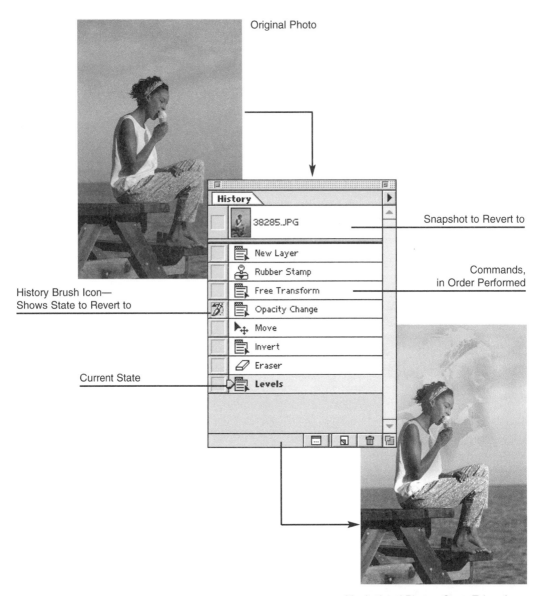

*Figure 1–30: The History palette.*

Manipulated Photo—Steps Taken Are
Remembered in the History Palette

You can make a snapshot of your image at any point and revert back
to in similar fashion. From the Palette Tool, choose New Snapshot,
and name it if you like. The snapshot will save below the picture of
your original image, above the solid black line. As you
continue to manipulate your image, just double-click on your
snapshot to revert back to it.

In the palette, each state of manipulation is given its own title, such as "Paint Bucket" or "Blur Tool," and are stacked downward in the order that they are completed. By clicking on any title in the palette, your image will go back to that state. The History palette will hold 20 states as its default (changing the default is discussed soon)—any states after that will be added at the expense of the oldest states.

Once you revert to an older state, all of the states that came afterward will disappear. This is the default, but we will soon learn how to change this.

# Settings

Choosing History Options from the Palette menu brings up a dialog box. The following options will be available to you:

◆ Maximum History States: You can set the number of states that the History palette will remember. The maximum number allowed is 100. There are obviously advantages to having more, but the more you have, the more memory you'll be wasting.

◆ Automatically Create First Snapshot: Checked by default, this is what causes the History palette to save the original image as a constant for instant reversion (see above for more details). Remove the checkmark and the palette won't automatically save your starting point as a snapshot.

◆ Allow Non-Linear History: As I explained earlier, once you revert to a state, all of the states that were created afterward will gray out. By checking this button, you will be able to revert to one state, but keep all subsequent states intact. This is a great feature, but it also consumes memory.

**In Photoshop 5 and 5.5, you could also use this dialog box to change the maximum number of history states. But apparently someone the Photoshop development team thought that would be too easy, and they moved this feature. Now, if you want to change the number of history states, you have to choose Edit -> Preferences -> General Preferences. This history states value area is kind of hidden off to the middle right of the dialog box.**

# Bad Things Happen...

There are some negatives that are associated with the History palette, the two most prominent of which are:

◆ **Megatonnage:** The History palette takes up *a lot* of memory. You're likely to run into a lot more "out of memory" errors than you did in previous versions of Photoshop. To reduce the possibility of running out of memory, or to regain lost memory, take one of the following steps:

  • Choose Edit -> Preferences -> General Preferences and reduce the number of states that the Palette will save

  • Choose Edit -> Purge -> Histories (You cannot undo this option, so make sure that you really want to do it before making this choice.)

◆ **Too Much of a Good Thing:** Don't get too comfortable with the idea of the History palette saving you from mistakes. I've fallen into the trap of continuing to make corrections to my image without saving, thinking that I can always go back to a previous state if I want to. But when I unhappily crash, my History palette is completely empty when I reopen my image. The information in this palette does not remain between uses of Photoshop.

## The History Brush

The History brush works in conjunction with the History palette. While clicking on one of the titles in the History palette will bring your image back to that entire state, the History brush will do the same, but only for the portions of your image that you paint over.

Each manipulation title in your image has a small empty box next to it on the left. Clicking in one of these boxes will cause an icon of the History brush to appear. That icon marks the state on the History palette to which you will revert. As you use the History brush to paint over your image, it will revert back to the marked state in the areas you brush over. Figure 1–31 illustrates this, as does Color Figure 1.

### *History, Monet Style: The Watercolor Brush*

I've never really been a big fan of fine art, although after a few quick visits to the Guggenheim, I'll take fine art over "modern art" any day. But either way, it's not really my thing, and since this is my book, I'm not going to spend too much time describing the Watercolor brush. Basically, this brush works the same as the regular History brush, but it turns your image into a virtual watercolor painting. Very, very exciting. Yawn.

# THINGS I MISSED

Of course there's more to Photoshop 6 than just what was covered in this chapter, and there are other features, such as the Channels palette, that deserve their space in this book as well. But trust me, everything that you will need to become a bang-up Web

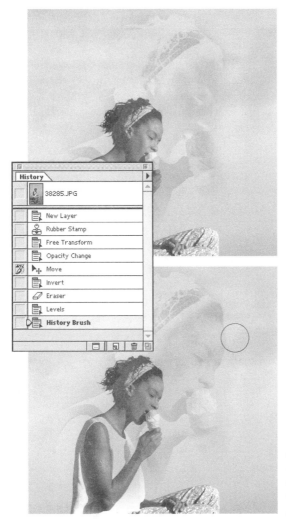

*Figure 1–31: The History brush, shown as the large circle in the lower picture, reverts just a portion of the picture to the point in the palette marked by the icon.*

designer and Photoshop expert will be covered in one place or another, depending on where they are most relevant. The four main features covered here—layers, actions, color, and the History palette—are more universal items that, when creating content for the Web, will apply in some way to nearly everything you do. Some features, such as layers, are unavoidable—you can do little in Photoshop without them. Other features, like actions, are universal in their convenience and will make your life easier and help to streamline your workload.

# SUMMARY

Photoshop takes practice—there's no doubt about that. However, by knowing the basics, and following the examples in the remainder of the chapters, you'll have enough tools at your disposal to create some great web graphics. Don't stop here, though—Photoshop 6 has such great depth as a graphic design tool that you'll be limiting yourself by not practicing continually and learning the aspects covered in this chapter in more detail, as well as the aspects of the program not covered in this book. It won't take long before you'll get the hang of the many functions Photoshop has to offer, with the basics serving as your springboard. Combine this knowledge with some of the unique aspects of the Internet that we'll see in upcoming pages, and you'll be on your way to a profitable and productive experience in web design.

# PREPARING IMAGES
# FOR THE WEB

Creating anything is always a blast. Whether you're working in a kitchen cooking up a great meal, sitting at an editing system splicing together a movie, or sweating it out in a woodshop building furniture, there's nothing more satisfying than watching your own work come to life.

Well, that is, almost nothing as satisfying—cashing the check for watching your work come to life enjoys a slight edge.

Unfortunately, no matter what your medium—food, video, wood, or any other—the creation process cannot begin without a certain amount of tedious preparation. At some point, the chef needs to shop for food and preheat ovens, the video editor has to digitize footage, and the wood worker has to ... well, I don't really know what the wood worker has to do to prepare, but I'm sure it's not fun.

Anyway, Web graphics are no different. The Photoshop part is a limitless challenge of creativity and talent. And for the most part, this book reviews techniques and aspects of design and Web creation that are fun. But unfortunately, before you get to that, there is some really boring, tedious information you must know first. Color palettes, file types, image sizes—all of these are important aspects of the "infrastructure" of Web design, and will be vital to you as you forge ahead in creating Web sites.

So just keep telling yourself that the best part is still ahead, and you'll be able to ease through this chapter. Although I am only providing the bare bones of what you need to know, you'll find this information an important resource to your work.

# CHALLENGES, OLD AND NEW

As stated in the introduction to Chapter 1, the web has changed a lot in the span of the last couple of years. These changes have been both cosmetic and technological, and have also changed the hurdles that web designers face. Two years ago, when I wrote *Web Photoshop 5 To Go*, problems included slow modem speeds, Color palette issues, spacing and differences between Netscape and Internet Explorer (which was still relatively new at the time) and sub-par AOL web-browsing capabilities.

Today's web designers work in a whole new landscape. This section goes into the major categories in question, explaining which old issues are no longer a big deal, and which new issues have emerged to replace them.

## Modem Speed

Modem speed is still an issue, but hardly as limiting as it was just a year or so ago. The biggest problem facing designers today is the bandwidth discrepancy between Internet connections in people's homes and in their offices. As the Internet changed from a business luxury to a (perceived) necessity, corporate America made the move to high bandwidth connectivity. Even 56K modems seem out of place in most modern offices, as DSL, ISDN, T1, T3, and cable have become all the rage.

Homes, however, haven't made the change as quickly. Current government regulations (or lack thereof) haven't put a lot of pressure on the local phone company (and its veritable monopoly) to push high bandwidth products into the home aggressively, which in turn have not put pressure on local cable companies to do so, either. The additional legal trouble that AT&T faced when it purchased major cable players also slowed the spread of cable modems into most homes. So homes have languished behind their corporate partners, at least in the "speed" category, with later year 2000 averages putting most homes at about 36.6bps modem speed.

But as more and more people report that their major use of the Internet is from work, and with the steep increase of business-to-business (B2B) web sites, many developers have started to worry a little less about how heavy their web sites are in file size. At the same time, as design style has changed to a less "in your face" approach of crazy background colors to a more subdued, almost "less is more" style, even reaching the 36.6 modem people has become less of an issue.

Does that mean that you should go out and create graphics without any thought at all to their file size? Of course not. It just means that you have a lot more liberty to be creative, without a very low ceiling to hold you back.

# Color Palettes

Once upon a time, a really big deal was made out of color palettes, and which were the right colors to use in your web sites. It was bad enough that we were limited to small graphics that were sent over 14.4bps speed modems, but were we really limited to only 256 colors, too?

Sadly, yes. Learning different color palettes was enough of a hassle to make any "wanna-be" web designer take up accounting, instead. Which colors could be used where, which were best for what, how do you avoid unwanted dithering on the monitor of idiots who didn't know they even had the ability to see more that 256 colors on their monitor?

Happily, this really isn't an issue anymore. Most monitors now ship with higher color settings, and owners of older monitors seem to have found out how to change their color settings to allow for thousands or millions of colors. Of course, there is still the download time to think about. For sites that use a lot and/or very large graphics with flat colors, using the GIF format (discussed later) helps to reduce the file size. GIF images only allow for 256 colors, and trying to determine which colors to use was an effort and a half in Photoshop 5 and lower. But Photoshop's Save for Web feature, introduced in version 5.5 and improved in version 6 is so easy to use that it's really not worth the effort any longer to know everything possible about adjusting colors for the GIF format's maximum of 256. Photoshop kind of does it for you.

The only real issue that remains, then, is the discrepancy that occurs between Mac monitors and Windows monitors. Basically, the problem is that Windows computers tend to see colors darker than their Macintosh counterparts. There's really no way to avoid this, but when creating your graphics, just keep in mind that maroon on a Mac will look brown on a PC, a navy blue will look black, and so on. And even though you might be creating your web site on a Mac (and if you are, you're probably a die-hard, cult-like fanatic), most of the rest of the world is viewing your work on a Windows PC.

# Browser Issues

When Microsoft introduced Internet Explorer (IE for short), the web design community let out a collective groan. Netscape was more than fine. But IE was a reality, and it wasn't going anyplace. So we sucked it up, and learned how to compensate for the fact that they each seemed to space things out a little differently—enough that it would often make a mess of your web layout in one browser or another. And the AOL browser was a complete mess.

But that was back in the day when designers also wrote their own HTML text, carved up graphics manually, and used single pixel tricks to try to fool one browser or the other. But development has become more sophisticated, and today, if you want to hard code your site in HTML manually, you may as well also break out your parents old 8 track tapes, because it's about as common. WYSIWYG (what you see is what you get) programs, with Macromedia's DreamWeaver leading the way, have joined Microsoft's FrontPage and even (to a lesser extent) Adobe's ImageReady programs to make web layout simple, with all coding done for you. At the same time, these "do-it-for-you" programs have eliminated any spacing problems that may happen between the major web browsers. And in the meantime, advancements in the AOL browser have occurred to make it much more friendly with traditionally designed web sites.

Now, the only real problem left between Netscape and IE are issues that go beyond Photoshop and HTML, and definitely beyond the scope of this book. These problems include the way each browser reads DHTML and other languages, which can some-times cause layout frustrations.

But as we saw with speed issues, the solution to old problems does not mean the solution to all problems. For right now, designers can enjoy a quiet time of develop-ment, with few inter-browser problems. But in the next couple of years, we're going to be faced with issues that will make the old Netscape/IE problems seem laughable. I'm talking about viewing the web on television. The threat was almost here already, with the mass marketing push of WebTV. Sales of the unit were slow, and the product seems to have slowed its push as Microsoft (owner of WebTV) targets an older audience. But new products are being developed all the time, and eventually, when cable modems are more prominent and digital TV has really taken hold (Congress keeps pushing the dead-line back for digital television, to accommodate small stations that don't have the funds for expensive upgrades, but that won't go on forever), web on TV will be a reality.

So would that really cause design problems? If WebTV was any indication, the answer is a resounding "yes." Primarily, color problems would be emerge, as TV screens differ from computer monitors. The former doesn't handle reds and yellows very well—they tend to bleed, while both look fine on the latter. Fonts, too, would be a problem, as 12 pt or even 10 pt font sizes are acceptable on a computer monitor, which is viewed at an average of 12 inches away. But TV screens, located in living rooms and bedrooms, are viewed at 12 feet away. There's no way in the world a person sitting a foot or more away is going to read a sentence at 10 pt font size.

Worst of all will be the inevitable layout issues. Resolution, which seems to have largely stabilized at 800 x 600 for most computer monitors, is 720 x 486 on television monitors, making web layouts not fit very well. This might not be so bad, except that, at least in the case of the WebTV product, there was no horizontal scrolling.

The bottom line is that, for right now, there is peace in the web world, at least where browser issues are concerned. But keep an eye out for a rapid popularization of Internet TV units in the coming months or years. The potential for nightmare-level problems is looming.

# ESTABLISHING A LEAST COMMON DENOMINATOR

So the field is more open, and there is plenty of room to stretch your legs, get comfortable, and even play a little. But until nearly everyone has cable modems and the most up-to-date browser versions are instantly installed on people's computers while we are sleeping, it's important to set some boundaries for design. Loose boundaries, but boundaries just the same.

Setting a "least common denominator" is a means of establishing these boundaries. Basically, what you're doing, is analyzing your audience, and asking, "OK, what are the lowest specifications that I need to design for to make sure that the largest number of people possible can view my site?"

In my initial book, *Web Photoshop 5 To Go*, I listed that my first least common denominator, when I started developing sites, was:

◆ 14.4 modem, 640 x 480 monitor resolution, AOL 2.5 browser

Wow, that was a long time ago (at least in web years). By the time I was writing that last book, my LCD had been upgraded to:

◆ 56.6k modem, 800 x 600 monitor resolution, IE or Netscape 4, FLASH compatible

Now, with the web and technology changing as quickly as it has, I have altered my LCD again (it's really an ongoing evaluation). I actually have two general LCDs, one for B2B sites and one for B2C (business-to-consumer) sites, although in reality I re-evaluate the LCD for each new site I build.

**B2B Sites:**

ISDN, 800 x 600 monitor resolution, IE 4 browser

**B2C Sites:**

36.6 modem, 800 x 600 monitor resolution, IE 4 browser

You'll notice that the only real difference between the two is the modem speed, but it's a major difference, and can affect the types of images and the number of alternative applications (such as audio files, Director movies, etc.) that I put on the site. Also of significance is that version 4 and higher of both the IE and Netscape browsers are compatible with Macromedia's FLASH, as the plug-in is preloaded. That might not really affect your Photoshop work, but it has already changed the way we view the web.

# FILE TYPES FOR THE WEB

When it comes to flat, 2D images, there are really only two file formats to consider: JPEG and GIF. A third, PNG, meant to be a combination of the other two really hasn't gained popularity.

**Even though PNG hasn't made a place for itself directly on the web, it is a popular format among FLASH developers when importing certain JPEG images into movies. PNGs prove useful in certain instances because they support partial transparency.**

Before we get into the reality of both formats, let's take a quick look at what makes each of them different from one another. See Table 2–1.

*Table 2–1: GIF Versus JPEG Formats*

| GIF Format | JPEG Format |
|---|---|
| GIF uses a color index, and supports 8-bit color (up to 256 colors). | JPEG supports 24-bit color (16 million colors). |
| GIF images can be transparent and made into basic animations. | JPEG images cannot be made transparent. |
| The GIF format is lossless compression, meaning that it does not lose information when you save it. | JPEG uses a lossy compression,which eliminates what it considers to be useless information. Each time you open and resave a JPEG image, the quality will deteriorate. |
| GIF will work better with images that have a high amount of specific detail that is important to the success of the piece. | JPEG is a better bet with photographs, or other images that use a lot of colors. |

◆ Do you want to place an image without the rectangular edges and corners? Then you'll want to use GIF for its transparency support.

◆ Is your image photographic, or continuous-tone with gradual gradations and changes of color? Then you'll most likely want to use JPEG.

◆ Do you want to make sure that the colors stay the same cross-platform? Then use the Web-safe color palette in the GIF format (Web-safe color is discussed later in this chapter).

◆ Are you trying to create something on your Web site that has some movement? Then use GIF to create a small animation.

◆ Do you have an image with text, or other elements with hard, detailed edges? JPEG won't work as well as GIF.

In the past, the differences between GIF and JPEG were worthy of in-depth academic study. This was especially true of GIF images, the intricacies that went into creating them, and the precision needed for getting the colors just right. But three things have changed that: The first is the improved bandwidth conditions that have made file size less of an issue than it used to be (this has been discussed more in depth earlier in this chapter), the second is that most people now see thousands of colors on their monitors, and so the need to create GIFs for fear of unwanted dithering has been virtually eliminated. Lastly, with version 5.5, Photoshop has made it very easy to create either a JPEG or a GIF. They have literally made the creation of either format as easy as using a simple pull-down menu, reducing the creation time (for GIFs especially), from long minutes into scant seconds. Trial and error, which was a necessary evil with versions 5 and earlier, is eliminated with the Save for Web feature that will be discussed in the next section.

# SAVING GIFS AND JPEGS: THE SAVE FOR WEB COMMAND CENTER

I'm not an advocate of laziness, so I would not suggest using Photoshop 6's Save for Web option as an excuse for not learning the differences between JPEG and GIF. But it will make your life infinitely easier when you are saving your web graphics.

To access the dialog box shown in Figure 2–1 and Color Figure 2, choose File -> Save for Web. Color Figure 2 (which is actually B & W but is there for reference) will be the main image that you'll reference through the bulk of this chapter.

On the top of the dialog box you will see four tabs: Original, Optimized, 2-Up, and 4-Up. 4-Up would be my choice in nearly every case, as it gives you the greatest opportunity to tweak and play with the variables for your image.

Click on 4-Up to access the tab shown and labeled in Color Figure 2. The following section will explain each feature.

*Figure 2–1. The Save for Web dialog box.*

# Preview Window

The Preview Window is divided into four quarters. The upper left quadrant shows your original image. The remaining three quadrants show the same image in different states. By default, each of these quadrants is optimized to what Photoshop believes would be the best specifications. That will change in just a moment. Click in any one of the quadrants (except the upper left, which is the original—this cannot be manipulated in this dialog box). A dark black border will appear around the window. This indicates that the window is active, and that any changes you make will be made to that quadrant.

Below each image preview is useful information, based on the values you'll establish. The upper left quadrant, which contains your original image, provides the name of the image and its size. This won't change as long as you're in this dialog box.

Under the other windows, however, you'll see great information for comparing and contrasting your images. The left side tells you the type of image that each quadrant is set to (GIF, JPEG, or PNG), the size of the file using the variables that you'll set, and how long that particular file would take to download on a 28.8 speed modem (how cool is that?). On the right is a recap of the settings you've chosen for that particular image preview, including (for a GIF) the type and amount of dither, which palette you've chosen, and how many colors). If you are testing the JPEG format, the compression quality is reported in this area.

Although you can save images as PNG using this dialog box, you won't see any in the figures for this chapter, nor will they really be discussed significantly. PNG still isn't used by enough designers to make it a viable option yet.

## Toolbar

The upper left of the dialog box shows three tools: the Hand, the Zoom Tool, and Eye-Dropper. These work pretty much the same as they do in the general Photoshop interface, but the important thing to note here is that if you use the Zoom tool to magnify one quadrant, the other quadrants will magnify as well. This holds true for the Hand tool, as well.

## Preview Menu

In the tradition of "Big Brother," you can now see everywhere at once. This drop-down menu lets you see your images as they might appear with various browser's dither, or even color-compensated for different platforms. Colors can be a particular problem, and extremely different between the Macintosh platform (where most sites are created), and the Windows platform (where most sites are viewed). The primary difference between the two is that colors on a PC will look darker than they appear on a Mac. Use this pull-down menu to remove the guesswork and know in advance what your images will look like, no matter where they are seen.

You can also select different modem speeds (14.4, 28.8, or 56.6) by which Photoshop will calculate image download time at variable settings. More on this in just a bit.

## OK and Cancel Buttons

Are these your standard OK and Cancel buttons, as they appear on all other dialog boxes? Maybe, but not everything is as it appears to be. In a short while we'll see how these buttons can be more functional than just allowing you to accept or decline image optimizations.

## Output Settings Button

Since Photoshop 6 now incorporates ImageReady's slicing functions, and therefore writes more HTML than it did back in 5.5, the Output Settings dialog box plays a more complex and important role than it did earlier.

The pull-down menu at the top of the dialog box is set to HTML by default, but also lets you change settings for the Background, Saving Files, and Slices. We'll review each one individually.

## HTML

The HTML options allow you to format your HTML in specific ways that are more consistent with how you write HTML yourself. For example, when I write HTML (and yes, I still code by hand), I like to put all my HTML tags in uppercase instead of lowercase, which helps me see them quickly when I am scanning a page. The Formatting area of the dialog box allows me the opportunity to establish these settings.

The Include Comments checkbox, when checked, will simply include the information that you can set in the File -> File Info dialog box (not reviewed in this book—it's very simple, and I have no doubt you can figure it out on your own) on your HTML page.

Click the Generate Table radio button to have your slices arranged in a table. The other pull-down menus that accompany this option allow you to control whether or not the Table Width and Height are included in the coding, and what Photoshop should do with any empty spaces.

## Background

If you know how graphics work in HTML (and if you don't you can skip this section), then you are aware that the background graphic works differently than other graphics do. The background graphic doesn't appear just once, but instead, starting in the upper left corner, will tile downward and to the right infinitely, covering your entire browser window. Use this dialog box, shown in Color Figure 2 to set your image as a background by clicking the Background radio button.

## Saving Files

The Saving Files dialog box, shown in Color Figure 2, looks the most intimidating, but is really rather simple. The File Naming section at the top gives maybe a little too much control over how you name each slice, using eight individual pull-down menus to decide how you want to name them. Choose from Slice name; file name; a bunch of month, day, and year configurations; a few symbols; and so forth until you come up with the perfect naming convention for your files. The final pull-down menu gives you the option to use either uppercase or lowercase file extensions.

**Some servers where your web files reside might be case-sensitive. In general, you're usually better off choosing a lowercase file extension.**

The most important part of the Optimized Files area is the part that allows you to name the folder into which your images will be placed.

## Slices

The Slices options allow you to work with individual slices if you have made them in Photoshop. However, as I mention during other portions of this book, although creating slices is convenient, you're better off creating them in ImageReady, so we won't really look into this until Chapter 8.

# Settings

This is the heart of the Save for Web dialog box—the place where all the action is. Click on one of the quadrants in the preview window (except the original in the upper left). The black border around the image tells you that that image will be affected by any impending changes. Click on the Settings pull-down menu to access a number of GIF or JPEG presets to apply to that particular quadrant. The image will change accordingly, as will all of the information in the Settings area and the information listed in the preview window for that particular quadrant.

The variables in the Settings area will change depending on which preset you choose. If you decide not to use a preset optimization, or you change any of the preset variables, the Settings pull-down menu will read Unnamed.

# The Optimize Menu

The Optimize menu only has a couple of things to choose from, but one of them, the Optimize to full size, is especially powerful:

## Save or Delete Settings

This is fairly straightforward. If you have a configuration of settings that you are happy with, and you think that at some point in the future you may benefit from using those same settings again, you might want to save them. Once saved, you can access them via the Settings pull-down menu.

Similarly, if you have saved settings you know you will never use again, or you want to delete some of the Photoshop presets that have come with the program, you can choose the Delete Setting option.

## Optimize to File Size

This is the feature in this menu to write home about. Choosing this option opens the dialog box shown in Color Figure 2. In the Desired File Size value box, enter the file size (measured in K), that you would like your completed image to be. Then decide which settings you would like to start with. Starting with your current setting, Photoshop will at the very least keep some of the options you have chosen, such as the desired format. This option, however, will do the best that it can, but in cases where your desired file size is not possible given the starting parameters, it will come as close as it can without hitting the target.

Choosing Auto Select GIF/JPEG allows Photoshop to have complete control over the format and other optimization choices, giving you a better shot at achieving your desired file size goal.

Once you optimize to a certain file size, you cannot go back to the setting you had before. There is no Undo button in this function. While you could save your settings as described previously, the more efficient way is simply to hold down the Option (Alt in Windows) key before trying to Optimize to File Size. Holding the Option (Alt) button will change the OK button in the dialog box to a Remember button. Click Remember to temporarily save the current settings. If you do not like the results achieved when you Optimize to File Size, you can recover the previous setting by again clicking the Option (Alt) key. The Cancel button in the dialog box will change to a Reset button. Click Reset to revert back to your previous settings.

## Repopulate Views

Choose this when you want to start from scratch, and have Photoshop provide optimization values for all quadrants in the Save as Web dialog box.

# The GIF Settings

If you do not choose a preset, you can decide on a format by selecting any of the choices in the Format pull-down menu (the top left pull-down menu in the Settings area).

Color Figure 2 shows the Settings area when the file format chosen is a GIF. Naturally, these settings are different than what would appear if the Format pull-down menu were set for JPEG. We'll look at the Settings that are available for GIF first in the following sections.

## Color Reduction Algorithm

This lets you choose the palette for your image. Choose from a number of different palette options:

◆ *System (Windows or Macintosh)*

Will use either the Windows or Macintosh default 8-bit color palette, respectively. Based on a uniform sampling of RGB colors, it could be a good choice if you're creating an intranet that will only be seen on one platform.

◆ *Web*

Saves your image with the browser-safe web colors. Described in greater detail earlier in this chapter, the browser-safe color palette consists of 256 colors, and will most often be seen as you intended by both Netscape and Internet Explorer web browsers.

◆ *Adaptive*

A popular method, and my personal favorite, the adaptive method does an excellent job of analyzing your image and assembling a palette consisting of the best possible colors. This choice will give you the best possible results with the least amount of work on your part. Although this one will cost you the most in terms of file size, you'll want to use it when working with photographic or other continuous-tone image work that originally contained more than 256 colors.

◆ *Custom*

The custom method lets you use your own palette for your image. The menu in the Swatches palette allows you to save swatches for later use, and the custom method in the Index Color dialog box allows you to choose any saved color palette.

◆ *Previous*

This feature lets you use the same palette on multiple images. It cannot be accessed unless you have already converted an image using either the adaptive or custom method.

## *Dithering Algorithm*

If you look at a printed piece through a loupe (a small magnifying glass), you can see that the cyan, magenta, yellow, and black are printed in certain patterns, too small for the human eye to see without help. The patterns and close proximity of the colors create an illusion of other colors that are not printed. Photoshop uses the limitations of the human eye to do this with index color palettes as well. When 256 colors are not enough to accurately represent your image, Photoshop will use its dither feature to create the illusion of a color in graphics consisting of various hues.

The Index Color dialog box gives you the option of turning the dither feature on or off. You'll have to judge for yourself when dithering is appropriate. If your image is made up of just a few colors, it may not be necessary and may cause your file to grow unnecessarily large in file size. Additionally, if you are using large blocks of colors, as shown in Figure 2–2, dithering may have a negative effect on the overall appearance. Conversely, dithering is a definite must if you are indexing an image with a wide tonal range, multiple color hues, or subtle shading. Figure 2–3 shows the difference between dithering and not dithering images that require it.

In addition to the standard dithering options, the new Noise dither has been included in version 6. The Noise dither creates a random pattern, without diffusing the pattern across neighboring pixels.

**In the next section we'll explore slicing images into segments. When optimizing any one portion of a sliced graphic, using a diffusion dither can make the seams between segments very apparent. To the seam effect in this scenario, choose Noise.**

*Figure 2–2: Dithering doesn't work well with large blocks of color. The left image is the original, red text on a yellow background, in RGB. The right image is the result of indexing the colors, using the Web palette, and a diffusion dither.*

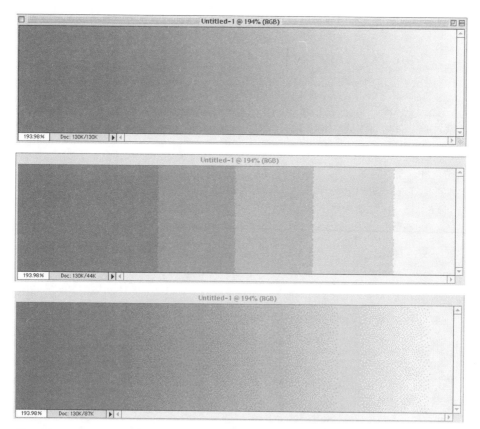

*Figure 2–3: Top image: shows an extreme gradient in its original TIF format.*
*Center Image: Index Color, Web palette, no dithering.*
*Bottom Image: Index Color, Web palette, diffusion dithering.*

## Transparency

If you have made a portion of your image transparent by using any of the methods discussed later in this book, click this checkbox to activate the transparency. If this area is not checked, whatever color is chosen in the Matte option (discussed in just a few moments), will fill in the areas that were made transparent. This color is white by default.

## Interlacing Images to Relieve Web Frustration

Graphics on a Web site can download in two ways: annoying and not annoying. The annoying way has them downloading from the top downward, making the user wait until it's completely finished before deciding whether or not the image is important. The not annoying way is called interlacing. Interlacing, in a nonscientific description, allows the image to appear as a whole immediately, but very blurry. As it downloads, it becomes more clear, so that the user can tell more quickly whether or not they want to wait for the full picture. Figure 2–4 shows an illustration of how an interlaced GIF appears in a browser.

Click the Interlace option to allow your GIF image to interlace. It'll add a few seconds to the download time, but it's worthwhile.

*Figure 2–4: Interlaced GIFs load gradually.*

## Lossy

A brand-new algorithm that Adobe created for this version, the Lossy slider allows you to compress your GIF file to reduce your file size by up to 50% (sometimes even more!). It does this by eliminating repetitious and unnecessary colors from your image. Obviously, there is a point on the slider when you are eliminating too many colors, and there will be an unwanted deterioration, but often you can compress up to 15% before seeing any real effect at all.

**The Lossy slider is not available when either the Noise or Pattern Dither algorithm has been chosen, or when your image will be Interlaced.**

## Colors

As described earlier, reducing the number of colors will also reduce the size of your image, but will also reduce the quality. Play with the value to use as few colors as possible without taking away too much quality from your image. Clicking on one of the small arrows in this area will reduce the value one digit at a time, or use the pull-down menu for values associated with different bit depths. Or, as with any value area, you can enter a numeric value manually.

## Dither

The Dither control allows you to place a value anywhere between 0%–100% when your selected Dither method is the Diffusion algorithm. Previous versions of Photoshop only allowed you to have the Dithering on (100%) or off (0%). Now you can decide for yourself how much Dithering will occur. The closer to 100% that you choose, the higher your file size will be (but also the clearer your image will be).

## Matte

If you have transparency in your image, and the Transparency checkbox is not clicked, the Matte color will replace the transparent areas with the selected colors. If the Transparency checkbox is clicked, the Matte color you choose will place a thin border of your selected color around the edges of your images. Choose the same color as your web page background to help your image blend in more easily, or choose None from the Matte pull-down menu to not use any colors at all.

## Web Snap

The new Web Snap slider works in conjunction with the Color table, which we'll explore later in this chapter. Use this to help control browser dither. Although we've already helped to control the Photoshop dither by choosing the appropriate algorithm and the dither percentage, the Web Snap feature allows you to control the amount of browser dither. Photoshop dither allows you to arrange the colors so that the eye is tricked into seeing more colors than are otherwise available in an 8-bit image. Browser dither, however, occurs when the web user is seeing your site with an 8-bit monitor (256 colors), and the browser will try to simulate the colors as best as it can, usually with unwanted results. By taking advantage of the web-safe color palette (discussed earlier), you can ward off harmful browser dither. Pulling the Web Snap slider to 100% will force all of your colors to shift to web-safe colors. It won't affect your file size or download time, but it will have an effect on the way your image displays. More on this topic will be discussed later, when we explore the Color table.

# The JPEG Settings

Figure 2–1 shows the settings area if the chosen format is JPEG.

## Compression Quality

Use this pull-down menu to choose the amount of compression for your image quickly. The higher the compression quality, the better your image will be (because more colors will be preserved), and the higher your corresponding file size will be. Notice that as you change the Compression Quality setting (Low, Medium, High, or Maximum), the numeric value in the Quality slider (discussed later in this section), also changes. Typically a middle-of-the-road approach is the way to go with this option, but, as always, it depends on the individual image.

## Progressive

Click this checkbox to make your image downloads much like an interlaced GIF. Instead of downloading one line at a time from top to bottom, the image will appear in your user's browser all at once, but very blurry. The image will clear up little by little through a number of scans. This will allow your user to get the feeling for what the picture is rather quickly and decide sooner whether or not it is an image that is vital to look at, or whether he or she can bypass it and move on to another page.

This option will add a little bit of weight to your file size and increase download time (look at how the information in the preview window changes when this box is clicked or not). Also, keep in mind that not every browser can read Progressive JPEG's, so be prepared to alienate at least part of your audience by clicking this box.

The Progressive option must be used in conjunction with the Optimize option, discussed later. Turning one on automatically turns on the other.

## ICC Profile

Although this book goes into color management systems to an extent, I fully cover establishing color space and the ICC profile in my second book, *Digital Publishing To Go*. That's because, this has been primarily a printing concern. Basically, the ICC (International Color Consortium) profile format assists you in recreating the same colors in your image from one platform to another, to various output devices, or from one ICC-compliant application to another (such as when you move images between different Adobe products).

For a more detailed look at how to set up the color space (this is not necessary, just an available option), you might just want to leaf through the book I just told you about. Don't get offended—I'm not trying to get you to buy another book … chances are you're sitting in the Barnes and Nobles café reading this one for free, anyway, so all you have to do is read the other one for free as well. If you do establish a color profile, and want it to be attached to the image, simply click on the ICC Profile checkbox, but anticipate an increase in download time for your image.

## Optimized

Click on this checkbox to enhance your image but also reduce your file size. This can be especially helpful if you are using a high compression quality setting.

**The effects you'll see by clicking on the Optimize checkbox will usually be minimal, and some browsers may not read this type of image. In my opinion, unless you know for sure that it will be viewed on a certain browser, you'd be safer to leave it unchecked.**

## Quality

Click the small arrow on the right of the number field to access the Image Quality slider, or fill in your own value manually. A higher value will maintain the detail in your image, but reduce the amount of compression, with the result being a higher file size. A low compression will significantly reduce the image detail and quality, but will provide great compression, so that your file size and download time will both be low.

The nice thing about this feature being part of the Save for Web dialog box is that you can see in real-time how the various compressions will affect your image. Before version 5.5, you couldn't visibly see how different compression values were affecting your image without closing and reopening the image. With this dialog box, you not only see the results immediately, but can set two quadrants to two different compression settings to compare and contrast one against the other.

## *Blur*

By blurring a JPEG image, you can reduce the number of colors, and thereby reduce both the file size and download time. Like the Quality option, Blur allows you to fill in a numeric value, or access a slider through the small arrow on the right-hand side.

While blurring your image in the name of file size reduction is a good idea, I'm not excited about the limitations of having to blur the entire image at once.

Much of the photography that you will use in your Web pages will contain a main subject, surrounded by supporting data. Figure 2–5 shows my original picture of a man and a woman sitting in what appears to be a hay field or a hay truck. They are obviously the main subjects of the image and everything surrounding them is necessary for the idea behind the picture but should not be in focus.

Figure 2–5 is the picture in its original state, saved as a JPEG with a quality compression setting of 8, saved as Baseline (Standard) for a resulting file size of 140K. However, when I make a selection around everything but the two people, feather it with a feather radius of 2, and apply a Gaussian Blur (choose Filter -> Blur -> Gaussian Blur) with a blur radius of 2, the resulting file size is only 120K. Comparing this picture with the original shows a negligible difference in photo quality—Figure 2–6 shows the slight blur on everything but the people, reducing the size to 120K. Apply an additional blur of 1 to the entire image and the file is reduced even more, down to 100K (Figure 2–7) with still very little visible difference to the image quality.

You'll notice that the Save for Web dialog box gives you an option for blurring your image before saving it as a JPEG. This will blur your entire image, not just the background area. I'd recommend doing your blurs manually before choosing Save for Web.

## *Matte*

As we'll review in an upcoming chapter, the techniques used for creating transparency in an image have been radically changed with the inclusion of the new masking tools that appeared in Photoshop 5.5.

JPEGs, though, as I said earlier, don't support transparency. If your image has any transparent portions, use the Matte option to access the Color Picker and choose which color will appear in place of the transparent portions. You'll likely want to use the same color that you are using for the background of your web site.

Since JPEGs don't support transparency, you're probably better off filling in the transparent areas before you save the image for the web.

*Figure 2–5: The original picture saved as a JPEG with a quality of 8 has a file size of 140K.*

*Figure 2–6: By blurring the background slightly, the file size is reduced to 120K, with no major quality loss detectable.*

*Figure 2–7: File size is reduced further to 100K when the blur is expanded to include the main subjects.*

# Lower Tabs

There are two other tabs in this dialog box beyond the tab that changes the preview windows. These are located below the Settings area, and they allow you to manipulate and review both the size and Color table of your image.

## *Image Size Tab*

One of the two tabs below the Settings area, the Image Size tab, shown up-close in Figure 2–1, is yet another great addition to this "everything but the kitchen sink" dialog box. As you've probably guessed, this tab will let you resize your image, with a more streamlined version of the main Image Size dialog box. In the Image Size tab, you can change the width and height of your image, but not the resolution. With the Constrain Proportions checkbox clicked on, changing either the width or the height will change the other proportionately.

You can also change the size by percentage (50% of its current size, for example), and decide through the Quality pull-down menu how the image resize should be accomplished. The options here are:

◆ *Bicubic* for the smoothest but slowest resize

◆ *Bilinear* for the fastest, but not quite as smooth, resize

◆ *Nearest neighbor* to let Photoshop delete or duplicate pixels as it feels necessary

Keep in mind that, like the Zoom and Hand tools in this dialog box, any image resizing that you do will happen in all quadrants, and not just the one currently selected.

## *Color Table Tab*

The Color Table tab, shown up-close in Color Figure 2, displays all the colors that comprise your GIF image. Unlike working with color in earlier versions of Photoshop, working with this Color table allows you a lot more flexibility.

**For the purposes of interest only, I'll go into how the Color table works, but as I had mentioned earlier, manipulating colors for the sake of low resolution monitors or to save a few K in file size isn't really worth the effort. In most cases, the colors that Photoshop chooses for GIF images are more than fine.**

### Sorting Colors

How you view the colors in the table is completely up to your discretion. Depending on what is easiest for you, you can sort image colors by hue, luminance (lightness/brightness), or popularity (frequency of color in your image). You choose how to sort the colors from the Color table menu, located under the black arrow in the upper right of the table.

### Adding Colors

If your image fewer than 256 colors, you may add colors that you feel were left out or are necessary to complete your image. To add a color to your image:

1. Choose the Eyedropper tool (from within the Save for Web dialog box, not the standard Tool palette).

2. Select a color that you want to add by clicking on the color in your image.

3. Choose New Color from the Color table menu.

4. The new color will appear in the palette. Its position will depend on how you have chosen to sort your colors. The small white square with the red middle that appears in the lower right corner tells you that that color is locked. (Locking colors is described later in this section.)

### Selecting, Editing, and Changing Colors

There might be times when you want to change the colors that appear in your image. To begin this, start by selecting the color or colors that you wish to change:

◆ With the Eyedropper tool, click a color in your image. The corresponding color swatch in the Color table will indicate that it has been selected with a white border.

◆ Click the desired color in the Color table. Hold the Shift key down to and select another color. All colors in between will be selected as well. To select two or more colors without the colors in between being selected, make your selections while holding the Command (Ctrl in Windows) key.

◆ Choose Select All Colors from the Color table pull-down menu.

◆ To select all web-safe colors that appear in the table, choose Select All Web Safe Colors from the pull-down menu, or choose Select All Non-Web Safe Colors for the opposite selection.

To change a color in your image, double-click on the selected color to access the Color Picker. Select a color from the picker to replace the selected colors in your Color table. Each new color appears in the table with a tiny black diamond in the center.

### Locking Colors

In attempting to reduce the file size of your GIF, you may try to reduce the number of colors in your image. However, there may be certain colors that you do not want to be eliminated from your image. In these cases, you can lock certain colors to ensure that they will be preserved.

To lock a color:

1. Use the methods described earlier in this section to select one or more colors that you want to lock.
2. Click the Lock icon (the second from the left at the bottom of the Color table—it looks like a lock) or choose Lock/Unlock Selected Colors from the Table menu.
3. A small white square with a red center will appear in the lower right of the locked colors.

### Deleting Colors

Deleting colors that are of minimal importance or are completely unnecessary will help reduce the file size of your image. When you delete a color from your GIF, however, two things will occur:

1. The deleted color will be replaced in your image by the nearest color available in the existing color palette.
2. The palette will automatically change to Custom. If you change the palette back to Adaptive, Perceptual, or Selective, the deleted color will be replaced.

To delete a color, simply select the color in the Color table, and either click on the Trash icon at the bottom of the table or choose Delete Color from the table pull-down menu.

## Saving an Image With Slices

Because you can slice up an image in Photoshop now using the same slice tool that originally appeared in ImageReady, Adobe obviously had to provide a way to optimize each slice individually.

But as I'll mention in other areas throughout this book, slicing your images is best left to ImageReady, due to the fact that optimizing each slice is easier, faster, and provides for animation and rollover states. Because of this, I'm not going to bother with detail about how to save images with slices in Photoshop. You'll be better off doing it in ImageReady. Chapter 8 describes this process in further detail.

## And Rounding Up the Features...

Some helpful features are added to the bottom of the dialog box, which will help make your design creation a bit more convenient.

### *Magnification*

Enter a magnification value manually in the text area, or click the small arrow on the right to access the slider. This will change the zoom levels of all quadrants at once.

## Info Bar

The Info Bar gives you information regarding the RGB and hexadecimal color values of any individual pixel.

## Browser Options

This pull-down menu will open your image in the browser of your choice, so that you can see automatically what your image will look like in various browsers before taking the final step and saving your image.

**You have to have the browsers actually installed on your system. Photoshop does not come with either Netscape or Internet Explorer, so if you don't have these in your system already, you won't be able to view your images on them.**

# Saving the Image

When you are content with the settings you have chosen, click in the quadrant of your choice and click OK to access the dialog box shown in Figure 2–1. This is your standard Save As function, with one slight twist—there is a small checkbox at the bottom of the dialog box marked Save HTML File. Click this checkbox, and Photoshop will include with the image an HTML code that you can paste into your own HTML pages. This is a very convenient way of getting the program to write a few lines of otherwise tedious code.

# SUMMARY

There have been tons of changes in both the way the web works and the way Photoshop deal with graphics for the web. We're still just in the second inning of this game, but so far it looks like the real winner is the designer. Photoshop has made working with web graphics easier, and the advancements seen in the web have given designers more room to play and be creative. Setting the file sizes and adhering to a lowest common denominator may still seem like a laborious chore compared to the actual creation process, but if it has to be done, be thankful that it has not nearly as bad as it used to be.

# chapter 3

# TRANSPARENCY

## NOW YOU SEE IT, NOW YOU DON'T

How useful would it be if you had the ability to make unimportant things suddenly disappear? By one touch, any undesirable thing in your life would no longer hold any significance or be in your way? Credit card bills, toxic waste, mimes, and children who cry on airplanes would suddenly vanish as the world breathed a sigh of relief, wondering whether we could get rid of Barbra Streisand records just as easily.

I'm sorry—I got lost in a personal daydream. Obviously, these things can't happen. To better illustrate my point on transparency, I'll provide a better example:

See that white space directly above? Well, it's not really white space—it's a transparent paragraph. I wrote it, but decided that because it was boring and unnecessary to the rest of this chapter, I'd make it transparent. It's still there, but you can see the white of the page in its place. I've saved myself the cost of the ink that would have been used to print it, and it is no longer able to detract from my primary message.

Transparency on the Web works in much the same way—you make a portion of your image vanish, so it is no longer visible. It will still act as a placeholder, but, like my transparent paragraph saved the cost of the ink I would have used to print it, transparent portions of my Web graphics save me the cost of large file sizes, and they help my images download faster.

As we discussed in detail in Chapter 2, however, time marches on and things change. The properties of transparency still hold true, but do they have any real value? As a tool to reduce file size, they are only beneficial in certain cases. For example, Chapter 4, which deals with backgrounds, will use transparency to significantly reduce excess file size from tiled backgrounds when creating borders or sidebars. But it's no longer as important when dealing with removing a few small areas of flat color in individual images. Let's say that you could save 10K of file size in an image by making a color transparent. Well, a year or two ago, most designers wouldn't create a page that was heavier than 100K, at the most. Saving 10K meant saving a minimum of 10%, or more in a lot of cases. That's pretty significant. But today, it's not unusual or detrimental for a page to be 300K or even more. Cutting 10K of file size, in that case, only saves you a small percentage. Not really worth the effort.

But there is always the case where you'll want something behind the image to show through your image in certain places. Say, for example, you have a picture of a soccer ball on a white canvas, but want the green grass color of the web browser background to surround the ball—a soccer ball in a big white square over a field of green isn't very attractive. Making the white background transparent in this instance is necessary for effect. So while the reasons for using transparency on the web may have decreased a little, they haven't "disappeared" completely (get it? Disappeared? Transparency? Well, I thought it was funny, anyway).

# TRANSPARENCY MADE EASY

It wasn't that long ago that making a portion of an image transparent was kind of a chore, involving a now-outdated dialog box called GIF89a. Since Photoshop 5.5, though, there are a number of ways that we can create transparency in our images, all of which are a lot easier and more effective than earlier transparency solutions. Now, the only reason you might ever open the GIF89a dialog box again would be strictly for nostalgia … kind of like playing an old Donny and Marie album, just to torture yourself with bad memories of the past.

The new tools for transparency creation, the magic eraser, the Background eraser, and the Extract function, each help make transparent desired portions of your image which can later be translated for direct web use in the Save for Web dialog box.

*Figure 3–1: The Magic eraser tool at work. The sky in the image on the right has been made transparent. (By default, the transparent areas will appear as a checker board.)*

# The Magic Eraser

The Magic eraser, shown in Figure 3–1, works just like the Magic Wand tool, with one distinct difference: Instead of creating a selection of certain pixels, it makes those pixels transparent. Simply click on a pixel of any color you choose, and all contiguous pixels (by default) within a certain shade of that color will become transparent. Figure 3–1 demonstrates this.

The Options palette for the Magic eraser tool, shown in Figure 3–2, allows you to manipulate how the tool works. Access the Options palette as you would for any other tool by double-clicking on that tool, or by simply selecting the tool and hitting the Return key (Enter in Windows). Click on the Contiguous checkbox to keep the erased pixels contiguous to the selected pixel. Click it off to allow non-contiguous pixels of the same or similar shades to be erased.

You can also manipulate how many shades of the selected color will be affected. Set the tolerance by manually entering a value in the Options palette to make your transparent area smaller or larger. A small value, say 10, in the tolerance area will mean that when any pixel is clicked on, the only pixels that will become transparent will be those that fall within 10 shades of that particular color. A higher number will allow more pixels to be affected.

*Figure 3–2: The Magic eraser Options palette.*

*Figure 3–3: The Options palette for the Background eraser.*

 Even though this is an eraser tool, you do not need to worry about a brush size—this is a point-and-click tool, and you will only be clicking on one pixel at a time.

## The Background Eraser

The Background eraser, also new as of version 5.5 and shown in Figure 1–1, works much like the Magic eraser if it were crossed with the Airbrush tool. To make an area of your image become transparent with the Background eraser, simply select your desired brush size and drag your mouse over the areas of your image that you wish to make transparent. It's just as simple as that, really. There is a cool twist, though—a small center point in the middle of your Background eraser brush will determine the color of the pixel you click on. As you drag around your image, pixels of that same color will also become transparent.

The Option palette for the Background eraser, shown in Figure 3–3, allows you to choose which type of eraser you want to use:

◆ Find Edges will help maintain the integrity of the edges of an object, while erasing contiguous areas of the same color.

◆ Contiguous will erase all areas in an image that contain the selected colors that are next to each other.

◆ Discontiguous erases all areas in an image that contain the selected colors. These areas do not have to be next to each other or touching.

*Figure 3–4: The result of using the Background eraser on my image.*

The Tolerance slider works the same way that it does in the Magic Wand tool. The higher the tolerance, the more color tones will be eliminated based on the selected color.

You can also choose Protect Foreground to make sure that any areas in your image that contain the foreground color will not be erased.

Figure 3–4 shows the result of using the Background eraser tool.

## Extract Image

This cool feature was introduced in version 5.5, and it gives you better masking control to create transparency in hard-to-define areas, such as around hair, fur, etc. It's a good tool, and helpful, but, well ... you know how the hamburger that you actually get served never really looks *quite* as good as the picture of it in the menu? Well, it's kind of the same thing here. The advertisements and magazine reviews make it look like this is an infallible way to make a good mask, but it can take a few tries to get it right for any particular image.

To use the Extract Image command, follow these steps:

1. With your file open, choose Image -> Extract to access the dialog box shown in Figure 3–5.

2. Make the Edge Highlighter tool active by clicking on it. The Edge Highlighter tool works just like the Paintbrush tool—just drag your cursor to create a stroke. However, with this tool, you're not as much applying paint as you are isolating an edge.

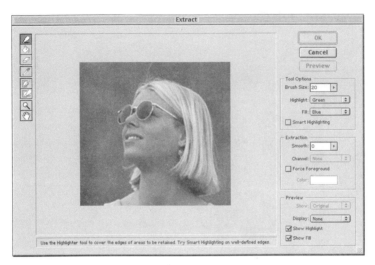

*Figure 3–5: The Extract dialog box.*

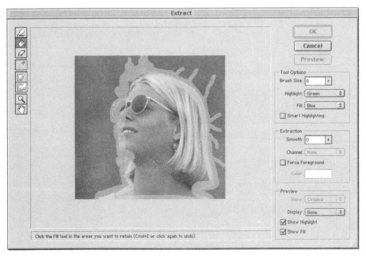

*Figure 3–6: The Edge Highlighter tool is used to trace around the image. I used a larger brush for the main area, and small brushes for the wisps of her hair.*

3. Create an edge around the object you want to extract—remember, everything outside your edge will become transparent. If necessary, you can increase or decrease your brush size by adjusting the Brush Size slider on the right (sorry—no Brushes palette here!). Figure 3–6 illustrates this task.

For very hard-to-define edges, such as those shown in the figures for this example, select a fairly large size brush, and create your edge outline so that the highlight color overlaps both the image that you want to extract and the background that you want to make transparent.

4. You can change the color of your highlight by selecting from the Highlight pull-down menu. Red, green, and blue are available as presets, or you can access the Color Picker by choosing Other. Once you have created a highlight around the entire edge, activate the Fill tool (the same paintbucket icon that appears in the regular toolbar). Fill the inside of your edge selection by clicking on it. Make sure that the edge is completely closed before you click, or you will fill your entire canvas.

You can edit either the fill or the edge highlight by using the Eraser tool. You can start over from scratch, too, by holding the Option (Alt in Windows) key, and pushing the Reset button (formally the Cancel button).

5. You can change the fill color by using the Fill pull-down menu. Decide how precise you would like your extraction to be by changing the Smooth slider in the Extraction area. Choose a lower number for less precision, and a higher number for greater precision (although this will take a few moments longer to complete).

6. Click the Preview button to see your extracted piece. Cool, huh? Figure 3–7 shows a sample of what this should look like.

You might notice that the Preview button is grayed out and not available until you fill your selection. If you would like to make an extraction of just the highlighted area (I'm sure that with six billion people in the world, *somebody* will find a reason to do this), click the Force Foreground button. The color that is chosen in the accompanying color display will be the color in the highlight that is retained. Click this display to access the Color Picker, or make a direct selection using the Eyedropper tool and selecting a color from your image.

7. To see your edge highlight and fill again, click the appropriate checkboxes to make each appear. Re-edit if necessary.

8. By default, the transparent areas will appear as a checkerboard. You can change this by selecting a Matte color from the Show pull-down menu (customize your color in the Color Picker by choosing Other, or see your results as they would be represented in a channel by choosing Mask).

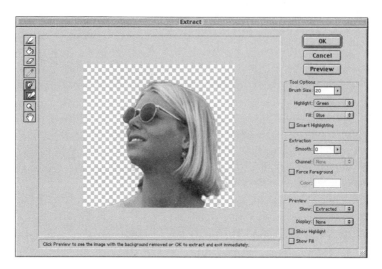

*Figure 3–7: My image when the extraction has been made.*

9. To go back to your original image, choose Original from the View pull-down menu. Return to the extraction by selecting Extracted from the same menu.

10. If you already have a selection saved as an alpha channel, you can use this as a starting point, by loading it from the Load Highlight pull-down menu.

11. Click OK when you are happy with your extraction.

### Setting Transparency for the Web

After you've used one or more of these tools to create your transparency, you'll be able to save it that way for web use through the Save for Web dialog box that we reviewed in Chapter 2. Choose GIF for your desired format (GIF is the only format other than the rarely used PNG that supports transparency), then click the Transparency box to turn the transparency on. If you want to create a smoother transition from your image into the browser's background color, set the Matte option to your desired color by clicking on it and choosing a color from the pop-up menu.

# SHADOWS, GLOWS, AND TRANSPARENCY

There are some who claim to have developed fairly elaborate methods of preserving shadows and glows when they are part of a transparent GIF. The truth is, however, that there is really just one basic rule that must be followed: Put your shadowed or glowing image or the average color of your background texture over your background color and hope for the best.

*Figure 3–8: Placing images or text with drop shadows or glows over patterned backgrounds creates a pretty ugly effect.*

This kind of "dirty" look, as shown in Figure 3–8, may be partially to blame for a severe decrease in both multicolored, wallpapered backgrounds, as well as the number of drop shadows that appear on the web (that, and the possibility that somewhere along the line, designers developed a sense of taste).

# SUMMARY

If you take a look at my earlier book on Photoshop 5, you'll see that just a couple of years ago, creating transparent files was far more of a chore. New tools introduced in Photoshop 5.5, as well as an improvement of style in general web creation, have made transparency on the web a little easier to deal with, even if you won't necessarily need to use it all that much.

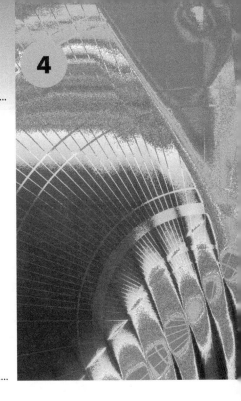

# chapter 4

## CREATING BACKGROUND GRAPHICS AND EFFECTS

While the web has gone through a lot of changes, one of the most visibly noticeable is probably the backgrounds of many sites. For a long time, hideous wallpapered backgrounds plagued the web with as much class as a Jersey diner. But as designers became more sophisticated, so did the Internet, and today it's pretty rare to find very many sites with any type of background at all. Savvy web developers and marketers have come to understand that the most important part of a web site is legibility and that users come to a site to find information, not to marvel at the great Photoshop work that went into creating a background or elaborate border design.

That being said, most backgrounds in modern web times tend to be either flat colors or, at the most, a very plain, flat border either on the left side or toward the top. But having anything on the site that gets in the way of the content is a definite taboo, and although you never can tell when the pendulum will swing back and retro designs will be back in fashion (even bell bottoms made a brief reappearance in the late 1990s), it doesn't look like the trend toward ease of use and readability is going to die anytime soon.

So use this chapter as an overview to more modern backgrounds, the importance they play in a web site, and how to use Photoshop to make them work with your site ... or at least make sure they don't work against your site.

# HOW BACKGROUNDS WORK IN A BROWSER

Whether you are doing your own hard coding of a site, or putting your site together with DreamWeaver or even ImageReady, there are a few basic, universal rules that apply to background graphics. It'd be a good idea to keep these in mind when setting up your site, just like it'd be a good idea to have at least a rudimentary knowledge of HTML, even if you are using a WYSIWYG program to put the site together for you.

**The "universal" truths that follow are for using 2D graphics saved as either JPEGs or GIFs. Images that are created in other programs and saved as different formats may not adhere to traditional rules of background images. Applications like FLASH or Shockwave, or sites that are created in DHTML and use layers, often work differently.**

◆ The background image and/or color is set in the <BODY> tag. If you're using an image as part or all of your background, it's the only image that is referenced in this tag, and there can only be one.

◆ The background image is the only image that can be connected to the browser window. All other images will usually come no closer than about 15–20 pixels from the edge of the browser window.

◆ The background can't be animated.

◆ Backgrounds don't print. So if your background color or image is dark, and you use white lettering, people who try to print your page will print white text on white paper. In other words, they'll get a blank sheet. Solve this by adding a link to a printable version, where just the text is presented in black on a white background.

◆ Background images don't appear only once in the browser window. Instead, the image is placed in the top leftmost corner of the window, and tiled (repeated) infinitely down and to the right.

It used to be that that last point played a major role in how sites appeared. When it was more common to have a wallpaper background (in which an image was manipulated in Photoshop a certain way as to look like a seamless, larger image in the browser window due to the tiling), designers needed to be careful how they created their designs. It was usually time-consuming enough just to make the image appear without seams when tiled together in the browser window. If the right side didn't line up with the left side or the top with the bottom, it was very obvious where the tiles were being created.

At the same time, there was a size issue. If the physical size of the tiled image was too small, the repletion would be too obvious. But if the tile was too large, then the file size would eat up a significant amount of the standard 100K maximum file size for any one page.

As we've seen in Chapter 2, it's no longer necessary to keep the file size of a page that low anymore. Bandwidth speeds have increased, and there can be more flexibility. But style and taste have changed enough that the extra file size considerations really don't matter much in terms of backgrounds.

# CREATING VARIOUS BACKGROUNDS

OK, so the style of the web has changed. Designers have gotten more "sophisticated" and most sites don't really have anything in the background. At most, they'll use a left or upper border to help organize certain information. But does that make it right to discuss wallpaper backgrounds as though we had just recently discovered them while on an archaeological dig? Trends change, and while it doesn't seem that the intrusive backgrounds of a few years ago are poised to make a comeback anytime soon, it'd be wrong to say that there will never be a use for them again, or that there aren't still some sites floating around out there today that make use of more colorful backgrounds than those to which we're accustomed.

So, in fairness, I'll use this section to show an example of how to create a wallpapered background, a tiled border background, and how to change the color of a background without any images at all. After that, we'll take a look at a few modern sites, and see how they treat their backgrounds. Determining what to put there will be explored in more detail in Chapter 4, when we walk through the building of a whole web site, from beginning to end.

## Saving Files as Backgrounds

When you create any of the following (or other) images for use in a web browser, use one of these two methods for saving the file:

1. If you are going to use a program like DreamWeaver to build your site, then use then Save for Web command that we reviewed in Chapter 2 to save your image as a GIF, the put the background together in the construction program of your choice. This is also the way you would save your file if you were going to hard code the site yourself.

2. If you want to stay with Photoshop and ImageReady then, with your image still open, push the button at the very bottom of your toolbar to launch ImageReady (using ImageReady will be reviewed in more detail in Chapter 8). Within ImageReady, choose File -> Output Settings -> Background. In the dialog box that opens, choose the radio button marked Background, and hit OK. Then choose File -> Save Optimized As, and name your file.

You'll want to Optimize your image first, the method for which is very similar in ImageReady to the way it is done in Photoshop's Save for Web dialog box. How it's done will be reviewed further in Chapter 8.

You'll notice that the file extension is not a standard file format, like .jpg or .gif. Instead, it's the .html format. ImageReady will not only save your image in the format that you designate when you optimize it, but it will also write and save the HTML file for you, with the Background tag filled in. Open the HTML file in a browser to see what your background looks like.

## Creating a Seamless Tiled Background

If you are going to create this type of background, let me first advise you to do it more for your own personal use, and not for corporate site development. But more importantly, make sure that the designs you use are subtle. Wallpapered backgrounds can become very intrusive and make type very difficult to read. Remember, people are coming to your site to get information, not to marvel at your Photoshop abilities. Sometimes you say more by saying very little at all.

1. In Photoshop, open a new file, 200 pixels wide and 200 pixels deep.

For all of the images you will be creating for the Web, you'll want to open new documents as RGB images at 72 ppi (pixels per inch) with a white background (unless you will be using black as your background color).

2. With black and white as your respective foreground and background colors, fill your canvas with clouds by choosing Filter -> Render -> Clouds. You now have a canvas filled with clouds, which, if you were to use it as your background, would look something like what you see in Figure 4–1. As you can see, it is very obvious where the seams are.

3. Choose Filter -> Other -> Offset and change the settings so that your clouds are offset 100 pixels to the right and 100 pixels down (half the distance of your canvas in both directions). Make sure you choose Wrap Around. Figure 4–2 shows how this filter changes the clouds picture. The edges in our pictures are now aligned to create a seamless tile, but as you can see in Figure 4–2, the middle of our picture has very apparent lines.

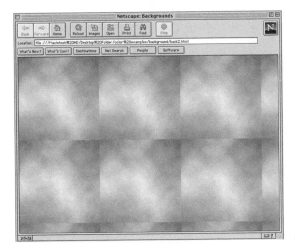

*Figure 4–1: The seams are obvious.*

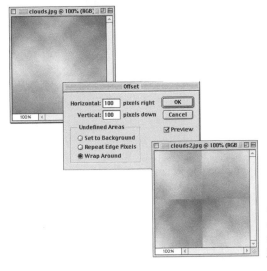

*Figure 4–2: The Offset filter at work. Lines in the center are apparent, although the edges will now wrap properly.*

**4.** Use the Rubber Stamp tool or the Blur tool (or a combination of both) to carefully erase the lines in the middle. Be careful not to touch the edges of the picture. (For more information on these tools and how they work, see Chapter 1.)

**5.** Choose one of the means to save your image described in the previous section.

Your browser window should now look similar to the one in Figure 4–3.

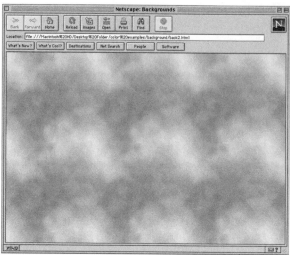

*Figure 4–3: Seamless texture in the browser.*

# USING HEXIDECIMALS TO CREATE A SOLID COLOR BACKGROUND

If corporate web design will be your career, solid color background will probably be the types of backgrounds that you use most often. They're en vogue, and extremely easy to create.

Any color that you can create in the RGB color mode can be used as a web background color. From a programming standpoint, this is done by translating the RGB values for any color or shade into a series of six digits, otherwise known as their hexidecimal value. In Photoshop 5 and earlier, and before the popularization of WYSIWYG programs like DreamWeaver, calculating the hexidecimal value was a bit of a chore. On a Mac, you needed to open a separate Preferences dialog box in the Finder. Windows users had to endure Intro to Calculus flashback while using an extended calculator to determine the values.

Today, there really is nothing to the determination of any hexidecimal value. If you're using a program like DreamWeaver, all you'll need to do is click a small color swatch, pick your desired color, and the program will fill the necessary hex value into the HTML script for you. If you want to figure it out from Photoshop, they've made that easier since version 5.5. As Figure 4–4 shows, the Color Picker has a small box right below the RGB values. This shows the hex value for any color or shade that you choose. It doesn't get more simple.

If you are hard coding your site, just plug the hex value found in the Color Picker into the <Body> tag, like so: <BODY BGCOLOR=#XXXXXX>

And that's all there is to it.

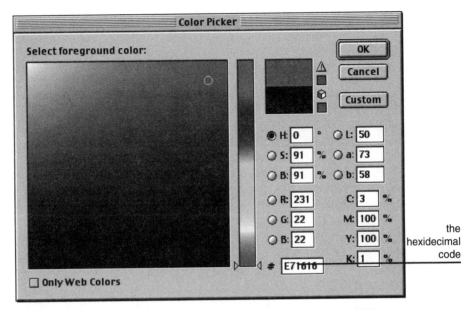

*Figure 4–4: The Color Picker provides the hexidecimal values of any RGB combination.*

# CREATING A TOP BACKGROUND BORDER

As I said earlier, although the trend has been to move away from obtrusive back-grounds, you can still find many instances in which a top or side border is used. They may have become less elaborate over the years, but it remains a convenient way to seg-ment off a site's navigation area, or headline stories, company name, and so forth.

If you understand that backgrounds are tiles in a web browser, how hex values work to create a flat background color, and how transparency (discussed in the last chapter) works, you can combine all of these elements to make a simple border with almost no file size weight.

1. Open a file in Photoshop that is 72 pixels wide and 1,440 pixels deep. Make sure you have the rulers turned on.

2. With the square Marquee tool, start from the top and make a box 72 pixels wide and 72 pixels deep.

3. Choose a color from the Color Picker or the Swatches palette, and fill in your box with that color.

4. Save the image in one of the two ways described in earlier in the section called "Saving Files as Backgrounds."

As we discussed earlier, background images are placed in the upper left corner of the browser window and are tiled infinitely downward and to the right. When you view this image in your browser, you see that this infinite tiling gives you what looks like a border at the top of your browser, similar to the page shown in Figure 4–5.

It's easy to see why the border is created, as the image tiles infinitely to the right. But if it's also tiling infinitely downward, shouldn't we also see the band again at the bottom of the browser? Well, we would, if the page scrolled down long enough. But since the image is 1,440 pixels high, there is little danger of that.

If you do have significant enough scrolling on a page to cause the border to repeat again in an unwanted area, go back to the original image and make the strip even higher by adding more white to the bottom.

## Combining Backgrounds and Hexidecimals: Transparency Factors

With Photoshop's Save for Web feature, you can see that the file size for this graphic is extremely small—measured in bytes! Years ago, when designers created GIFs manually, the file sizes tended to be much larger, and we used transparency (which holds no file weight) to significantly reduce the file size. The idea was to take the white portion of the border image, where most of the pixels are, make them transparent, and use hex values to make the background white. You'd see the white background through the transparent pixels, but still have your color border at the top. The length of the image would be retained, to ensure that you didn't repeat the border at the bottom of the browser window, but the file size of the image would be a fraction of its original size.

Without file size being a worry any longer, is there a need anymore to make the white pixels transparent? Actually, there is. It's more of a convenience reason than anything else. Use the methods described in Chapter 3 (try the Magic eraser tool) to make the white pixels transparent. Use the Save for Web dialog box and, with the Transparency button checked, save your image as a GIF. Use this as your background graphic. Now, using whatever method you want to write the HTML program, you have

*Figure 4–5: A narrow but long background image will tile repeatedly to give the effect of a border at the top of your Web page. By exaggerating the height, you reduce the risk of seeing the border repeat again at the bottom.*

free reign in choosing a background color. If you want to make the home page background white, that's enough. But if you want to make the interior page backgrounds a cream color, it's far easier to change the hex value for those pages than it is to open your background image in Photoshop again, change the white pixels to cream, and resave it under a different name.

# More Interesting Border Effects

Even though the trend has been toward simplicity in backgrounds, who's to say you have to follow the trend? There is a lot more you can do with borders than just a flat color. Try the following examples. Even if you don't use them in your web pages, they may spark some ideas of your own.

## *Creating a Border With Shadows and Ridges*

1. Open a new file 72 pixels by 1,440 pixels.

2. Add two new layers to your image. Do this by first opening the Layers palette by choosing Windows -> Show Layers, or by pushing the F7 button. Figure 4–6 shows that you can quickly create a layer by clicking the Add Layer button at the bottom of the palette. The new layers will automatically be named Layer 1 and Layer 2, respectively, with the newest layer also being the topmost layer.

3. Click on Layer 2 to make it the active layer.

4. Use the Square Marquee tool to make a box about 108 pixels wide, and 72 pixels deep (the entire height of your image).

5. With the Color Picker or the Swatches palette, choose a color you like for your foreground color. Fill the square marquee with this color by pushing Option + Delete (Alt + Backspace in Windows).

6. Make Layer 1 your active layer by clicking on it.

7. With your square still selected, push the right arrow key three or four times to move your selection on Layer 1 to the right of the selection on Layer 2 as shown in Figure 4–7.

8. Feather your selection by choosing Select -> Feather, or by hitting Command + Option + D (Ctrl + Alt + D in Windows). Feathering makes your edges soft instead of hard.

9. Choose to feather your selection by 3 pixels and hit OK.

10. Make black your foreground color and fill your selection with it. Play with the opacity slider to select an opacity that gives it a realistic shadow look. Your image should look similar to the image in Figure 4–8.

11. Now that we have our color field with a shadow under it to give it some depth, we'll put ridges on the edges to make it pop even more. Make Layer 2 your active layer again by clicking on it.

12. Add two new layers the same way you did earlier. These new layers will be at the top of the Layers palette and will be named Layer 3 and Layer 4, respectively. Make Layer 4 the active layer by clicking on it.

13. With the Square Marquee tool, start at the top and make a selection approximately 72 pixels high by 18 pixels wide.

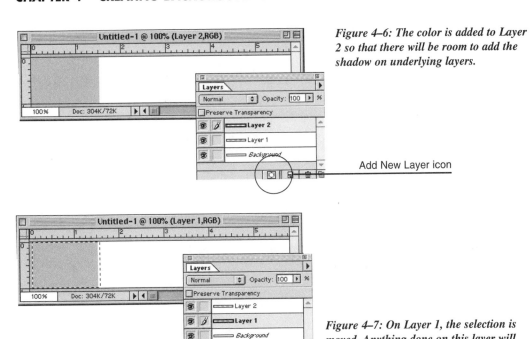

*Figure 4–6: The color is added to Layer 2 so that there will be room to add the shadow on underlying layers.*

Add New Layer icon

*Figure 4–7: On Layer 1, the selection is moved. Anything done on this layer will not affect the green box on Layer 2.*

14. Make black your background color. For your foreground color, use the same color that you used to fill your initial selection. (If you need to recapture that color, use the Eyedropper tool and click anywhere on the field of color in your canvas.)

15. Click on the Gradient tool. As with all other tools in Photoshop 6, the Options palette for the Gradient tool will open automatically at the top of your screen, as shown in Figure 4–9.

16. The available gradient will be, by default, a Foreground to Background gradient. Open the Gradient editor (shown and described in Figure 4–10) by clicking once on the gradient preview in the Options palette.

17. The gradient bar will show a smooth transition from your foreground color to your background color, with arrows (markers) both above and below the gradient preview bar, at either extreme. The arrows on top represent transparency, while the arrows underneath represent solid color.

18. Click on any of the markers to activate it. You'll see that the tip of the marker turns black to show that it is active. Slide the markers along the gradient preview bar to reposition them, and change the overall gradient. If you have activated a Transparency marker (along the top of the bar), you'll have the ability to change the opacity, increasing the transparency of the color in the area. If you have clicked on a Color marker, you can change the color in that area. Do this either by choosing Foreground or Background from the Color pull-down menu (the marker will

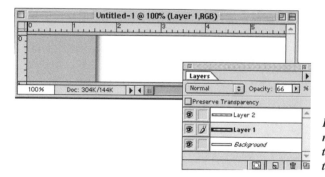

*Figure 4–8: The shadow, made realistic by feathering the selection, adds depth to the border.*

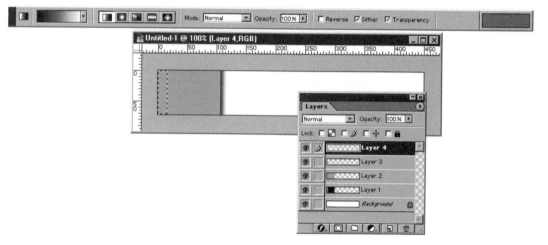

*Figure 4–9: The Gradient tool options palette, shrink up above the canvas. The canvas shows the selection that was last made.*

have a checkerboard in it if you choose either of these options), or customize the color by accessing the Color Picker. You can access the Color Picker either by clicking on the color swatch in the dialog box, or by double-clicking on the marker that is currently activated. The marker will change to whatever color you select.

19. You can add color or transparency by clicking anywhere above (transparency) or below (color) the gradient preview bar just by clicking. This will add a new marker. Add one color as close to the middle of the gradient preview bar as you can. Change all the colors of the available markers until the two extreme markers are black, and the center marker is a medium gray, like the gradient preview bar in Figure 4–10 on the next page.

20. Click OK to go back to your image.

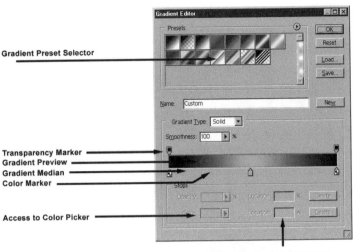

*Figure 4–10: The Gradient editor.*

21. With the Gradient tool, start on the left of your marquee selection. Hold the Shift button, to ensure a straight gradient, and pull over to the right of your marquee selection. You will have what looks like a ridge at the top of your image.

22. Put the same ridge at the right of your color field by hitting "v" to select the Move tool. Position your cursor over the ridge and, holding the Option key to access the copy feature and the Shift button to restrict movement, drag downward until you come to the end of your color field. The result will look like Figure 4–11.

23. If you like, use Layer 3 to put a shadow under your ridges by using the techniques taught earlier. This is illustrated in Figure 4–12.

24. Flatten your image and turn change modes to index color. Make the white body of it transparent, and save it as a GIF. When you put it in your <HTML> document, the resulting background will look like the browser shown in Figure 4–13.

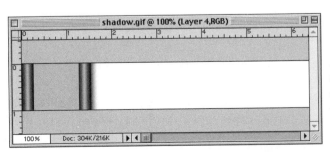

*Figure 4–11: After applying the gradient, copy the ridge by selecting the Move tool and dragging while holding the Option/Alt + Shift keys.*

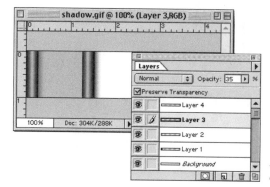

*Figure 4–12: Add a shadow on an empty layer.*

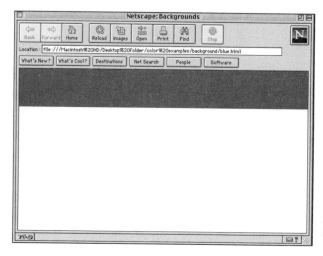

*Figure 4–13: Simple border in a browswer.*

## Ripped, Crinkled Paper Border

1. Open a new file 216 pixels by 216 pixels.

2. With black and white as your foreground and background colors, respectively, choose Filter -> Clouds. Keep hitting Command + F to redo the filter until you get clouds that have a good amount of contrasting areas, such as those shown in Figure 4–14.

3. Save your file in Photoshop format and name it Clouds.

4. Open a new file, 1,440 pixels by 144 pixels. Create a new layer.

5. Make a square selection at the far left of your new canvas, 144 pixels by 144 pixels. Fill your selection with a light brown/beige color.

6. Choose Filter -> Texture -> Texturizer to access the dialog box shown in Figure 4–15. Choose Load Texture and select your file named Clouds. Set the scaling to 100% and experiment with the Relief control (depending on how your clouds looked, and the exact shade of brown that you chose, the exact amount of relief you'll need will vary). The preview window should show your brown plane as having "crinkles" in it. Hit OK.

*Figure 4–14: Clouds will form the basis of the paper texture.*

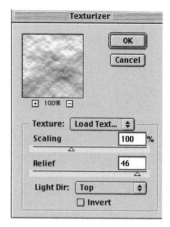

*Figure 4–15: Texturizer filter.*

7. Use the Free-Form lasso tool to select the right edge of the paper jaggedly. Hit Delete.

8. Select the paper edge by first using the Magic Wand tool to select all the white on the right side of your canvas. Press Command + Shift + I (Ctrl + Shift + I in Windows) to select the inverse.

9. Give the edges of your paper a "burnt" look. Choose the Paint Brush tool with a 50% opacity (manipulate this with the Opacity slider in the Options palette). Click the Wet Edges box in the Options palette. Brush along the edge of the crumpled paper border to give it a "burnt" look. Figure 4–16 illustrates this.

10. What you have at this point will not be a seamless tile when you place it in your browser. And because of the odd canvas size, you won't have much luck using the Offset filter described earlier. Create a rectangular selection around the bottom half of your image.

11. Copy your selection, and paste it back into your image. It will paste back into the area that held your selection but on a new layer.

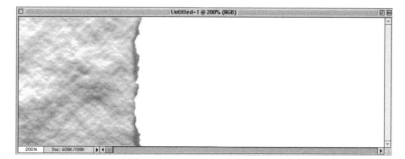

*Figure 4–16: Cut the edges for the ripped effect, and use the brush with Wet Edges to create a "burnt" edge.*

**12.** Select Edit -> Transform -> Flip Vertical. Move the pasted image to the very top, so that the outer edge kisses the top and left border of your image, as shown in Figure 4–17 on the next page.

**13.** Lightly erase the bottom of the pasted image so that it blends in with the rest of the paper border.

**14.** Add a drop shadow as described earlier in this chapter. The final image in your browser will look similar to that in Figure 4–18 on the next page.

# USING FRAMES TO DEVELOP BACKGROUNDS

Figure 4–19 (also Color Figure 5) shows a site that my agency created for Your-FlowerMarket.com. The client wanted it built in such a way that the background outer ring of flowers would remain stationary, while the interior was scrollable to view various products. To accomplish this, we used frames.

The challenge when it comes to frames, though, is making sure that the graphics are cut up in such a way that when they are distributed over the individual frames, they match up properly. This particular site would have been extremely difficult a few years ago, but with the combination of the Slice tool (in either Photoshop or ImageReady) and DreamWeaver, creating frames and making seamless backgrounds behind them is pretty easy.

To help with this, the Slice tool was used to carve up the background image. As we'll see in Chapter 8, the Slice tool is more often used in ImageReady. The complex graphic can be saved with different slices either optimized differently or assigned different functions (such as rollovers or hyperlinks). In this case, the Slice tool was used just to help make the selection, since each portion had to be saved as a separate image to be referenced in a different HTML page.

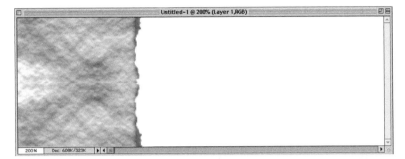

Figure 4–17: Notice the mirror effect of copying, pasting, and inverting the bottom half of the wrinkled paper. Erase a portion to ensure a seamless quality.

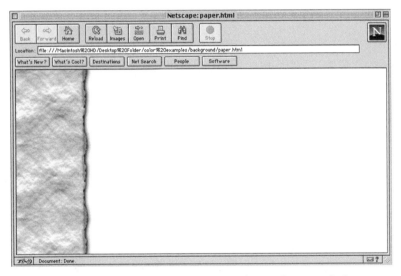

Figure 4–18: The wrinkled paper look as a border in a browser window.

Of course, when you save an image that has been sliced apart, the different slices are saved as individual images. But Photoshop or ImageReady will save them in a separate folder called Images and apply their own default name to each slice — it's kind of a pain to change, so in this case I'm going to just save each slice individually myself.

Once the slices were made (again, Chapter 8 goes further into this), I made a selection of each slice by choosing Select -> Make Selection from Slice. Then the selection was copied and pasted into a new canvas.

Top Frame

Left Frame

Right Frame

Main Frame

*Figure 4–19: The frames in this site made it tough to create the background.*

When you create a new canvas with a copied or cut image on the Pasteboard, the measurements of that new canvas will automatically be the measurements of the image on the Pasteboard.

This was done for each slice, except the main slice where the information would be placed, and the slices were saved as individual files. In DreamWeaver, the Frameset document was created, and each image was placed into its own individual file within the Frameset.

# SUMMARY

Once upon a time, the background was the first thing you would see when you came to a site. Fortunately, that's no longer true. Like the Clinton economic policy, backgrounds are almost nonexistent. Designers have figured out that content is king, and a too elaborate background actually gets in the way of the reader's ability to gather information. But that doesn't mean that you can't have some fun, buck a trend or two, and understand how backgrounds play a part in the overall web site aesthetic.

# chapter 5

# CREATIVE

# TEXT

# EFFECTS

No one who needed to write a book, dissertation, report, article, or even a shopping list ever sat down at her computer and opened Photoshop as her word processor of choice. Text has never been, and never will be, Photoshop's core competency. But it's fine for laying out small amounts of type for certain effects, or color manipulations that you can't achieve in QuarkXPress or with simple HTML text. So, Adobe keeps trying to perfect it.

And while there is nothing wrong with striving for greatness, sometimes trying too hard can lead to missteps. Photoshop 5.5 was the best version yet. Using the same Text editor concept that had always been used, 5.5 for the first time allowed multiple font styles and sizes to be placed within one block of copy. All of the text, no matter how long or how large, could be forced to fit within the editor window, text could be moved around the canvas while being placed just by dragging the cursor outside the editor, and the ability to force bold italic and underline returned to the program (they disappeared in 5). Most importantly, all of the necessary options were easily accessible and conveniently located within the Text editor. Sure, the editor box itself was a little bulky, but you typed what you wanted, hit OK, and you were done.

Well, they say that all good things must come to an end, and in my opinion, this good thing ended with a crash landing. I say "in my opinion" because if you read the reviews of the text upgrade for Photoshop 6, you will get the impression that every major design guru loves the changes that were made. Then again, most of these reviews appeared in publications in which Adobe is also an advertiser. Now, I don't want to imply anything, but ...

The bottom line is what was finally a convenient way to place type on a canvas is now gone. In its place is the new Type tool. As we'll see in the upcoming section, the few benefits of this upgrade scarcely make up for its shortcomings.

# THE NEW TYPE TOOL: A BRIEF EDITORIAL

If you read this whole book cover to cover, and have any sense of insight, you probably get the feeling that 6 is not my favorite upgrade. You can't please everybody, right? It's not that this is a bad upgrade and, like the Layer sets that we read about in Chapter 1, it has a few good points. But for the most part, the changes made just seem kind of extraneous. I was happy enough with the Options palette the way it was before, and I really kind of liked being able to access the Brushes palette even if I wasn't using a painting tool. The Shape tool was a nice addition, but I run out of breath trying to create my own custom shape, and I really don't understand the need for Shape layers and Photoshop's sudden affinity for paths. And the new Liquify feature ... well, that's really nothing more than Kai's Power Goo repackaged and made less interesting.

But those things are just the kind of stuff that makes you shake your head and wonder if each upgrade is about improvement, or just an excuse to get users to spend more money. Where I have a problem is the areas in which they have dismantled something that was fine to begin with, and rebuilt it to be worse than it was before.

As I wrote in the introduction to this chapter, type has never been particularly easy to place in Photoshop. But while the traditional Text editor may have been a bit bulky, by the time Adobe release Photoshop 5.5, they had it working really well—all of the options were there in front of you, you had far more control over the size and style of the text you were placing, the Move tool worked in conjunction with the editor, changing type you had placed was as easy as double-clicking the layer it was on and (for me, at least), the fact that the editor was open forced you to finish what you were typing before you moved on to perform other functions.

Photoshop 6, however, has abandoned the Text editor completely. Now when you want to place text, you just activate the Type tool, click the area of your canvas where you want to place your text, and begin typing. It seems like a great idea, but start working with it a bit, and you'll likely get frustrated. The options available, like color, font style, size, and so forth, are spread out over three separate palettes, one of which is the Paragraph palette. Who writes entire paragraphs in Photoshop?

Simple things have been changed, also. The oft-used "force" attributes, like underline, bold, and italics, which went from nonexistence (in version 5), to prominence (in version 5.5) to obscurity (version 6), hidden in a submenu of one of the three palettes. Were these a little too simple to find before? Nothing like some adventure when designing under a deadline.

Re-editing your type has changed, as well. In earlier versions, double-clicking on a Type layer, regardless of what tool was active, opened the Text editor and allowed you to change the copy you'd placed. In 6, you first have to activate the Type tool again then click within the Type that you placed to do any revisions. Maybe that's simple enough, but if you want to place new type on your canvas, don't inadvertently click on the canvas within 10 pixels of any other body of type, or you'll find yourself editing copy that you didn't mean to change.

But the worst part of all is the fact that the new Type tool works contrary to the way most long time designers have trained themselves to work. Photoshop is primarily a keyboard-command program. Even though you need a mouse of some sort to paint, draw, and so forth, the program is really much faster and richer if you liberally use keyboard commands and shortcuts. Use any tool in Photoshop, and you can immediately activate any other tool by pressing a single button. Say you're using the Airbrush, for example, and suddenly need the Lasso tool. Just release the mouse button and push the L key. This is simple enough and is universally true for every tool in Photoshop. But the Type tool is not like every other tool. In the past, you wouldn't think to access the Lasso tool while the Text editor was open. But the lack of an editor box in 6 creates the impression that the Type tool is like any other, and more often than not you'll find yourself trying to access the Lasso tool only to type a long series of Ls on your canvas. It's annoying.

Lastly, and along the same lines, designers like me, who are used to keyboard shortcuts, are prone to working without any palettes open and in Full View mode, without the menu bar. Try to place type on your canvas under these conditions. Then try to change the font. It's an extremely frustrating process.

It's unfortunate that a program like Photoshop, which has been largely responsible for the advanced state of modern graphic design, doesn't know when to stop. Hopefully this lackluster upgrade and a retreat from the last best attempt to provide a decent Type tool is more of an unfortunate glitch, rather than an indication of what's to come.

# PLACING TEXT

In version 6, text is placed much more directly than in previous versions. Simply activate the Type tool, click on your canvas in the area that you wish to place your text, and start typing. As in previous versions of Photoshop, the text will appear on its own layer, marked by a large T. Every new piece of text that you write (each time you click in a unique location with the Type tool) will be placed on its own layer.

To go back and edit any text that you have placed, activate the Type tool and click any place within your desired copy. The layer for that text will be activated, and you can begin typing, deleting, or otherwise editing any area of what you wrote.

**It might be silly to remind you of something so obvious, but remember: When you're placing text with the Type tool, don't try to use the keyboard commands for other tools. You'll end up typing those letters instead of activating the other tools.**

To move your copy to another area of your canvas while you're placing or editing text, move your cursor slightly off the text itself to temporarily access the Move tool. Drag the text to the new location.

One of the nice new features with this text setup is that you can now change the color of individual words or letters within any one body or type. You do this by highlighting the text in question and selecting a new color from the color swatch icon in the Options palette (shown in Figure 5–1). This palette works in conjunction with two other palettes, all of which are reviewed in further depth in upcoming sections.

**You can also use the Options palette to select the type of anti-aliasing you want to use. Since version 5.5, we've had more choices than just turning anti-aliasing on or off. We can now choose to make the anti-aliasing crisp, strong, or smooth. There's only a slight difference among the three choices, and you can test each out to decide for yourself which works best for you (smooth tends to work best for very small text). But whichever one you choose, you'll probably never want to choose None (which turns anti-aliasing off completely). As Figure 5–2 shows, the result of turning it off usually isn't pretty.**

## The Character Palette

Any "tweaking" or cosmetic settings that you'll make to your text will be done through the Character palette, as shown and described in Figure 5–3. Fairly straightforward, this palette allows you to establish the font(s) you'll use for your copy, as well as any attributes (such as bold, underline, or italics).

*Figure 5–1: The Type Tool's Options palette.*

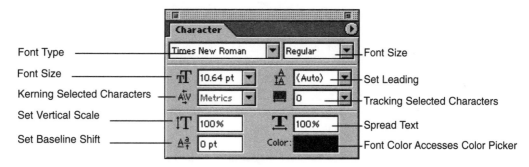

*Figure 5–2: Aliasing is on top; anti-aliasing is on bottom.*

*Figure 5–3: The Character palette.*

Anyone who was happy to see the return of the forced bold, italic, or underline features in version 5.5 doesn't have to panic—they're still here, just not as prominent. These options, plus options for strikethrough, superscript, and subscript are available in the Character palette's Options menu.

Other areas of the Character palette provide new features for text, none of which really needs a rocket scientist to understand. The center command area of the palette lets you set the values for the characters themselves, and how they will relate to one another. These include setting the point size of the text, as well the pixel distance between lines and the letters themselves. Each option gives you the chance either to insert the value yourself, or to use the drop-down slider.

The lower command area contains the more aesthetic adjustments to your copy, including color adjustment and the somewhat pointless horizontal and vertical text stretch areas (pointless because you can achieve better results more quickly by using the Free Transform commands).

You don't need to settle for one set of values for any one area of text that you create. Instead, you can set lines of text one at a time, with varying fonts and sizes, kerning, tracking, stretching, color, and so forth.

To change any of the settings or attributes on text that you have already placed, simply use the Type tool to highlight the copy that you wish to change, then make your changes in the Character palette.

## The Paragraph Palette

The Paragraph palette, shown in Figure 5–4, is a new feature to version 6. In earlier versions of Photoshop, your only real options in terms of placing multiple lines of copy were to justify left or right or to center. What was always missing was the ability to justify both left and right at the same time, with the ability to choose the justification for the last line (either left, right, or centered). Those choices have now been added, and they appear in the Paragraph palette.

What has also been added are features that you'd be more likely to find in a standard text editor or page layout program, such as MS Word or QuarkXPress. These include paragraph indents on the left or right, indentation of the first line of copy, or adding a set value of space before or after a paragraph. The Paragraph palette's options menu even provides the opportunity to make the first character in a paragraph larger.

The problem here, as I see it, is that there really shouldn't even be paragraphs in Photoshop. Photoshop is a bitmap program and should primarily be used for graphic

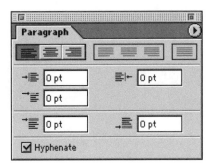

*Figure 5–4: The Paragraph palette.*

design—not for writing book reports or brochures. Typical text that is placed in Photoshop should be for effect only and used sparingly. These new features are good to have around and to understand on a "just in case" basis, but my advice to you is not to allow yourself to get lazy and begin placing too much copy within Photoshop itself. For printed pieces, text will come out a lot sharper if it's set in a page layout program such as QuarkXPress (and it will be easier to adjust in the long run) and, for web sites, setting as much text as you can in standard HTML will help keep your file size down, as well as make changing content a lot easier in the future.

# NOW YOU CAN REALLY MANIPULATE YOUR WORDS!

Although Adobe's other monster product, Illustrator, is a key graphics tool in its own right, one of the main reasons a lot of designers would use it is for special text effects. Curving text, waving it, bloating it—none of that was ever very easily or successfully accomplished in Photoshop until version 6 hit the shelves. The new Shape button in the Type tool's Option palette calls up the dialog box and menu shown in Figure 5–5. These options allow you the freedom to manipulate your text more creatively without having to render the layer (as you would need to do if you wished to use a filter on your text, which we'll review in the next section).

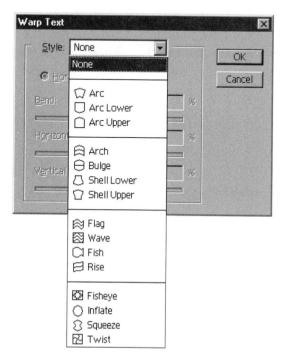

*Figure 5–5: The new Shape dialog box gives plenty of options for manipulating your text.*

To use one of the options on your text, simply place your text in your canvas and, with the Type tool still selected, press the Shape button and choose the shape you wish to apply to your copy. Sliders and other standard dialog boxes will appear with any shape that you select to help you adjust the shape accurately. Figure 5–6 shows a few sample shapes, their respective dialog boxes, and the values that were used.

# GREAT WAYS TO COMBINE TEXT AND LAYER ATTRIBUTES

Apparently, the term Layer effects didn't accurately describe the drop shadows, bevels, and other effects that you could instantly create, as introduced in Photoshop 5. So they changed the name to Layer attributes.

*Figure 5–6: Examples of text manipulation.*

Frivolous changes aside, the ability to create fairly common features found in both web sites and printed pieces instantly has been a boon to developers who can save hours of design time by not creating these effect by hand.

Although, as we'll see later in this book, Layer attributes can work with any object and be a big help when creating buttons and navigational pieces, they really shine when used on text. We'll see how these commands help text to pop off a page and add depth, as well as how they might differ from more manually created effects.

**In earlier versions of Photoshop, these commands were accessed through the upper menu bar. In Photoshop 6, you can access them by pushing the Layer attributes icon at the bottom far left of the Layers menu.**

## Drop Shadow: Creating Drop Shadows With Layer Attributes

1. Open a new file, 360 pixels wide by 144 pixels high.

2. Select the Type tool and click anywhere on the canvas.

3. Within the Type editor, choose a light color for your text and, using either a bold Helvetica or Arial font, set your font size to 70 points.

4. Type "Web Page" and manually position the words in the middle of the canvas, toward the top.

5. Click OK and your canvas looks something like Figure 5–7.

6. Choose Drop Shadow from the Layer attributes pop-up menu at the bottom of the Layers palette. You will get a dialog box similar to that in Figure 5–8.

7. Set your angle to 135 degrees, the distance to 5 pixels, and leave the Spread at its default value of 0. Spread is a new control in 6, that allows the drop shadow to expand and harden its edges at the same time. The last slider, called Size, is really

*Figure 5–7: The text is placed on the canvas.*

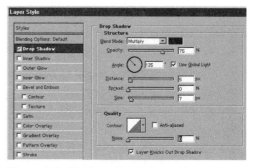

*Figure 5–8: Layer attributes: Drop Shadow.*

the old Blur slider from previous versions. Set this to 7. You can see the drop shadow as it is being made. Before clicking OK, play around with some of the sliders and watch the different effects that each one has.

8. Click OK, and your canvas will look something like the canvas in Figure 5–9.

And there you have it: instant drop shadow courtesy of Photoshop 6's idiot-proof drop shadow attributes menu. The really cool part is that Photoshop 6 will preserve the layer attribute within its own sublayer. Later in this chapter we'll review how to change any settings you've made, or hide or eliminate an effect completely.

If you move the text on your layer around your canvas, you'll notice that the drop shadow (like all the Layer attributes) will follow it around as if stuck by glue. Sometimes, though, it will be necessary to separate the effect from the original image, as illustrated in our next example.

1. Working from the previous example, make sure that the layer named "Web Page" is the active layer.

2. Choose Layer -> Layer Style -> Create Layer. Figure 5–10 shows the differences in the Layers palette. Although you've gained an extra layer and can manipulate your drop shadow at will, that ability did not come without its price—namely, that your text layer will no longer retain the Layer attributes information to apply to future objects, nor is it editable anymore.

## Adding Dimension to the Text

An effect that is very easy, and quite effective in certain situations, is to add dimension to your text simply by doing the following:

1. Using the same document from the last section, add a layer between the shadow and the text.

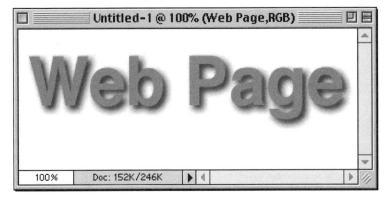

*Figure 5–9: Drop shadow created with Layer effects.*

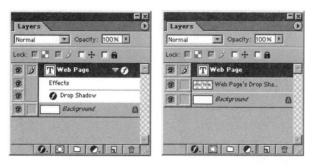

*Figure 5–10: The Layers palette before and after separating effects. Notice the circled "I" is gone in the latter, and the drop shadow has its own layer.*

2. Press the Command key and click your mouse (Ctrl + click in Windows) on the "Web Page" layer in the Layers palette to get the selection of your text.

3. Press the M key to make the Marquee tool active and use the arrow keys to move your selection down and to the right by two pixels.

4. Fill your selection with black. You may want to reduce the opacity of your shadow a bit, and maybe drag your shadow farther away from the text. The result is shown in Figure 5–11.

That was a super-easy illustration of an addition you can make by creating your drop shadow the traditional way. Here's another:

1. Make the shadow layer active by clicking on it.

2. Choose Edit -> Free Transform (in Photoshop 5+, the Free Transform and Transform options are located in the Edit menu, as opposed to Photoshop 4, in which they were located in the Layer menu).

*Figure 5–11: Adding more depth.*

**3.** Your shadow will now have a box around it with "handles" on the corners and the sides, as shown in Figure 5–12. Grab one of the bottom corner handles with your cursor and, holding Command and Option (Ctrl + Alt in Windows), drag the corner inward and upward slightly. Continue dragging until your shadow looks like the one in Figure 5–13. Get a distance effect by using a feathered, low-opacity eraser over the far end of the shadow.

# EVEN MORE EXCITING LAYER ATTRIBUTES

Drop shadows aren't the only effect you can create. These commands, introduced in Photoshop 5, also include inner shadows, glows, bevels, and embosses. With Photoshop 6, not only have the dialog boxes and functionality changed, but there are a few new effects, as well. Although some of these effects are less than thrilling, we will briefly review each of them. At the end of this section, look for a condensed, bulleted list that reviews some extra, important points about Layer attributes.

*Figure 5–12: Selecting Edit -> Transform.*

*Figure 5–13: Dragging the shadow for a depth effect.*

# Inner Shadow

The new Inner shadow feature gives you an easy way of creating a really cool depth effect.

1. Type in text.
2. Choose Inner Shadow from the Layer attributes pop-up menu at the bottom of the Layers palette.
3. Figure 5–14 shows the effect with the default setting, except the angle, which was changed to 135°.

This effect works best with sans serif fonts set at a large point size.

## *Adding Depth to an Inner Shadow*

1. Choose Layer -> Layer Style -> Create Layer to separate the inner shadow into its own layer.
2. With the Inner shadow layer active, press Command and T (Ctrl + T in Windows) to activate the Free Transform feature.

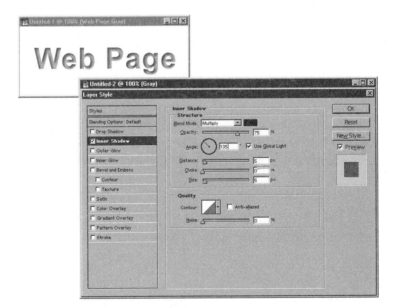

*Figure 5–14: The Layer Attribute Drop shadow.*

3. Hold down the Option key (Alt in Windows) and drag one of the corner handles in slightly. Next hold the Command, Option, and Shift keys (Ctrl + Alt + Shift in Windows) to gain control over the perspective, and drag one of the top corner handle bars in slightly. If even more depth is desired, drag the top center handle bar down slightly. Figure 5–15 illustrates the process.

## Outer Glow

Like Drop shadow, there may be instances that you find it's important to separate the Layer attribute into its own layer.

1. Lay out text.
2. Choose Outer Glow from the Layer attributes pop-up menu at the bottom of the Layers palette.

*Figure 5–15: Separating the Inner shadow from the actual text allows you to manipulate it with the Free Transform feature, and to give the piece greater depth.*

3. Figure 5–16 shows the effect with the opacity set to 85%, the blur to 18 pixels, and the intensity to 352. I also changed my glow color to a bright yellow. (This effect looks the most natural using bright, glowing colors on darker backgrounds.)

## Inner Glow

The least exciting of all the effects, Inner glow puts a glow on the inside edges of your selection.

1. Type in text.
2. Choose Inner Glow from the Layer attributes pop-up menu at the bottom of the Layers palette.
3. Figure 5–17 shows the effect with an opacity setting of 85%, a blur of 6 pixels, and an intensity of 184. (This effect works best with brighter glows within dark objects.)

## Bevel and Emboss

This really cool feature all but negates any need for the Emboss filter found in the Filters menu. There are four separate Bevel and Emboss effects for you to choose from: Outer bevel, Inner bevel, Emboss, and Pillow emboss.

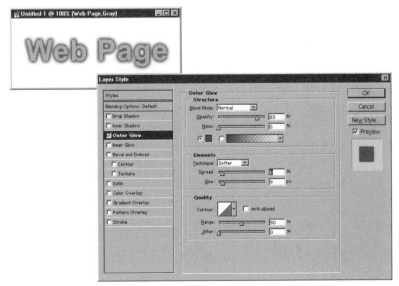

*Figure 5–16: The Layer Attribute Outer glow.*

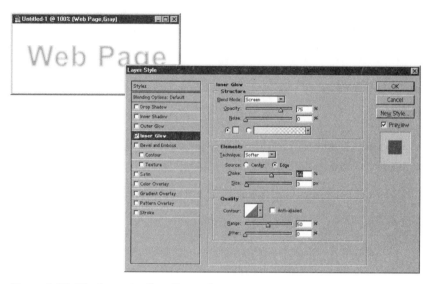

*Figure 5–17: The Layer Attribute Inner glow.*

## Outer Bevel

1. Lay out text.
2. Choose Bevel and Emboss from the Layer attributes pop-up menu at the bottom of the Layers palette.
3. Choose Outer Bevel from the Style pull-down menu.
4. Figure 5–18 shows the effect of the default setting, except the depth, which has been increased to 221% (Photoshop 6 measures depth in percent rather than pixels, as earlier versions did—this allows you to create far greater bevel effects), and the size (previously called blur) which has been increased to 8.
5. Play around with the opacity settings for both the highlight and the shadow to get a clean, hammered-out effect for your text, especially when you have a photograph in your background.

## Inner Bevel

1. Type in text.
2. Choose Bevel and Emboss from the Layer attributes pop-up menu at the bottom of the Layers palette.

3. Choose Inner Bevel from the Style pull-down menu.

4. Figure 5–19 shows the effect with the default settings, except the depth, which is set to 520%.

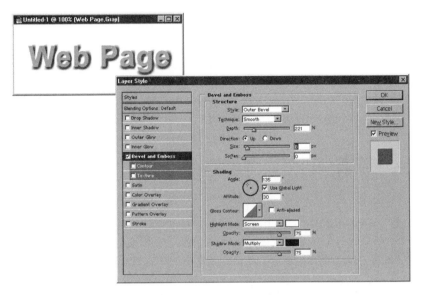

*Figure 5–18: Outer level, as found in the Layer attributes menu.*

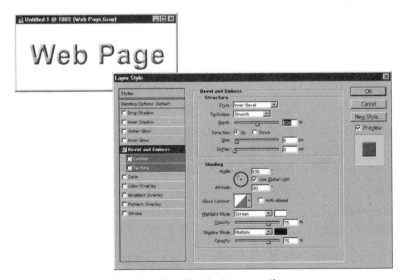

*Figure 5–19: Inner bevel, as found in the Layer attribute menu.*

## Emboss

1. Type in text.
2. Choose Bevel and Emboss from the Layer attributes pop-up menu at the bottom of the Layers palette.
3. Choose Emboss from the Style pull-down menu.
4. Figure 5–20 shows the effect with the default for all settings. The result looks similar to the Inner Bevel effect, with the addition of a slight drop shadow and highlight added.

## Pillow Emboss

1. Type in text.
2. Choose Bevel and Emboss from the Layer attributes pop-up menu at the bottom of the Layers palette.
3. Choose Pillow Emboss from the Style pull-down menu.
4. Figure 5–21 shows the effect with the default for all settings except the depth set to 740%, the size set to 13 pixels, and the technique to Chisel Hard.
5. Like the Outer Bevel attribute, experiment with the opacity settings for your highlight and shadows as the key to getting a realistic look for your Pillow emboss, especially on top of photographic backgrounds.

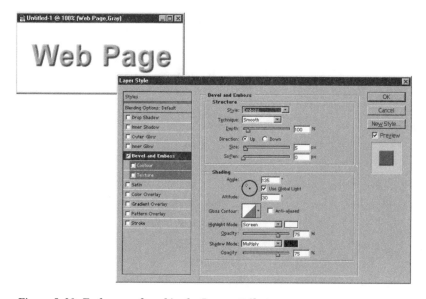

*Figure 5–20: Emboss, as found in the Layer attribute menu.*

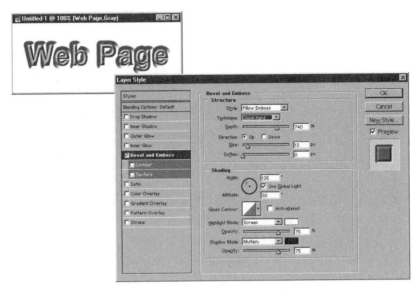

*Figure 5–21: Pillow emboss, as found in the Layer attribute menu.*

# NEW LAYER ATTRIBUTES IN VERSION 6

Version 6 comes with a few new Layer attributes that weren't available in previous versions of the program. Although an unremarkable set of new offerings, some of them may be at least a little beneficial to certain projects. Each of these can be accessed by using the Layer attributes button at the bottom of the Layers palette.

## Satin

As it sounds, this effect is meant to give the objects on a layer a satiny look by manipulating interior shadows based on the shape of the objects. Figure 5–22 provides a sample.

## Color Overlay and Gradient Overlay

Both of these are so extraneous that I'm not going to even bother showing examples. Basically, the Color overlay allows you to fill in the objects on your layer with any color and to set your blend mode from the same dialog box. The Gradient overlay does pretty much the same thing, but with a gradient instead of a solid color. No big deal here—just a bit of a time saver versus the way you might have otherwise filled in a color or a gradient without these features.

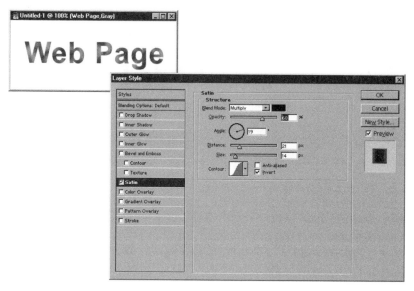

*Figure 5–22: Satin gives the objects on a layer a satiny look.*

## Pattern Overlay

The Pattern overlay stands out mostly because of the preset patterns available and the ability to scale them instantly within the given objects. The dialog box shown in Figure 5–23 shows a fairly simple number of options, with the main focus on the Pattern drop-down menu, which allows you to choose from preset patterns or to save your own custom pattern, and the Scale slider, which lets you adjust the pattern within the layer objects.

## Stroke

This one is actually really cool. The ordinary Stroke function, accessed by choosing Edit -> stroke, allows you the bare minimum of control over any stroke you make. Besides choosing the Blend mode, you can pretty much just choose the color, pixel width, and position of your stroke (inside, outside, or center). But the Stroke Layer attribute gives you complete control over the strokes that you create.

You can use a slider to see how any particular stroke width will affect the layer in question—a far cry from the Edit -> Stroke way, which lets you fill in one numeric value, hit OK, and hope for the best. Better yet, the Fill Type drop-down menu lets you instantly access the Gradient fill and the Pattern fill and apply either of them to the stroke itself. The example in Figure 5–24 shows a stroke with a gradient fill applied to it.

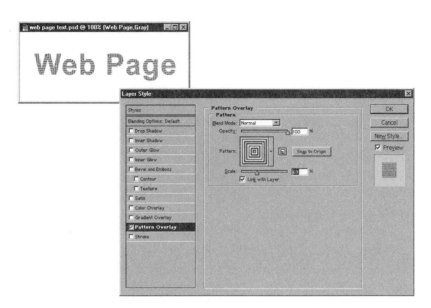

*Figure 5–23: The Pattern overlay dialog box.*

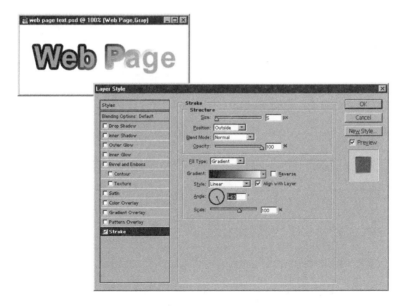

*Figure 5–24: The Stroke dialog box.*

# A FEW LINGERING POINTS ABOUT LAYER ATTRIBUTES

As Layer attributes have evolved into Version 6 Layer attributes, they've become complex enough to deserve a chapter all to themselves. In my other book, *Photoshop 6 Primer*, I've dedicated a whole appendix to the topic. But while a full chapter or even an appendix might be beyond the scope of this book, the following list should provide you with the last few remaining points you'll need to assist now in using attributes.

◆  In earlier versions, Layer attributes were indicated with a small icon (a white "f" in a black circle) on the layer in which they were created. To edit the variables for any effect, you double-clicked on the icon to reopen the dialog box for the last effect that you created.

With 6, the icon still exists on the layer where you created the attributes. But now a small triangle also exists next to that icon. Clicking the triangle will open sublayers. Each sublayer contains an individual attribute that you've created—one sublayer for each attribute.

◆  Edit the settings for any attribute by double-clicking on its sublayer.

◆  Temporarily hide one or more attributes by clicking the Eye icon for that sublayer, just as you would hide any layer in the Layers palette.

◆  Delete an attribute by dragging the sublayer to the Trash icon at the bottom of the Layers palette.

◆  If you change the angle of light for any one Layer attribute, the direction will change for all other attributes on your canvas—even if they reside on a completely different layer. This a failsafe method to ensure that you don't have conflicting light sources in your image. To turn this off and allow conflicting light sources, click off the checkbox marked Use Global Angle in the attribute you are creating or editing.

◆  When you create attributes on any given layer, everything on that layer will be effects. For example, say that you have a drop shadow and emboss attribute on a layer. Later on, you paint a thick red line on that layer. That line that you paint will automatically have a drop shadow and emboss attribute associated with it.

◆  You cannot create Layer attributes on the Background layer.

◆  To create multiple attributes at one time, you no longer have to use the pull-down menu inside the dialog box as you did in the past. Now, just click the names of the new attributes you want to create in the list at the left side of the dialog box.

# LAYER ATTRIBUTES IN THE REAL WORLD

Although Photoshop 6's Layer attributes make developing certain design aspects rather simple, you're by no means strictly limited to filling in a dialog box to achieve your end result. Combinations of Layer attributes together, as well as other Photoshop tools, can put creativity back into the creation process.

Figure 5–25 shows the top portion of a web site my agency is currently creating for a client, an osteologist who wants us to help release information on the formation of bones and the human anatomy. The figure also includes a magnification of the portion of the titlebar that utilizes the Layer attributes.

Although the subject matter is serious, our client wants the site to reflect his own personality, which is lighthearted and fun. Part of what we have done is to create the illusion in the titlebar of words that reflect their meanings through imagery. In the full title of the site, "Bones & Your Body," a combination of Layer attributes, the Lighting effects filter, and the Paintbrush tool was used to make the word Bones look as though

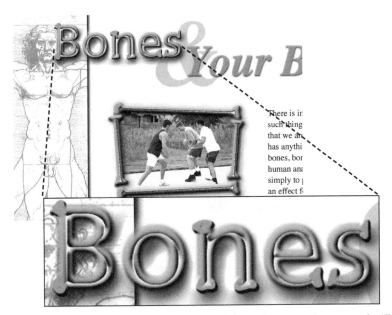

*Figure 5–25: A combination of Layer attributes and other tools was used to create the illusion that the title in this upcoming web site is made out of bones.*

it is made up of actual bones. The following shows the steps necessary to create this effect:

1. Open a new file, 720 by 290 pixels. Create a new layer, "Layer 1," to begin.

2. With the Type Mask tool, type *bones* in a Helvetica or Arial font, large enough to fit in the center of your canvas, as shown in Figure 5–26.

3. Feather your text selection by pressing Command, Option, and D (Ctrl + Alt + D in Windows) and set the Feather radius to 3. Click OK.

4. Fill your selection with a light to medium gray color, as shown in Figure 5–27.

5. Choose Inner shadow from the Layer attributes pop-up menu at the bottom of the Layers palette to access the dialog box. Change the settings to:

   | | |
   |---|---|
   | Opacity: | 95% |
   | Angle: | –48° (with Use Global Angle checked) |
   | Distance: | 5 pixels |
   | Blur: | 1 pixel |
   | Intensity: | 105% |

   Your image will look similar to Figure 5–28.

6. Before clicking OK, choose Bevel and Emboss from the main pull-down menu in the dialog box. Choose Outer bevel from the subsequent Style pull-down menu. Keep the Highlight and Shadow options at their default settings, and change the remaining settings to read:

   | | |
   |---|---|
   | Opacity: | 95% |
   | Angle: | –48° (with Use Global Angle checked) |
   | Distance: | 5 pixels |
   | Blur: | 1 pixel |

   Click OK and your image will now look similar to Figure 5–29.

7. If your image is no longer selected, select it now by holding down the Command button (Ctrl in Windows) and clicking Layer 1.

8. Choose Select -> Modify -> Contract and contract your image by 8 pixels.

9. Establish the selection as an Alpha Channel by choosing Select -> Save Selection. Make sure that the Channel pull-down menu is set to New, and click OK. The selection is now saved as an alpha channel and can be viewed in the Channels palette.

10. Select Filter -> Render -> Lighting Effects to bring up the dialog box shown in Figure 5–30. In the Texture Channel pull-down menu, choose Alpha 1 and pull the Height selector over to Mountainous. Make sure the White is high checkbox is left unchecked and that the light source is coming from the northwest direction as shown in Figure 5–30. Click OK, and your image will look similar to Figure 5–31.

11. Deselect your selection by pressing Command and D (Ctrl + D in Windows).

Figure 5–26: The Type Mask tool sets the selection marquee for the title.

Figure 5–27: After the selection is feathered and filled with color, the edges take on a soft edge.

Figure 5–28: The Layer attributes Inner shadow, when used on a selection with a soft edge, creates an interesting "puffed up" effect.

Figure 5–29: The addition of the Outer bevel from the Bevel and Emboss Layer attributes arsenal, accentuates the letters.

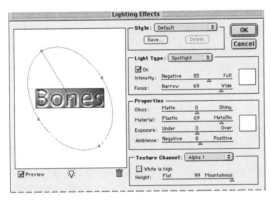

Figure 5–30: The Lighting Effects dialog box.

Figure 5–31: The Lighting Effects filter on the Alpha Channel creates the bone frame.

12. Add the cartoonish bone ends onto the letters to complete the effect. Do this by selecting the Paintbrush tool with a small, hard-edged brush, and paint the ends onto each letter. Because you're painting in Layer 1, which retains the Layer Attribute settings, those same settings will apply to your newly painted additions. The final effect can be seen in the close-up provided in Figure 5–32.

# BEYOND LAYER ATTRIBUTES: CREATIVE TEXT DESIGN

Although you can be endlessly creative with Photoshop's Layer attributes, especially when they are used in combination with one another as shown in the preceding section, "Layer Attributes in the Real World," don't forget that there's an entire world of design beyond Layer attributes. The next few pages will show how you can use combinations of tools and filters to create some really outstanding looks and special effects that will help your web page come to life and stand out. Hammered emboss plus great techniques for creating fire, ice, and 3D text are just the beginning of what Photoshop can do to enhance your web sites.

## Creating a Hammered Emboss Effect

The preceding section touched on the power of the Lighting Effects filter. This example takes it a step further, illustrating how to give your text the illusion of having been hammered out from the other side of your canvas.

1. Open a new file 360 pixels wide by 144 pixels high.
2. Set your foreground to a rich shade of blue and your background color to bright red.
3. With the Gradient tool, create a diagonal gradient from the top left corner to the bottom right, as shown in Figure 5–33.
4. Choose the Type Mask tool and type "Text Fun" in a Helvetica or Arial font at a point size of 75 points. (This effect tends to look better with sans serif fonts.) Click OK and

*Figure 5–32: Painting the end caps of the bone helps to develop its structure.*

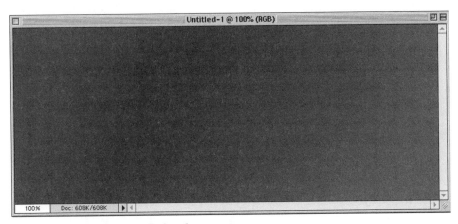

*Figure 5–33: A gradient applied to the canvas.*

center your text. Notice that while Photoshop ordinarily places text on its own layer and preserves the components, this does not hold true for selection text. Selection text is placed on the active layer and does not retain information for editing.

5. Choose Select -> Feather, and set the Feather radius to 3. Click OK. Your text selection now looks a little round at the edges.

6. Choose Select -> Save Selection to bring up the dialog box shown in Figure 5–34. For Channel, choose New and name it if you'd like. If you don't name it, it will automatically be called Alpha 1.

7. Choose Filter -> Render -> Lighting Effects. Figure 5–35 shows the Lighting Effects filter, one of the most interesting, but complex, filters that Photoshop 5 provides for you.

8. With the Lighting Style set to Default and the light type set to Spotlight, choose Alpha 1 as your texture channel. The preview window will show the emboss effect on your text.

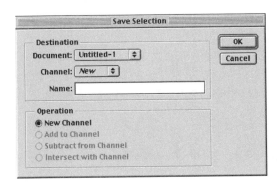

*Figure 5–34: The Save Selection dialog box. Saving your selection creates an Alpha channel.*

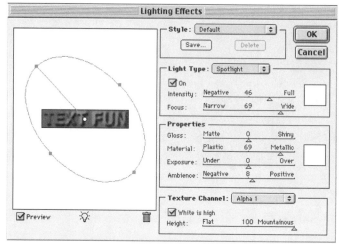

*Figure 5–35: The Lighting Effects dialog box.*

9. Turn the light source so that the spotlight is shining down from a northwest direction, giving your text a more universal shadow style. Make sure that the spotlight area is wide enough that none of your text is lost in dark shadows. Click OK. Your image now looks similar to Figure 5–36.

 For a deeper emboss, go back to when you were in the process immediately after Step 6, and use the arrow keys to move your selection up about six spaces. The result will be similar to Figure 5–37 and will add some dimension to your image.

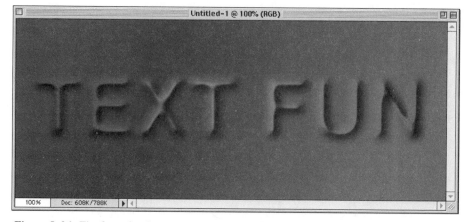

*Figure 5–36: Final result when using a Lighting Effects filter on a saved feathered selection.*

*Figure 5–37: Moving your selection before using the Lighting Effects filter can create a deeper embossed effect.*

# Creating Burning, Melting Text: Technique One

This effect comes from a combination of artistic talent (yes, even though Photoshop makes some effects very simple, you still need some artistic ability!) and one of Photoshop's native filters.

1. Open a new file 360 pixels by 144 pixels.

2. Choose the Type Mask tool and type "TEXT FUN" in all caps, in a Helvetica or Arial font, at a point size of 70 points, and in Bold. Click OK and center your type selection. Notice that while Photoshop ordinarily places text on its own layer and preserves the components, this does not hold true for the selection text. Selection text is placed on the active layer and does not retain information for editing.

3. Create Layer 1 so that you are not working on the background layer.

4. Choose Select -> Save Selection and save your selection as an Alpha Channel.

5. Choose Select -> Feather and set the Feather radius to 2.

6. Choose a bright red for your foreground color and a medium to dark orange for your background.

7. With the Gradient tool set to Foreground to Background, hold the Shift key down for constraint and drag from the top of your selection to the bottom. Your canvas will look something like Figure 5–38.

8. Create a new layer over the currently active one.

9. Choose Select -> Load Selection. Figure 5–39 illustrates the Load Selection dialog box. Make sure that the Channel option is set to Alpha 1 (or any other name you may have chosen for the selection you saved earlier).

10. Make your foreground color white. Hit the J key to activate the Airbrush tool.

*Figure 5–38: A gradient (from red to orange) into a feathered text selection.*

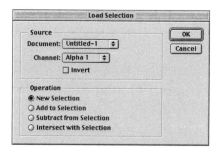

*Figure 5–39: Load Selection dialog box.*

11. In the Airbrush Options palette, set the Airbrush opacity to 30. (You can do this by pressing the key or by using the palette's Opacity slider.) The opacity slider is marked Pressure on the Options palette. Select a soft brush with a diameter of 100 pixels.

12. Swish through the selection so that various parts of your text will appear in a faint white, as shown in Figure 5–40. Deselect your selection when you are through.

13. Choose Filter -> Distort -> Ocean Ripple to pull up the dialog box illustrated in Figure 5–41. Use the default settings and click OK. Your faded white letters will now be very curvy, as shown in Figure 5–42.

14. To create the fire and give the illusion that your text is melting, make Layer 1 (your red to orange gradient) your active layer by clicking on it.

15. Choose the Smudge tool (located by scrolling through the choices under the Blur tool—see Chapter 1, "Overview to Photoshop"), and with a soft brush with a diameter of 27, drag the top of your gradient upward to smear the color. Do this over the top of all your letters. With a smaller brush, make the flame details by smearing the gradient in smaller sections. Your image will look similar to Figure 5–43.

16. For a more authentic flame, try adding some yellow to the middle of your red to orange gradient.

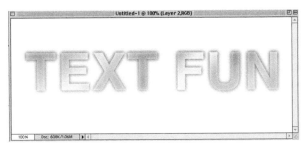

*Figure 5–40: After swishing through with white.*

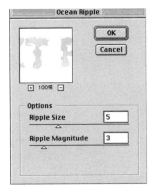

*Figure 5–41: Ocean Ripple.*

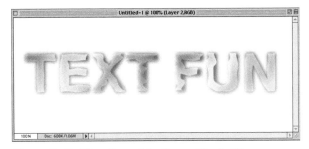

*Figure 5–42: The effect of the Ocean Ripple filter.*

*Figure 5–43: The final result after using the Smudge tool.*

## Creating Burning, Melting Text: Technique Two

This technique is a little more realistic looking; however, it is also different to achieve on a white background. It will take a little bit of work on your part to achieve a decent burn and have your text remain legible.

1. Open a new file 360 pixels wide by 360 pixels deep.

2. Fill the background with black.

3. Use the Type tool to place the word "TEXT" in the center of the canvas. Use white for the letters.

4. Flatten your image and choose Image -> Rotate Canvas -> 90° CW to turn your image 1/4 turn to the right.

5. Choose Filter -> Stylize -> Wind for the dialog box shown in Figure 5–44. Choose Wind for the method and From the Left for the direction. Click OK.

6. Hit Command and F (Ctrl + F in Windows) twice to exaggerate the effect of the filter.

7. Rotate your canvas 90° CCW to its original position.

8. Select Filter -> Blur -> Motion Blur to bring up the dialog box shown in Figure 5–45. Set the angle to 59° with a blur of 4 pixels and click OK.

9. Choose Filter -> Distort -> Ripple and maintain the default settings. Click OK. Your canvas will look similar to Figure 5–46.

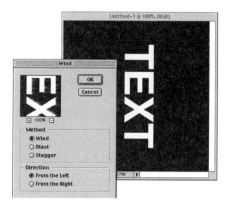

*Figure 5–44: The Wind filter dialog box. Text has to be turned because the Wind effect only goes left and right.*

*Figure 5–45: Apply a Motion Blur filter.*

10. Add a new layer and fill it with a bright yellow. Change the layer mode to Overlay. Add another layer and fill it with bright red. Also change this layer's mode to Overlay. The final image is shown both in Figure 5–47 and in Color Figure 6.

## Creating Icy Letters

This is a pretty "cool" text effect (sorry, I couldn't resist).

1. Open a new file 360 pixels wide by 360 pixels deep.
2. Fill the background with black.
3. Use the Type tool to place the word "TEXT" in the center of the canvas. Choose an icy sky blue color for the letters.

*Figure 5–46: After the Ripple filter is applied.*

*Figure 5–47: A realistic burning effect. See Color Figure 13.*

4. Flatten your image, and choose Image -> Rotate Canvas -> 90° CW to turn your image 1/4 turn to the right.

5. Choose Filter -> Stylize -> Wind for the dialog box shown in Figure 5–48. Choose Wind for the method and From the Right for the direction. Click OK.

6. With the Wind effect, you're going to be placing your icicles, so press Command and F (Ctrl + F in Windows) two or three more times until your icicles are as long as you'd like them.

7. Rotate your canvas 90° CCW to its original position.

8. Choose Filter -> Brush Strokes -> Accented Edges for the dialog box as shown in Figure 5–49. Set the Edge width to 2, the Edge brightness to 38, and Smoothness to 5.

9. Create a new layer, and with the Airbrush tool brush randomly over the text, as shown in Figure 5–50. Make sure that you have white as your foreground color, and choose a brush size of around 35 pixels. When finished, set the Layer mode to Overlay. Figure 5–51 and Color Figure 7 show the final image.

## Creating Dotted Text

For any member of Generation X, the dotted effect is a must (at least that's what advertising agencies seem to think).

1. Open a new file 504 pixels wide by 144 pixels deep.

2. With the Type Mask tool, place the words "TEXT FUN" in the center of your canvas.

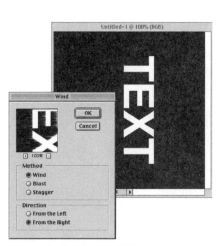

*Figure 5–48: The Wind filter again gets us started.*

*Figure 5–49: Apply the Accented Edges filter.*

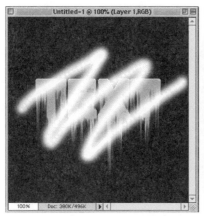 

*Figure 5–50: Airbrushing with white on a new layer set to Overlay will help provide light hits on the ice.*

*Figure 5–51: The final image.*

3. Choose Select -> Feather and set the Feather radius to 4. Fill the selection with any color you choose.

4. Deselect all.

5. Choose Filter -> Pixelate -> Color Halftone to bring up the dialog box. Lower the maximum radius to 4 and click OK. Figure 5–52 and Color Figure 18 show the result.

## Creating Neon Text

1. Open a new file 504 pixels wide by 144 pixels deep.

2. Use the Type Mask tool to write "TEXT FUN."

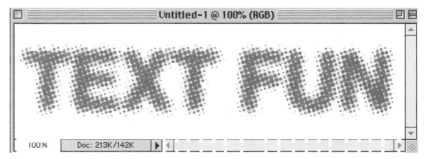

*Figure 5–52: Dotted effect achieved by using the Color Halftone filter.*

3. Choose Select -> Feather and set the Feather radius to 3 to soften the edges.

4. Fill your selection with black. It will look similar to Figure 5–53. Deselect all.

5. With black and white as your foreground and background colors, choose Filter -> Render -> Difference Clouds. Your canvas will look like Figure 5–54.

6. Choose Image -> Adjust -> Invert.

7. Overlay any color and your image will look similar to Figure 5–55 and Color Figure 9.

## Creating Quick 3D Text

1. Open a new file 576 pixels wide by 144 pixels deep.

2. With the Type tool, type "TEXT FUN" and center it on your canvas.

*Figure 5–53: Feathered text filled with black.*

*Figure 5–54: Applying the Difference Clouds filter.*

*Figure 5–55: Invert the image for the neon result above.*

3. Text is put on a new layer that retains all of the text specifications for editing later. However, no luxury comes without its price. While the layer retains the settings, there will be certain things you cannot do to it, such as use traditional filters or change the perspective. To change this, Choose Layer -> Rasterize-> Type. This will turn your text into a regular graphic, giving you access to all of Photoshop's effects, but eliminating your ability to edit the text. (See? I told you everything had its price!)

4. Choose Edit -> Free Transform. (Notice that the Transform and Free Transform items are located under the Edit menu, as opposed to the Layer menu in version 4.)

5. Grab the bottom right corner handle and, while pressing the Shift, Option and Command buttons (Shift + Alt + Ctrl in Windows), drag outward. Drag one of the top corner handles and drag inward, until your text looks similar to Figure 5–56. Hit Return (Enter in Windows) or double-click on the text to apply the transformation.

6. In the Layers palette options menu, select Duplicate Layer to access the Duplicate Layer dialog box. Click OK to accept the default setting, and the new layer will appear just above your original. This new layer automatically becomes the active layer. Make the previous layer the active layer by clicking on it.

7. Choose Filter -> Blur -> Motion Blur. Set your angle to 90° and your distance to 75. Click OK.

8. With your Move tool, move the blur down until it fits below your letters and looks like Figure 5–57. You may have to play with the Transform feature to fit it more exactly.

## Creating Bubbled Text

One of the coolest new toys introduced back in Photoshop 5 is the 3D Transform filter. Although it is a bit clunky (mark my words, future Photoshop versions will undoubtedly add improvements to this filter), it can still do some pretty amazing things. Mostly meant for changing perspectives of 2D images (such as a picture of a box of cereal or a soup can), this effect can manipulate text in some neat ways as well.

*Figure 5–56: Text with a perspective transformation applied to it.*

*Figure 5–57: Duplicating the layer and applying a motion blur create a 3D effect.*

1. Open a new file 576 pixels wide by 144 pixels deep.
2. With the Type tool, type "TEXT FUN" and center it on your canvas.
3. Choose Layer -> Type -> Render Layer.
4. Select the letters by pressing Command and clicking (Ctrl + clicking in Windows) on the text layer in the Layer palette. Save your selection as a channel.
5. Deselect all and choose Filter -> Render -> 3D Transform to access the palette shown in Figure 5–58.
6. Using the sphere tool, create a sphere around part of the letters. Use the trackball tool and rotate the sphere upward just a bit as shown in Figure 5–59. Click OK.
7. Erase the bottom of the sphere.
8. Create a new layer in between the background and your text layer. Load the Alpha Channel you created earlier.
9. Choose Select -> Feather and feather your image by 4 pixels. Fill it with black.

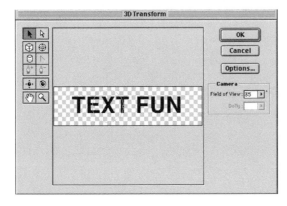

*Figure 5–58: The cool new 3D Transform filter.*

Erase
bottom of
sphere

*Figure 5–59: The effect of the 3D Transform filter on the text.*

*Figure 5–60: The final effect after the bottom ring is erased and a drop shadow is placed.*

**10.** Lower the opacity on your layer to around 30% and move your shadow just a little off center. The final image is shown in Figure 5–60.

# Filling Part of Your Text With an Image (Working With Masks)

**1.** Open a new file 576 pixels wide by 144 pixels deep.

**2.** With the Type tool, type "TEXT FUN" and center it on your canvas.

**3.** Choose Layer -> Type -> Render Layer.

**4.** Press Command and click (Ctrl + click in Windows) the text layer to grab the selection and save the selection as a channel named "Alpha 1."

**5.** In the Channels palette, shown in Figure 5–61, click on the channel marked Alpha 1. You'll notice that your canvas has changed—your background is now black and your text is white to show where your selection is.

*Figure 5–61: The Channels palette.*

6. You'll also notice that no matter what colors were in your Color palette, they are black and white now. That is because by selecting the channel Alpha 1, you have turned off the other channels that hold the color values. With the Gradient tool, hold the Shift key for constraint and make a gradient from top to bottom, white to black. Your canvas will look like Figure 5–62.

7. Choose Select -> Load Selection, and choose Alpha 1. Click OK. You'll see that only the upper half (the white half) of your text is selected now. Click on the channel marked RGB to load the selection into the color channel. Your canvas and Color palette go back to normal.

8. Open an image on a separate canvas. In this example, I used the image of an island resort (where I'll be writing my next book ...) shown in Figure 5–63. Copy the image to your pasteboard.

9. Back in your original canvas, the top of your text is still selected. Use the Paste Into command to paste your image into your selection. You'll see that, as in Figure 5–64, your image is 100% opaque on top and gradually fades to 0% as it goes down your text. As long as the channel that you loaded is selected, the same effect will happen to any effect you use.

*Figure 5–62: Setting a gradient within the channel selection.*

*Figure 5–63: The image I will use to fill partially my text selection.*

*Figure 5–64: The final text after being partially filled.*

# SUMMARY

I think I've done enough bashing of the new Type tool at the beginning of this chapter that I don't need to repeat myself here. So while I'm not a fan of the tool, I'll end by saying that I still believe that Photoshop offers more than its share of ways for designers to create great effects. From what you can accomplish using Layer attributes, traditional tools and filters, and a combination of the two, you'll find it remarkably easy and a lot of fun to bring your web text to life.

The History palette includes the following items:

- 38285.JPG
- New Layer
- Rubber Stamp
- Free Transform
- Opacity Change
- Move
- Invert
- Eraser
- **Levels**

**COLOR FIGURE 1**
*The History palette.*

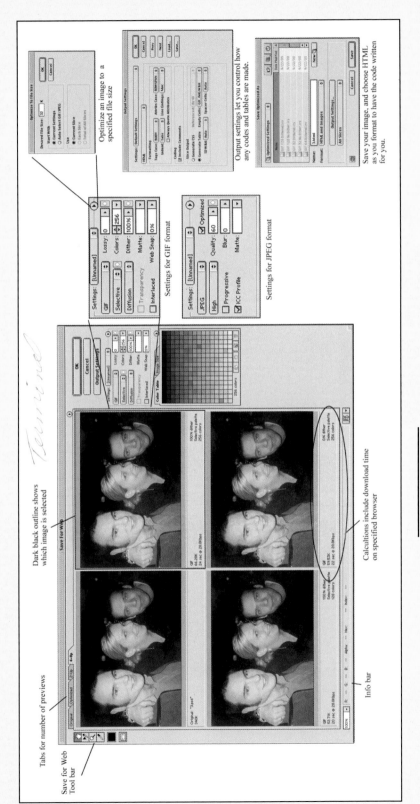

**COLOR FIGURE 2**

*The many and varied Save for Web dialog boxes.*

Optimize an image to a specified file size.

Output settings let you control how any codes and tables are made.

Save your image, and choose HTML as you format to have the code written for you.

Settings for GIF format

Settings for JPEG format

Tabs for number of previews

Save for Web Tool bar

Dark black outline shows which image is selected

Save For Web

Info bar

Calculations include download time on specified browser

**COLOR FIGURE 3**
*The Background Eraser erases based on the color value of the first pixel that is selected.*

**COLOR FIGURE 4**
*The Extract dialog box makes it easy to remove the background from an image, even if the image you are saving has difficult items to mask, such as hair.*

**COLOR FIGURE 5**
*The frames in this site made it tough to create the background.*

**COLOR FIGURE 6**
*A realistic burning effect.*

**COLOR FIGURE 7**
*A realistic "icing" effect.*

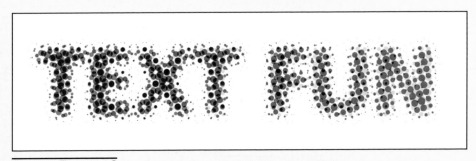

**COLOR FIGURE 8**
*Dotted effect achieved by using the Color Halftone filter.*

**COLOR FIGURE 9**
*Invert the image for the neon result above.*

**COLOR FIGURE 10**
*Various text effects.*

**COLOR FIGURE 11**
*Add a few extra drops on the fringe to make the puddle more realistic.*

**COLOR FIGURE 12**

*A tab system of navigation.*

**COLOR FIGURE 13**

*The buttons on this intranet site are small, cut-out photographs which help create the overall theme.*

## COLOR FIGURE 14

*This picture of my friend, Michali, came out washed out when I scanned it.*

## COLOR FIGURE 15

*After using the Color Balance adjustment, I was able to add red and yellow to her highlights, midtones, and shadows to give her picture more vibrancy.*

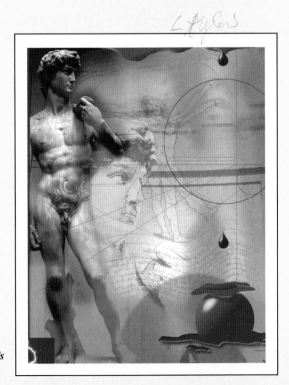

## COLOR FIGURE 16

*A collage created for one of my agency's brochures.*

## COLOR FIGURE 17
*The Tye-Dye Ring (left) and Spirograph Frame (right).*

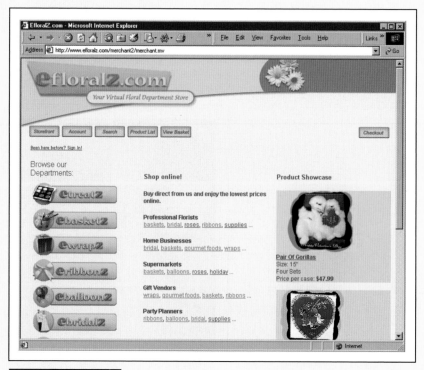

## COLOR FIGURE 18
*The site my company built for Union County Floral Supply.*

# chapter 6

# NAVIGATION, BUTTONS, AND BULLETS

In just one word, how would you describe the most widely accepted reason that the Web has become so popular so quickly? Here's a hint: It has nothing to do with the fact that insecure guys can shamelessly lie to faceless women.

That reason came in second.

No, the real reason the Web has grown so quickly is *hyperlinks*. Hyperlinks have allowed the virtual library to penetrate our everyday lives and make gathering information both simple and enjoyable. Rather than having to run to a card catalog every time you need to research a new reference, the Web puts all information just a click or two away.

As Web users began to realize the potential and convenience of the Internet, the importance of establishing effective navigation systems became evident to Web designers. Graphic artists have come to take advantage of Photoshop for button and navigation tasks, and today button art has almost become an industry all its own. Sites will often be judged more on their ease of navigation than on their aesthetic design, and the truly successful designers will combine creativity of shape, color, and texture with logic of layout and a well-thought-out site map.

In this chapter, you'll learn how and why buttons have become so important, quicker Photoshop methods for creating certain navigation staples, and exciting techniques for designing more interesting button and bullet styles.

# THE IMPORTANCE OF NAVIGATION

The fact that buttons can be any shape and size rather than just blue underlined words isn't that much of a secret anymore. But, amazingly, many web developers seem to overlook the importance of solid navigation as a factor of Internet success.

For years I've spoken at seminars and consulted at some of the nation's largest corporations preaching the necessity of navigation on a site. I tell them over and over that it's not so much about the design of a button or the shape of a navigation bar—it's about the ease of finding information. Regardless how nice your site is to look at, people are still visiting your site to gather information, and if they can't find that information, then the whole site is pointless.

Keep the following points in mind when developing the navigation for a site, no matter how large:

◆ Navigation can be placed anywhere on the page, but considering that monitor sizes and resolutions vary, the only reliable places to put it are either along the top or down the left side. Placing the navigational elements along the right-hand side or the bottom could possible cause unwanted scrolling, and you should never make a user scroll to find a main navigation button.

◆ Keep the primary navigational elements (the buttons that lead from the home page to the pages one tier down) visible at all times, no matter what page you're on. It's OK if they appear in one place on the home page, and then another place on all other pages (many sites will change layout and design between the home page and all other pages), but it's imperative that your primary navigation be visible throughout the site and except on the home page, should be in a consistent location.

◆ Secondary and tertiary navigation should be visible and placed in a standard, consistent location, as well.

◆ As a rule of thumb, you'll want to create your site so that any one page can be accessed from any other pages with three or four clicks, without having to resort to the Back button on the browser.

◆ Keep button names short and to the point, whenever possible. Remember, buttons are part of the overall graphics and layout, but they are primarily tools, not works of art.

◆ It always helps to layout the hierarchy of a site on paper before you start to build the site. Check out Chapter 10 for an example of this.

Figure 6–1 provides an example of a third tier of a web site that my agency created for the LPR Group (www.lprgroup.com). As you can see by the page provided, it's very easy to find your way around from one section to another without ever getting lost.

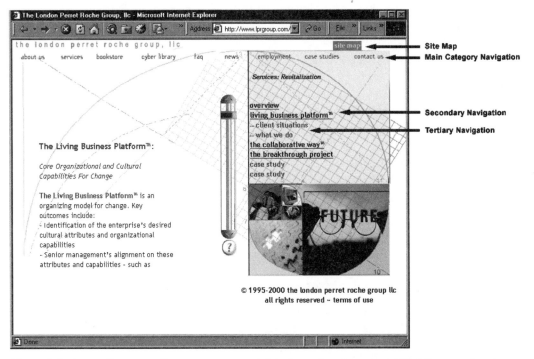

*Figure 6–1: A page from* `www.lprgroup.com`*. A lot of pre-planning ensured that the user almost never has to use the browser's Back button.*

# CREATING BEVELED BUTTONS

Beveled buttons have, in the last year or so, severely decreased in popularity. Once seen on practically every page on the web, they're kind of rare these days. So should we skip out on learning how to create them? If I were to write a chapter only on the latest fad or design trend, this wouldn't be a very long chapter: Most large, corporate sites use flat text in a colored bar as their primary navigation tool. They're elegant, easy to read, and, personally, I'm a big fan of this type of design. But when you're writing a book on web design, flat text in a color field doesn't make for a very interesting chapter on buttons.

So in case the trend starts coming back, or you just feel like being an individual, the next few sections will show you how to create various types of button designs.

# Using Simple Bevels to Create Buttons

1. Open a new file, 216 pixels by 72 pixels (yes, these are a bit big for buttons, but for this example, I'd like you to *see* what you're doing—we can resize later).

2. Create Layer 1 and make that the active layer (note: the Attributes features will not work on the background layer).

3. Choose a light shade of blue to fill your canvas.

4. Choose Bevel and Emboss from the Layer palette Layer attributes pop-up menu to get the dialog box shown in Figure 6–2.

5. From the Style pull-down menu, choose Inner Bevel.

6. For this example, set Angle to 120 degrees, Depth to the maximum 20 pixels, and Blur to 10. Click OK, and your canvas will look similar to Figure 6–3. Come back to this later and experiment with the different settings.

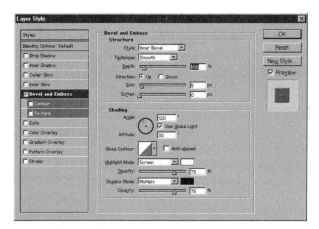

*Figure 6–2: The Layer Style Bevel and Emboss dialog box.*

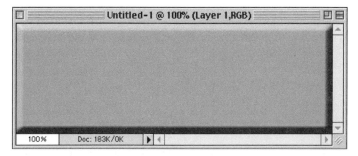

*Figure 6–3: Inner bevel with applied of depth 20 pixels, blur 10 pixels.*

# Creating Buttons With Dual Bevel

1. Working from the previous example, use the Rectangular Marquee tool to make a selection of the solid blue area in your button.

> **You may wonder why I'd suggest using the Rectangular Marquee tool instead of, say, the Magic Wand with a low tolerance. The answer is that Layer attributes will still read the entire layer as your shade of blue, and not distinguish the shadow or the light.**

2. Choose Select -> Modify -> Contract and choose a setting of 3. This will make sure that your selection is not interfering with the beveled edge you created. It will look similar to Figure 6–4.

3. We're going to put a new bevel on this selection. Since Layer attributes always applies to the entire layer, the fact that you have one particular portion selected won't matter much. Press Command and C (Ctrl + C in Windows) to copy your selection, and then Command + V (Ctrl + V in Windows) to paste it in the same spot but on a new layer.

4. Choose Layer -> Attributes -> Bevel and Emboss and, keeping the angle and the depth the same, push the Radio button for down instead of up, and lower the blur to 2. Your button will look like the button in Figure 6–5.

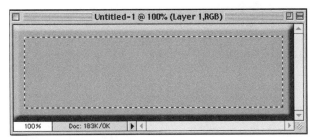

*Figure 6–4: Part of the main field was selected, copied, and pasted onto a new Layer, so a new Layer attribute can be applied.*

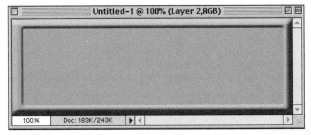

*Figure 6–5: A bevel effect applied to the new layer, this time beveling downward instead of upward. The result is a ridge around the edge.*

# Using Traditional Methods for Bevels

Depending on what you're looking for, you may want to use more traditional methods for creating a beveled button, which tend to be less limited.

1. Open a new file 216 pixels by 72 pixels.

2. Choose a color to fill your canvas.

3. Select All, choose Select -> Modify -> Border, and choose a border setting of 12.

4. Choose Select -> Save Selection, and choose New in the Channel pull-down menu (if you do not name them, channels will automatically default to "Alpha 1," "Alpha 2," and so on in your Channels palette). All color disappears, and even the foreground and background colors are now black and white. The Channel palette is shown in Figure 6–6.

5. Deselect all and choose Filter -> Render -> Lighting Effects to bring up the dialog box shown in Figure 6–7. In the Texture channel pull-down menu, select Alpha 1. Set the direction of your light to be similar to that of the figure.

6. Click OK, and your image will look like Figure 6–8.

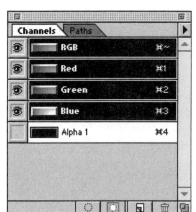

*Figure 6–6: The Channels palette. Alpha 1 is our selection.*

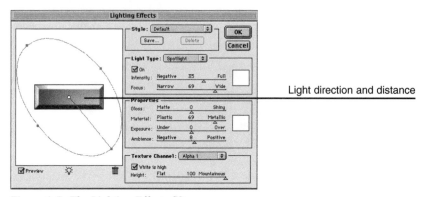

Light direction and distance

*Figure 6–7: The Lighting Effects filter.*

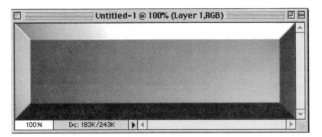

*Figure 6–8: A simple bevel created with the Lighting Effects filter.*

# Creating Traditional Dual Bevel

1. Still working from the previous example, open the Channels palette. Make Alpha 1 the active channel by clicking on it. Choose Select All by pressing Command and A (Ctrl + A in Windows). Choose Select -> Modify -> border and set the border to 24 (twice what our original border was).

2. Choose Select -> Save Selection. This time your new channel is automatically named Alpha 2. Make Alpha 2 the active layer by clicking on it.

3. Press Command and L (Ctrl + L in Windows) to open up the Levels dialog box, as shown in Figure 6–9. The Levels dialog box allows you to adjust both the input and output levels of your image or selection. While Input Levels allows you to increase the shadows and highlights and adjust the midtones, Output Levels lets you decrease the shadows and highlights.

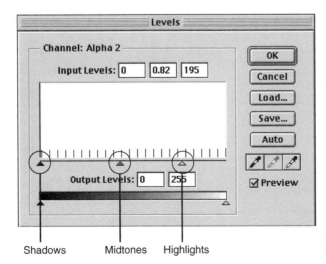

Shadows    Midtones    Highlights

*Figure 6–9: The Levels dialog box.*

Increase the highlights in Input Levels by moving the right slider to the left until it has a reading of 195. Adjust the Midtones slider, in the center, over to the right, for a reading of 0.85. This will make the neutral areas in your button darker, and the highlighted areas brighter.

4. Press Command and D (Ctrl + D in Windows) to deselect all.

5. Click the RGB channel to make your color channels active again.

6. Go back to the Lighting Effects filter and this time make sure that the Texture pull-down menu is on Alpha 2 and no longer on Alpha 1. Play around with the light until it looks like the light shown in Figure 6–10.

7. Click OK, and your image will be similar to that shown in Figure 6–11.

# CREATING CIRCULAR BEVELS

Another popular type of button is a circular one and, again, the addition of a bevel can help add to the depth and realism of your buttons.

## Creating A Simple Circular Bevel

1. Open a new file, 216 pixels by 216 pixels. You can reduce the size of the button later.

2. Create a new layer so that you start your button on Layer 1. We'll be using some of Photoshop's Layer attributes later, which don't work on the background layer.

3. Using the Elliptical Marquee tool, hold down the Shift key for constraint and drag to create a circle in the middle of the canvas, like in Figure 6–12.

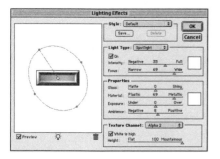

*Figure 6–10: The Lighting Effects dialog box.*

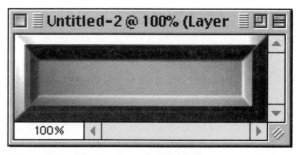

*Figure 6–11: The final result shows a deep outer ridge.*

4. Set the background color to black and choose some light shade of blue for your foreground color. Using the Gradient tool, with the options set to Foreground to Background, drag a gradient from the northwest position of your circle to the southeast position. This is illustrated in Figure 6–13.

5. Make sure the circle is selected and press Command and C (Ctrl + C in Windows) to copy it to your clipboard. Press Command and V (Ctrl + V in Windows) to paste it back again. It will automatically appear in its own separate layer.

6. Choose Edit -> Transform -> Rotate 180 degrees.

7. Choose Edit -> Transform -> Numeric Transform to access the dialog box shown in Figure 6–14. Make sure that Scale is checked, and reduce your selection to 80% on both axes. Click OK. The result will be similar to Figure 6–15.

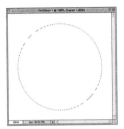

*Figure 6–12: A perfect circular selection, made by holding the Shift key while dragging with the Circle Marquee tool.*

*Figure 6–13: The gradient has been added.*

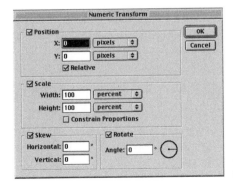

*Figure 6–14: The Numeric Transform dialog box.*

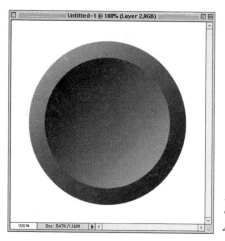

*Figure 6–15: An indent appears when the original gradient is made smaller and is flipped.*

8. Add a shadow to the button by making Layer 1 the active layer again, and choose Drop Shadow from the Layers attributes icon at the bottom of the Layers palette.

9. In the dialog box, select a distance of 10 and a blur of 20. Click OK and the drop shadow will appear as in Figure 6–16.

This seems to be as good a place as any to mention that any of the buttons shown here, especially the circular ones, can be used as bullets as well. The truth is, except for their size, many buttons and bullets are interchangeable—even the rectangular buttons described earlier in this chapter can be made into bullets if they are narrowed into squares instead of rectangles.

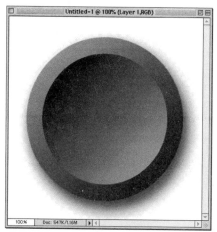

*Figure 6–16: The button gains depth with the drop shadow.*

## Creating a Pushed-in "Coat" Button

You know those big round buttons your grandmother was forever sewing onto something? Well, this exercise will make grandma's job a little bit easier ...

1. Follow Steps 1–3 from "Creating a Simple Circular Bevel" earlier in this chapter.
2. Fill your selection with a light shade of blue.
3. With your circle still selected, choose Select -> Save Selection, and save your selection as Alpha 1.
4. Within your Channels palette, make Alpha 1 your active channel.
5. If your rulers are not already showing, click Command and R (Ctrl + R in Windows) and pull a horizontal and vertical line from each ruler (by placing your cursor over the left ruler and dragging to the right) to establish a middle point on the circle, as in Figure 6–17. If you're still using Photoshop 3, you'll have to place guides by opening a new layer and using the line tool.
6. With the Radial Gradient tool selected, and the gradient range set to Foreground to Background in the Options palette, drag a gradient from your center point to the edge of your circle.
7. Press Command and L (Ctrl + L in Windows) to access the Levels dialog box. Set the Shadows level to 32, and the highlights level to 235. You'll see that your gradient is no longer as smooth as it once was.
8. Make the RGB channel active again by clicking on it. Note that you can see the color in your image again.

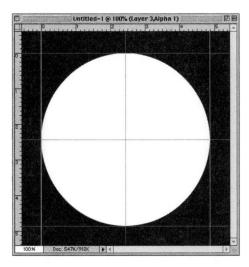

*Figure 6–17: Midpoint of the circle is located by using both the horizontal and vertical rulers.*

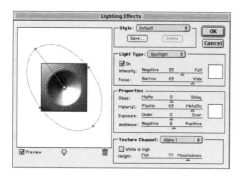

*Figure 6–18: The Lighting Effects dialog box previews the button.*

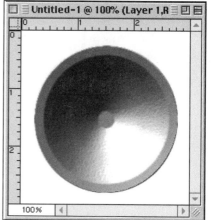

*Figure 6–19: Final product after setting lighting effects.*

9. Choose Filter -> Render -> Lighting Effects to access the Lighting Effects dialog box shown in Figure 6–18. Set your light type to Spotlight and move the direction to coming from the northwest. Make sure that the White is high option is clicked, and set your Texture channel to Alpha 1. Click OK.

10. Your button will look like the one shown in Figure 6–19.

# Creating a Pill-Shaped Button: Photoshop 5.5 and Lower

Pill-shaped buttons are a great effect that give you the personality of a round button, the rigidity of a rectangular one, but that leave enough space to write on. They're fairly easy to make and very functional. Version 6 now includes the Shape tool, which allows you to make squares with rounded corners, so the creation of pill-shaped buttons is quick and easy. Not an important enough feature by itself to make anyone run out to buy the upgrade, though, so for anyone still working with version 5.5 or lower, here's how to go about it:

1. Open a new file, 432 pixels by 216 pixels. This is too large for a button but, for the example, I'd like for you to see what you're doing—you can reduce the size later.

2. Open a new layer and, using the Elliptical Marquee tool, hold the Shift key down and make a circle toward the left side of your canvas.

3. Select the Paintbucket tool and fill your circle with a light shade of blue.

**Make sure that Anti-aliased is clicked off in the Paintbucket Options palette. Leaving it on can lead to an unwanted haloing effect.**

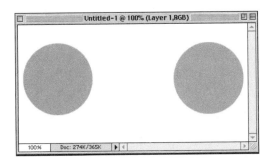

*Figure 6–20: Two identical circles will become the ends of the pill button.*

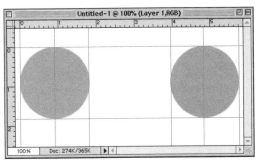

*Figure 6–21: Use the rulers to build the body of the button.*

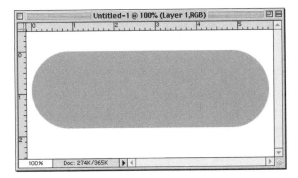

*Figure 6–22: Fill the body with the same color as the circles.*

**4.** Press the V key to select your Move tool and, holding the Option and Shift (Alt + Shift in Windows) keys down, drag a copy of the circle to the other side of the canvas. The Option key is what activates the copy function, while the Shift key restricts you to dragging in a perfectly straight line. Your canvas will look like Figure 6–20.

**5.** If your rulers are not already visible, press Command and R (Ctrl + R in Windows) to make them visible. Drag down two horizontal rules, one at the top and one at the bottom of your circles, and drag over vertical lines to pinpoint the center diameter of both circles, like Figure 6–21.

**6.** Select View -> Snap to Guides to make sure that your next selection will hug the rules you just made.

**7.** With the Rectangular Marquee tool, make a selection from the top left corner of your rules to the bottom right corner. Fill your new selection with the same color that you used to fill the circles. Your image should look similar to the image in Figure 6–22.

**8.** Hold down the Command key (Ctrl in Windows) and click on Layer 1 to select your entire image. Start a new layer so that you don't disturb the pill you just created.

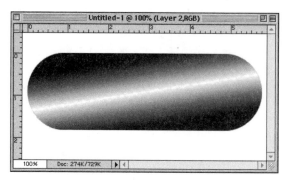

*Figure 6–23: Use the striped gradient tool to create a black to white to black gradient over the pill button. Choosing Soft Light as your layer mode will make your button appear to have a light hitting it.*

9.  Choose Reflected gradient as your tool and press the D key to change the foreground and background colors to black and white. Press the X key to switch the foreground and background colors. Starting from the middle of your selection, drag a gradient downward and just slightly to the right to create the diagonal gradient that you see in Figure 6–23.

10. In the Layers palette, select "soft light" for your mode. This will make the gradient blend in with the blue on Layer 1, making it seem as if there were a light going through it.

11. With Layer 2 still the active layer, choose Bevel and Emboss from the Layer Attributes pop-up menu at the bottom of the Layers palette.

12. In the Bevel and Emboss dialog box, select Emboss as your style. Figure 6–24 shows the pill button with different depth and blur settings.

## *One More Cool Example*

I cannot think up a good title for what this is, so I'll just say it's a cool thing that you can do to add flavor to the previous example.

1.  Make Layer 1 the active layer and select the pill button on it by pressing Command (Ctrl in Windows) and clicking on Layer 1.

2.  Choose Select -> Modify -> Contract and enter 16, which is the maximum.

3.  Choose Select -> Modify -> Border and choose a border of 10.

4.  Choose Select -> Feather and feather your selection by 2.

5.  Choose Select -> Save Selection and save your selection as Alpha 2.

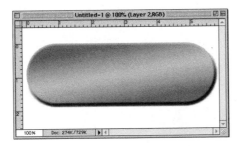

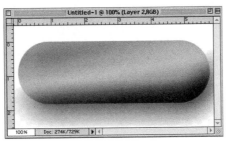

*Figure 6–24: Various Layer Attributes settings:*

Top left: Inner bevel, depth = 5, blur = 5
Top right: Inner bevel, depth = 20, blur = 10
Bottom center: Inner bevel, depth = 20, blur = 40

6. Choose Filter -> Render -> Lighting Effects.

7. Set the Texture channel to Alpha 2, and alter the direction of the light as shown in Figure 6–25. Click OK, and your image should look like the image in Figure 6–26, only cooler because yours is in color.

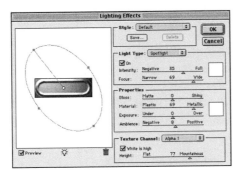

*Figure 6–25: Using the Lighting Effects options on the pill button to create a stark ridge toward the edge.*

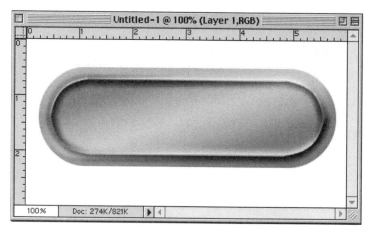

*Figure 6–26: An inner ridge gives the button increased depth.*

# CREATING BUTTONS WITH TEXTURE ADDED

Once you have gotten the hang of beveled buttons, you're probably going to want to put some texture on them, depending on the look or theme of the web site. The following are just some of the great textures that you can create in Photoshop 6. After that are some text effects to work with the texture we're creating.

## Creating Buttons With a Brushed Metal Texture

The brushed metal effect can be a cool texture for a button, but is probably a good technique to learn for other projects, too. Personally, even though you can do this particular effect at 72 ppi like all the others, I think it comes out nicer if you create the texture at 150–200 ppi and then scale it down.

1. Open a new file, 432 pixels by 216 pixels, 200 ppi. You can scale it down to proper size later.

2. Create a new layer to begin.

3. Make white your background color and a medium to dark gray your foreground color.

4. Make the Gradient tool active by clicking on it. From the Options palette, click once on the Gradient preview to access the Gradient editor shown in Figure 6–27.

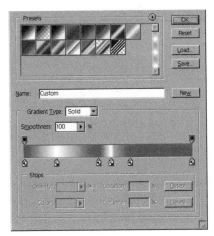

*Figure 6–27: Gradient editor.*

5. Create a gradient as shown in Figure 6–27 by alternating between the foreground color and the background color to simulate stripes. Click OK to leave the Gradient editor when you're finished.

6. Drag the Gradient tool crosshairs from the top left corner to set your gradient.

7. Your canvas should look as though there is light reflecting off it.

**If the stripes are too well defined, choose Filter -> Gaussian Blur and move the slider outward until the stripes are blended better.**

The result will look like Figure 6–28.

8. Choose Filter -> Noise -> Add Noise to access the dialog box shown in Figure 6–29. Set the noise Amount to 50, using a uniform distribution. Click OK.

9. Choose Filter -> Blur -> Motion Blur. Set the angle to match the direction that your light hits are going. Set Blur Distance to 110, and Click OK.

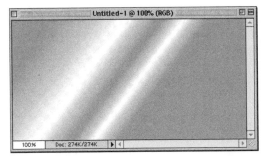

*Figure 6–28: The gradient placed into the selection.*

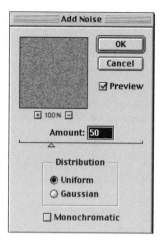

*Figure 6–29: The Add Noise filter.*

10. Choose Image -> Adjust -> Color Balance to bring up the dialog box shown in Figure 6–30.

11. In the midtones, move the top slider closer to Cyan until the first numeric color level reads -16. Move the bottom slider closer to Blue until the last number color level reads +28. Click OK.

12. Select Image -> Image Size and reduce your image to 72 ppi.

13. Bevel the button with one of the methods described earlier. (You may have to make your canvas a bit larger to get a decent bevel effect. If so, do this by choosing Image -> Canvas Size, and making each dimension just a bit larger.) I chose to use Layer attributes, with an inner bevel 20 pixels deep and 8 pixels blurred, as seen in Figure 6–31.

14. Using the Type Mask tool, open the text editor and type "HOME" in large letters and click OK. You'll notice that the selection text resides on Layer 1 and does not automatically start a new layer as regular text does.

15. We're going to use the Layer attributes options for our text. Because the attributes options automatically apply to everything on the layer and not just what you've

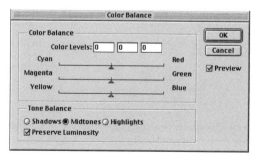

*Figure 6–30: The Color Balance dialog box.*

selected, we're going to have to work on a different layer. Move your text selection where you want it and push Command and C (Ctrl + C in Windows) to copy that part of the image to the pasteboard. Now press Command and V (Ctrl + V in Windows) to paste it back. You'll see that it pastes into a new layer.

16. Open the Bevel and Emboss dialog box from the Layers attributes icon in the Layers palette. Figure 6–32 and Color Figure 10 show how some different settings can look, each nicely complementing the brushed steel effect.

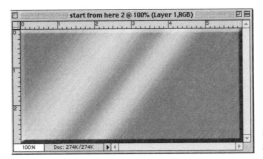

*Figure 6–31: The final product resembles a button made of steel.*

*Figure 6–32: Various text effects.*

Top left: Outer bevel, depth =5, blur = 5
Middle left: Emboss, depth = 20, blur = 7
Bottom left: Outer bevel, depth = 20, blur = 6, plus Inner shadow, default settings
Top right: Inner shadow, distance = 10 blur = 3

# Creating Water Puddle Buttons

This button design will help you make a splash on your web site (sorry—sometimes I cannot resist). Instead of each button having a hard edge, the Water Puddle button takes advantage of a variance in shape and texture to create its effect.

1. Open a new file, 600 pixels by 400 pixels, 200 ppi. You can scale it down to proper size later.

2. Create a new layer, Layer 1, to begin.

3. Use your Free Form lasso tool to make a wavy, elliptical selection, as shown in Figure 6–33, to create the outlines of your puddle.

4. Make white your foreground color and select a light shade of blue for your background color.

5. Choose the Radial Gradient tool and, starting from the center of the selection, create a gradient from white to light blue, as illustrated in Figure 6–34.

6. Press Command and D (Ctrl + D in Windows) to deselect your selection.

7. Open the Bevel and Emboss dialog box from the Layers attributes icon in the Layers palette. From the Style pull-down menu, choose Inner Bevel.

8. Set Depth to 10 pixels, and Blur to 20 pixels. Click OK, and the result will look similar to Figure 6–35.

9. Choose Filter -> Distort -> Zig Zag to access the dialog box. Set Amount to 34% and Ridges to 7%. Click OK, and your image will look similar to Figure 6–36.

10. Add a slight shadow by opening the Bevel and Emboss dialog box, from the Layers Attributes icon in the Layers palette. Set Opacity to 40%, Distance to 3, and Blur to 4. Click OK.

11. Place the button name on your puddle with the Text editor, as shown in Figure 6–37.

12. The text will need to be fluid as well and not as harsh as it currently appears. Before applying a filter, choose Layer -> Type -> Render Layer.

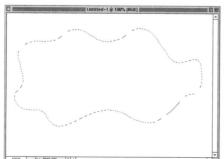

*Figure 6–33: A wavy, elliptical selection.*

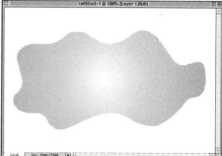

*Figure 6–34: Selection filled with white to blue gradient.*

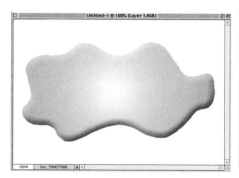

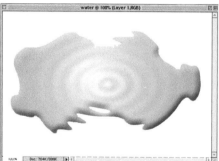

*Figure 6–35: The Inner Bevel effect.*

*Figure 6–36: The Zig Zag filter provides a pond-like ripple.*

13. Applying the same amount of the Zig Zag filter would distort the text too much and make it illegible. Instead, select Filter -> Distort -> Ripple and set the Ripple amount to 115% and Size to Medium.

14. Click OK, and your final button will look similar to Figure 6–38. Don't forget to reduce the resolution to 72 ppi before using it on your Web site.

 **For a more realistic puddle effect, add a few droplets around your button, as shown in Figure 6–39 and Color Figure 11.**

*Figure 6–37: Straight Text is too harsh.*

*Figure 6–38: The Ripple filter makes the text blend in better with the button.*

*Figure 6–39: Add a few extra drops on the fringe to make the puddle more realistic.*

# OTHER TYPES OF BUTTONS

There are a lot of buttons you can make with the examples given in this chapter. Of course, not all buttons are limited to rectangles, circles, and pills with bevels and embosses. There are plenty of other types of buttons that you can use, including image icons, tabs, and others. The following pages show just a couple examples that have been used on different sites.

## Tabbed Buttons

Creating folder tabs are a clever way to help your user navigate through a Web site. By using various intensities of shadows and/or various tab shapes, you can have the tabs come forward or backward to show which page the viewer is seeing.

In Figure 6–40 and Color Figure 12, I created a tab navigation system for Mac Products' Web site (`www.macproduct.com`). Each tab appears to come forward as the user clicks on a different topic.

## Buttons Made From Images

Buttons don't always have to conform to traditional expectations of what a button should look like. Sometimes the button can be small pictures—icon sized—to help add to an overall theme. Figure 6–41 and Color Figure 13 show a home page my agency created for a Novartis intranet. They wanted to go with an office theme throughout the intranet site. To enhance the imagery, especially in the lower-tier pages where graphics gave way to text, we created office-oriented pictures for each of the buttons. Rolodexes, briefcases, file cabinets, and other photographs played a part in not only the navigation, but in tying the concept together.

# COMPLEX BUTTONS: IMAGE MAPS AND ROLLOVERS

There aren't many sites on the web that you can still visit without running into at least one set of rollovers or an image mapped navigation system. Whether this trend is because they are useful or because they are simply easy to create is up for question (I have my opinions, but I'll keep those to myself this round). Either way, if you plan to make a web site longer than one page, you'll likely need or want to learn how to make rollovers and image maps.

As a quick refresher, for the few out there who might not know exactly what I mean by *image maps* and *rollovers*, I'll offer the following definitions:

*Figure 6–40: A Tab system of navigation.*

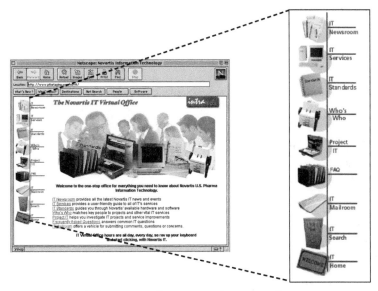

*Figure 6–41: The buttons on this intranet site are small, cut-out photographs which help create the overall theme.*

◆ *Image map*—An image map is one image that has been carved up into pieces and reassembled in an HTML table. Each of the pieces can act as a link to a separate URL, even though it is part of one image.

◆ *Rollover*—A rollover is a button or image that changes, or causes something else to change, when you move your cursor over it. A shadow might appear under it, for example, or maybe the button will change colors.

In the first edition of this book, for version 5, the explanation of how to do this spanned 10 pages, and was replete with math and programming code. This time, though, it's a lot simpler. In fact, it's really no longer even a Photoshop issue. Since ImageReady is now shipped as an integrated part of Photoshop, it has become responsible for more complex navigation such as rollovers and image maps.

**Truthfully, it's DreamWeaver, not ImageReady, that is responsible for more of the image maps and rollover effects. But this book isn't about DreamWeaver, so for convenience we'll just pretend that more of it is done in ImageReady.**

Technically, it is possible to create image maps in Photoshop. Version 6 has incorporated the Slice and Slice Select tools that once appeared only in ImageReady. Photoshop also allows a way for you to make each slice link to its own URL. But it's a far easier and more streamlined process in ImageReady, and should, at least for now, stay there. You can read more on how to use ImageReady to create these features in Chapter 8.

# SUMMARY

Buttons and navigation are what give people the ability to find their way through the Web. If a navigation setup is attractive and functional, it will not only become a major part of your site's overall appearance, but it will open up all of the other pages to your users. Poorly planned and designed navigation tools will hinder the user's ability to find sought-after information. Paying special attention to how you establish your buttons, image maps, and rollovers will prove worthwhile as people will extend their visits and really have the opportunity to find the information you have available.

# chapter 7

# INLINE GRAPHICS:
# IMAGE IS
# EVERYTHING

More and more often, Web designers are relying on graphic elements rather than text to get their messages across to potential visitors. As speeds of modems increase and users become more sophisticated, the images that are used in your site will play a more important role in presenting information. These images can be as simple as a photograph or an illustration, and as complex as a multiphotographic collage.

This chapter will briefly explore some of the available methods for getting images into Photoshop and techniques for retouching scanned, damaged, or otherwise problematic images. We'll then take a detailed journey into some of the Photoshop features—some tried and true, some brand new—that have helped turn good Web sites into great Web sites.

# GETTING IMAGES INTO
# PHOTOSHOP

Your Web site is all laid out in your head, and you've got a stack of family vacation pictures that you are dying to put online. So how do you do it? You can try to fold them up and shove them into your disk drive, but that rarely works. There are ways that are far more effective.

# Personal Scanners

There are many scanners on the market that do a great job of getting photographs into Photoshop. If you're not sure which scanner to buy, you might want to check out the following Web sites that offer reviews and descriptions:

◆ www.byte.com

◆ www.zdnet.com/pcmag/features/scanners/_open.htm

◆ www.inconference.com/digicam/scanners.html

◆ www.scanshop.com/scanner

Some of the above Web sites also give some useful inside tips to better scanning, so they're worth a quick glance.

Once your scanner is hooked up and all the necessary software has been installed into your system, you'll have to let Photoshop know that the scanner is there before you begin to scan. For this example, I am going to be using the HP 4C ScanJet. Other scanners will have a different interface, and may function differently, but the basic theory will remain the same.

1. Choose File -> Import -> Twain Select and choose the scanner that you installed. (Note: You will only have to do this once.)

2. In the scanner interface shown in Figure 7–1, the object that you are scanning will appear in the preview area. Create a marquee around the object or part of the object that you wish to scan.

3. From the Type pull-down menu, choose what type of scan you would like to make. In most instances, I usually choose "Sharp Millions of Colors." That way I get the most out of the image and can reduce colors later. Although most scanners have tools in them that you can use to manipulate your image, you're better off concentrating your efforts on getting a clean, raw scan and manipulating it in Photoshop.

*Figure 7–1: The interface of the HP 4C ScanJet desktop scanner.*

4. Because Web graphics don't need to be greater than 72 ppi, I change the scan resolutions by choosing Image -> Print Size to access the dialog box shown in Figure 7–2, changing all the variables to 72 ppi.

5. Use the slider to increase or decrease image size and hit Final or Scan.

The image will appear in a new canvas in Photoshop, ready to be manipulated.

**Scanning at higher resolutions will give you more detail in your image, but you may wind up scanning the actual texture of the original paper at higher resolutions. Later in this chapter I'll discuss how to fix these problems with the Gaussian Blur filter.**

Each scanner model will be different from other models and the models of other manufacturers. Interfaces, troubleshooting solutions, and work-arounds will also vary—too much, in fact, to really get into it in a book on Photoshop for the Web. Check out Robert Gann's book, *Desktop Scanners*, also published by Prentice Hall, for a really in-depth scanner discussion.

Unless you take extra good care of both your original image and the bed of your scanner, you'll almost definitely have a fair amount of dust particles on your scanned image. Later in this chapter I'll discuss how to get rid of these.

# Photo CD-ROMs

Today it's easier than ever to get your photos on a CD-ROM. CD drives are standard issue on most computers, and having your images on a photo CD can be helpful when creating your Web images. Some of the benefits of having your pictures on a photo CD include:

◆ You don't have to do your own scanning—professionals do it for you!

◆ A small additional price per image will give you a number of resolutions, so you can use them for anything from Web design to printing.

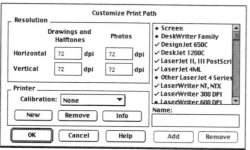

*Figure 7–2: The Print Size dialog box will change the resolution of the scan.*

◆ The CD will act as storage so you can use a minimal amount of hard drive space.

◆ Printed icons of the images on the back of the CD case will help catalog your images for future use.

To get your photos on a CD, simply bring them to any service bureau, or even to most one-hour photo developing shops. Depending on the place you bring them to, the average wait for your CD can range anywhere between 24 hours and one week. Prices, as of the time of this writing, usually fall between $2.00–$4.50 per picture depending on the desired resolution, plus $20.00–$25.00 for the CD.

**You can usually avoid the CD fee by supplying your own CD. If you've already gotten your photos on a CD, and you're getting more, just have them put the new images on the old CD, if there's still room.**

**Don't confuse the floppy disk that sometimes comes with your film for the Photo CD. The disks usually just contain icons of your photos, to make it easy to reorder—not hi-res images that are suitable for printing.**

# Stock Photo CDs

If you don't have any of your own photographs to scan or put on a CD, there are many companies that do all the work for you. Collectively, stock photo companies have millions of images that you can use in your designs, usually broken up into convenient categories for simple reference. Collections such as "Business Today," "Vacations and Leisure," and "North American Locations" provide you with both generic and specific images from which to choose.

The following companies are some of the ones that I use often when I need a picture but don't feel like dusting off the camera:

◆ Photodisc               `www.photodisc.com`

◆ Eyewire                 `www.eyewire.com`

◆ Corel                   `www.corel.com`

◆ Comstock                `www.comstock.com`

◆ Adobe Image Library     `www.adobe.com/newsfeatures/imagelib`

◆ Artville                      `www.artville.com`

◆ Digital Stock             `www.digitalstock.com`

Stock images are usually sold in one of two ways:

◆ You can purchase one CD that contains multiple images, any of which you have the right to use for one predetermined price per CD. (Different categories will have different prices.)

◆ You can choose a picture or set of pictures from a catalog or CD sampler and negotiate a price with the stock house. They will supply you with a transparency, negative, and so forth. Price is based on usage, distribution, and so forth.

◆ Low-res images can also be downloaded directly from the Web.

**Make sure you read the disclaimers and copyright material carefully for each company. Although you will have the rights to the photos you purchase, there may still be limitations on their usage.**

## Digital Cameras

Digital cameras have roared onto the scene and are continuing to gain popularity quickly. Although still a bit pricey, digitals allow you to skip the film aspect of photography altogether and send your image directly to your computer. Even more exciting is that digital cameras that come with a view screen allow you to check out your picture after you take it and decide to either save it or delete it.

Price ranges for digital cameras tend to vary; however, the lower priced units (under $1,000) do not really supply a high enough resolution for quality commercial printing. They are ideal for use on the Web, though, and are an increasingly popular source for Internet photography.

Because the features, prices, and abilities of digital cameras change too rapidly for me to write their specifications in this book, you may want to visit the following Web sites for articles and reviews:

◆ `www.zdnet.com/familypc/content/9706/fthw/index.html`

◆ `www.dcresource.com`

◆ `www.computers.com/cdoor/0,1,0-21-2,00.html?st.cn.re.story.co`

# RESIZING AND RESAMPLING IMAGES

When you bring an image into Photoshop, you're not obligated to keep it at its original size or resolution. In fact, as I will explain later, when scanning images for the Web, changing the size and the resolution will be necessary to achieve an optimal image quality to file size ratio.

Although you can make size and resolution changes in a few different ways (see "Cropping Image Edges" later in this chapter), the best way is to do the following:

1. With an open image, choose Image -> Image Size to access the dialog box shown in Figure 7–3 (7–3 shows the *resize* dialog box, Figure 7–4 displays the options used to *resample*). The top portion of the dialog box displays your image in pixel size (the default setting), as well as providing information on the file size. The bottom portion of the dialog box shows the size in terms of inches, or other desired measurements including percent, points, and picas.

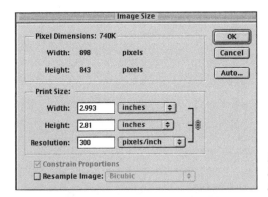

*Figure 7–3: The Image Size dialog box, set to resize the image (with the resample box unchecked).*

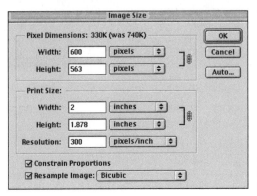

*Figure 7–4: The Image Size dialog box, set to resample the image (with the resample box checked).*

**2.** Decide how you want to change your image:

*Resizing* your image generally implies changing its physical size without changing the number of pixels. To do this, make sure that the Resample Image checkbox is left unchecked. The dialog box will look like Figure 7–4. You'll notice that the width and height dimensions in the pixel information section stay static—they cannot be manipulated. Beyond that, the Constrain Proportions checkbox, reflected in the chain link in the Print Size section links the width, height, and resolution.

Change the size of your image by manipulating any one of the available variables. If you reduce the resolution, the width and height will increase proportionately. Alternately, if you increase the resolution, the width and height will decrease. This practice holds true, too, if you increase or decrease either the width or height. In the end, the following mathematical equations will always hold true:

Width (Print Size) x Resolution = Width (Pixel Dimensions)

Height (Print Size) x Resolution = Height (Pixel Dimensions)

The file size of your image will not change, no matter what dimensions you choose. Figure 7–5 shows an example of a resized image and its file size, before and after.

Original Picture
7.707 inches x 5.087 inches
2,312 pixels x 1,520 pixels
300 ppi resolution
3.37M

Resized Picture
4 inches x 2.64 inches
2,312 pixels x 1,520 pixels
578 ppi resolution
3.37M

*Figure 7–5: The resized image. Notice that the pixels and file size stay the same, but the resolution and physical size change. The screen display, however, does not change, as the small physical size in the revised picture has a higher resolution.*

*Resampling* will actually change the number of pixels in your image and can be done by checking the Resample Image box. As shown in Figure 7–4, the dialog box differs from the dialog box for resizing your image in a few distinct ways:

◆ The width and height in pixels can be changed.

◆ The chain in the Print Size section only links the width and height.

◆ A new chain appears in the Pixel Dimensions section linking the width and height.

◆ The Constrain Proportions checkbox is made active (when unchecked, the chain links disappear).

◆ A pull-down menu with options for how you want to resample your image is made active.

Regardless of what you change in your image, the file size and the pixel dimensions will be affected. You will also have three choices as to how to resample your image, with each choice accessible through the Resample Image pull-down menu:

◆ *Bicubic* is the smoothest, but also the slowest.

◆ *Bilinear* is faster, but not quite as smooth.

◆ *Nearest Neighbor* will cause Photoshop to throw away or duplicate pixels as necessary.

You'll most often want to use the Bicubic option, even if it takes a few seconds longer. The quality increase is worth the almost insignificant wait. Figure 7–6 shows an image that has been resampled.

Original Picture
7.707 inches x 5.087 inches
2,312 pixels x 1520 pixels
300 ppi resolution
3.37M

Resampled Picture (Bicubic)
4 inches x 2.64 inches
1,200 pixels x 792 pixels
300 ppi resolution
929K

*Figure 7–6: The resampled image. Notice that the pixels and file size both change.*

Resampling up is usually not such a great idea and rarely has a useable effect. When you increase either the resolution or the physical size independent of each other, Photoshop is forced to add pixels to the image where there were none. Because Photoshop does not have any information as to what to put in these new pixels, an image that is resampled up usually looks blurry or pixilated (see Figure 7–7).

Resampling down, though, is a good idea, especially when creating Web sites. To make sure that scanned images have the maximum quality, scan each image in at 300 ppi (even 600 ppi depending on the details in your image). Then resample down to the 72 ppi resolution level. The number of pixels and the file size will both be smaller, but your image will have the best chance of retaining decent quality this way.

*Figure 7–7: The top image is 72 ppi, shown at 200%. The bottom image shows the same picture resampled up to 600 ppi, also shown at 200%. So much information has been forced into the picture that it is blurred almost beyond recognition.*

# PHOTO RETOUCHING TECHNIQUES

No matter what medium you're designing for, whenever you scan or otherwise import original photography into Photoshop, you'll most likely have to do at least a little bit of retouching. Retouching can include cropping a picture's edges, removing dust and scratches, or fixing the colors. Depending on your perspective, retouching can either be painfully dull or one of the most exciting parts of Photoshop—some companies have even developed their retouching talents to such an extent that that's all they do, and they make tons of money doing it.

## Cropping Image Edges

Sometimes it may be difficult to scan a picture without also scanning some unwanted edges. It is even more difficult to place a picture on the scan bed perfectly straight and have it stay that way after you close the top of the scanner.

There are other reasons for cropping images besides bad scanning. These include cropping to reduce file size for faster uploading of Web pages and cropping one image or a series of images to match the dimensions of another image. Whatever your reasons are, it is important to understand the various techniques you can use to crop in Photoshop.

### *Using the Crop Tool*

1. Choose the Crop tool from the toolbar. It's hidden under the Marquee tools.

2. Drag a selection around the portion of your image that you wish to keep. If you make a mistake, use the handles on the corners and sides of the crop selection to make changes. Holding the Shift key down while dragging will constrain the proportions.

3. Outside the selection, your cursor will look like a curved line with arrowheads at either end. Drag your mouse in the direction of either arrow to crop at the appropriate angle. Figure 7–8 illustrates this.

   To change the center of rotation, drag the point of origin (the center crosshair in the crop marquee) to another area of the image.

4. Press the Return/Enter button to crop your selection, or the Esc button to cancel your selection.

*Figure 7–8: You can rotate the Crop tool for diagonal scans or shots before making your final cut.*

## Using the Marquee to Crop

**1.** Use the Rectangular marquee to make a selection around the area you wish to keep.

**2.** From the menu options, choose Image -> Crop. (Easy, huh?)

## Changing the Canvas Size to Crop an Image

**1.** Decide the portion of your image that you wish to delete. Figure 7–9 shows an image with the guides marking off the areas I wish to crop away and the areas I wish to keep.

 You don't need to use the ruler or the guides to crop with this method, but it helps for accuracy.

**2.** Choose Image -> Canvas Size to access the dialog box shown in Figure 7–10. The information toward the top of the dialog box shows the Current Size (file size), as well as the current width and height. Below that is the area in which you can change the size of your canvas. If you increase the width and height, Photoshop will add pixels to your canvas, filling them in with your background color.

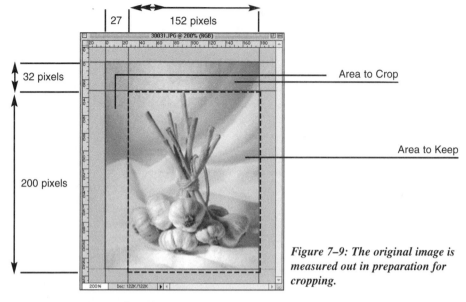

27 | 152 pixels

32 pixels

Area to Crop

Area to Keep

200 pixels

*Figure 7–9: The original image is measured out in preparation for cropping.*

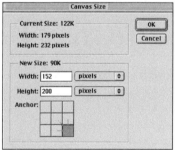

*Figure 7–10: The Canvas Size dialog box.*

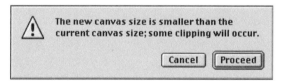

*Figure 7–11: The Warning reminds you that your image will crop.*

For this example, reduce the width and height by the amount that was measured out in Step 1.

3. The Anchor point in the dialog box represents the full image in nine separate squares. If you click the middle square (which is the default), the image canvas will increase or decrease around that portion of your image. Because in this example the entire portion of the image that you want to keep is in the lower right corner, click on the lower right box in the Anchor grid. Click OK.

A warning box (shown in Figure 7–11) will appear to let you know that the dimensions you have entered will cause your image to be cropped. Click Proceed. Your image will be cropped as shown in Figure 7–12.

*Figure 7–12: The cropped image.*

## Cropping to Make Sizes Match

This will prove especially helpful when you are trying to turn images into buttons that need to be the same size.

1. In the Crop Options palette (double-click on the Crop tool to access it), check the Fixed Target Size box, and enter the desired dimensions for width, height, and resolution. As you crop each image, your Crop marquee will resize your image to these dimensions.

or

1. Copy and paste one image into the canvas of another.
2. Choose Edit -> Free Transform, and drag one of the corner handlebars in or out until the posted image is the desired size.

# Removing Dust and Scratches

Figure 7–13 is a close-up of the corner of an image scanned from a personal flatbed scanner. You can see that there are dust, scratches, and rips on it, either from the original photograph itself or from the glass on the scan bed. Although they may seem minor, you'll want to get rid of these things, especially if you are working on a site for a client.

There are a number of different ways that you can get rid of dust, scratches, and even rips in your photographs when working in Photoshop.

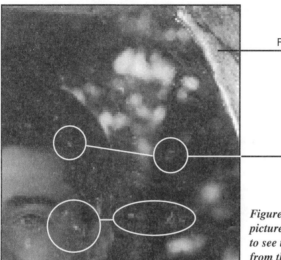

Folded & ripped corner

Dust specs

*Figure 7–13: Rips and dust litter this picture. Although this image is blown up to see the specs better, they still detract from the picture, even at normal size.*

## *For photos with a significant number of specks, dots, and dust...*

1. Use the Dust & Scratches filter. From the menu options, choose Filter -> Noise -> Dust & Scratches. You'll see the dialog box shown in Figure 7–14. Personally, I'm not crazy about this tool, but a lot of people like it.

2. Use the Radius slider to establish the extent to which the filter will seek out random pixels or noise within your image. You'll want to experiment with this, depending on both your image and the number and severity of unwanted noise: A higher Radius number will cause the image to be more blurry.

3. The second slider is to set Threshold, setting the amount of tonal difference between the affected pixels.

## *For just a few specks and dust particles, or as a follow-up to using the Dust & Scratches filter...*

1. Select the Rubber Stamp tool.

2. Zoom in on your image to 200% or 300% and take a quick glance over the entire image. Figure 7–15 shows the difference in the photo before and after using the Rubber Stamp tool.

3. Suck up a part of the image that has a similar color tone or pattern, use a soft-edged, small brush and clone acceptable parts of your image over the dust and scratches.

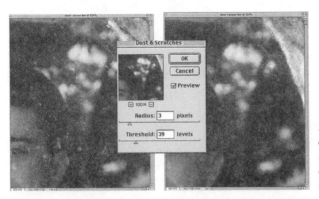

*Figure 7–14: Before and after shots using the Dust & Scratches filter. Obviously the rip in the corner is largely unaffected.*

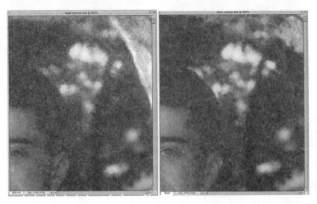

*Figure 7–15: Before and after shots using the Rubber Stamp tool. Notice the rip in the corner has been fixed, replaced by the trees from the image background.*

Try not to clone from an area too close geographically to the area you are correcting. Oftentimes a pattern will emerge that could look worse than the original dust and scratches.

# Removing Noise From an Image

There are any number of ways to remove large problems like noise from an image. In truth, the ability to bring photographs from a state of disrepair back to usable form is one of the more remarkable aspects of Photoshop. There is, in fact, such a variety of methods for cleaning up an image, especially when it comes to removing noise, that I could dedicate an entire chapter to the topic. But, since we only have a few pages to spare, I'll illustrate just a few of the more popular and effective techniques:

## *Using the Despeckle Filter*

Choose Filter -> Noise -> Despeckle to activate this tool. Unlike many other filters, this one does not have a dialog box associated with it. The Despeckle filter finds the edges of your image and preserves them, while blurring the rest of your image. An example of the results of the Despeckle filter is shown in Figure 7–16.

## *Using the Median Filter*

Choose Filter -> Noise -> Median to access the dialog box shown in Figure 7–17. The dialog box offers you the option of selecting a radius value between 1 and 16. As Figure 7–17 shows, the greater the radius value, the more severe the final effect will be on your image.

When you enter a value in the Radius selector, the Median filter will, for every pixel in your image (or specified selection), take an average of the colors of all the pixels that fall within the desired radius. It will ignore any extreme pixels that could tend to throw an accurate average off and apply the average color to the starting pixel. It will do this for every pixel in your image (or selection).

*Figure 7–16: Using the Despeckle filter.*

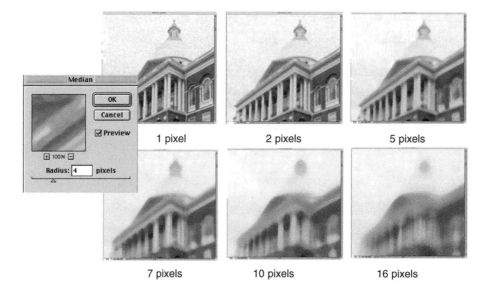

*Figure 7–17: Using the Median filter.*

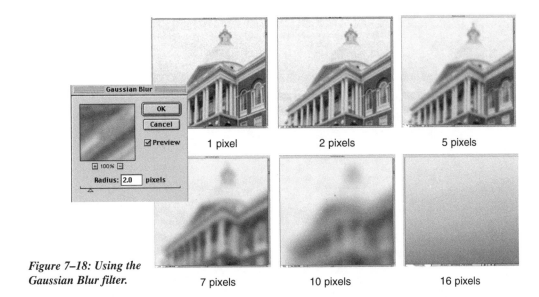

*Figure 7–18: Using the Gaussian Blur filter.*

## Using the Gaussian Blur Filter

This tool is widely considered the most powerful and most useful of the blur filters, as well as the most effective when it comes to eradicating noise from an image. You can access the dialog box (shown in Figure 7–18) by choosing Filter -> Blur -> Gaussian Blur. Like the Median filter, there is only one form of control, a radius slider, with which you can control the amount of blur you desire (from a minimum of 0.1 to a maximum of 250). As you can see in Figure 7–18, the higher the blur radius, the more severe the effect it will have on your image.

The Gaussian Blur filter works by blurring the number of pixels in the established Radius selector, following an internally devised Gaussian distribution curve. Although the higher end values will blur your image beyond recognition (hardly the solution for reducing noise), they are often useful in creating other effects.

## Sharpening Blurred Photographs

Quick editorial: The Sharpen tool is terrible. That's just my opinion, of course, and others may disagree, but I've rarely found it useful. There are effective ways, however, to sharpen a blurred photograph. As it often does in other instances, the Photoshop Filter menu comes to the rescue, providing the necessary tools to keep you from thinking that you need thicker glasses.

Within the Filter -> Sharpen submenu, there are four filters: Sharpen, Sharpen Edges, Sharpen More, and Unsharp Mask. Each of these filters works by affecting the contrast between the target pixel and neighboring pixels. The first three do not have a dialog box or any customizable options. Try each out on a blurry photograph and test

*Figure 7–19: The original blurry image before being manipulated.*

*Figure 7–20: Sharpen filter.*     *Figure 7–21: Sharpen Edges filter.*     *Figure 7–22: Sharpen More filter.*

the results. Figure 7–19 shows the original blurry photograph, while Figures 7–20, 7–21, and 7–22 show the results of each of the first three filters.

To really get a good sharpening effect, it's the fourth Sharpen filter that you'll want to master: Unsharp Mask. This filter yields the power of each of the other filters, in that it works to sharpen the entire image (Sharpen and Sharpen More), as well as the edges (Sharpen Edges), plus it gives more flexibility and control. So by now you're asking: If that's true, then why bother with the other Sharpen filters at all? Well, the answer is you don't have to. In that case, you'll ask, why did Photoshop put them there in the first place? The answer to that, my friend, is I just don't know.

The Unsharp Mask filter brings up the dialog box shown in Figure 7–23. The three sliders offered in the dialog box offer you a vast amount of control over how you sharpen your image:

◆   Set Amount to the percentage (1 to 500) you would like to sharpen your image. As you may expect, the higher the percentage, the more severe the sharpen effect.

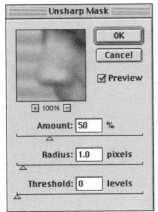  

*Figure 7–23: Unsharp Mask dialog box.*     *Figure 7–24: Unsharp Mask filter, correct adjustment.*     *Figure 7–25: Unsharp Mask filter, extreme adjustment.*

◆ The Radius slider, measured in pixels, allows you to set the thickness of the edges that are sharpened. Again, the higher the value, the more drastic the effect, with greater contrast in your image as a result.

◆ The Threshold slider works a bit differently from the other sliders, in that the greater effect on the image is realized when you have a lower value. As you set the level of the Threshold, you will determine the difference between the target pixel and its neighboring pixels that must exist before Photoshop sharpens those pixels.

The Unsharp Mask filter, because it has three separate control values, is difficult to master. You'll have to experiment with it to see how much adjustment you'll need to sharpen any given image. Keep changes to the sliders slight for images that are just a little out of focus, as the image in Figure 7–19 is. Figures 7–24 and 7–25 show the results of two different Unsharp Mask settings, one with an extreme effect and one that sharpens the image correctly.

## Color Correction Tools and Techniques

Because of differences in scanner settings and other variables, the colors in your scanned image may not look like your original photo. One of the scan results I've regularly come across is a slight grayish film over the image, or a lack of sharpness in the shadows and highlights. Other times your photograph might scan exactly as planned, but the original picture may need some color enhancements.

Figure 7–26 shows how flat the photograph of my office looks after I scan it. You can see that it lacks depth and seems flat. There are a couple of methods that I'll use to go about correcting this:

◆ By choosing Image -> Adjust -> Levels, I bring up the dialog box shown in Figure 7–27. It will let me manipulate the photograph and add necessary depth. This histogram in the center shows how the dark and light areas are distributed throughout the picture. The left slider adjusts the shadows, the middle slider adjusts the midtones, and the right slider adjusts the highlights.

As the histogram shows, there is a lack of shadow and highlight in my photograph. By moving the left and right slider in toward the edges of the histogram, I'll distribute the levels more evenly throughout the image. Figure 7–28 shows the effects of adjusting levels.

◆ For more precise tonal correction, choose Image -> Adjust -> Curves. This tool is more complex than Levels, but also more accurate. The Curves dialog box shown in Figure 7–29 displays a full tonal range graph of your image. Unlike the limited Levels command discussed above, which allows you control over only three ranges (shadows, midtones, and highlights), Curves will let you make adjustments at any point along the 255-point range.

Although a full explanation of how Curves works is beyond the scope of this book, the ultra-basic rule of thumb is that as you pull points on the diagonal downward, parts of your image will become darker, while dragging points higher than the diagonal will make the image lighter. Experimenting with levels can bring about some pretty surprising results! Figure 7–30 (on page 180) shows the curves associated with some final images.

*Figure 7–26: My office photograph came through the scanner with a gray film over it, leaving it looking washed out.*

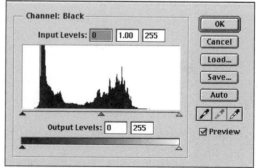

*Figure 7–27: The Levels palette before adjustments. Adjust the levels for brighter highlights and darker depth.*

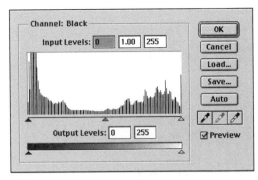

*Figure 7–28: The Levels palette after adjustments creates a more dispersed histogram. The image gains definition and sharpness after Levels adjustments.*

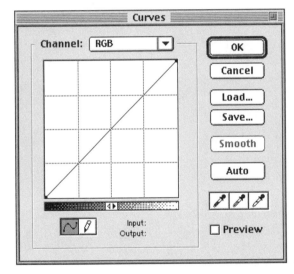

*Figure 7–29: The Curves feature gives you greater control than Levels.*

In the Layers palette, choose New Adjustment Layer and make your desired adjustment from there. The changes will happen on a separate "adjustment layer" so that you can make further changes later on, or even eliminate their effects completely.

Figure 7–31 (Color Figure 14 & 15) shows a picture of Michali, a friend of mine. Although she is always beautiful, this picture washed her out after scanning, leaving her in need of some color. I'll use Photoshop to tint the picture a bit and give her a tan. Because there is good contrast between her and the background, I chose to use the Magnetic Lasso to select her.

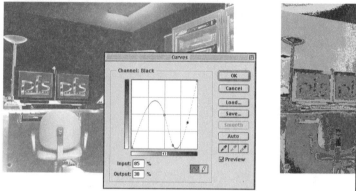

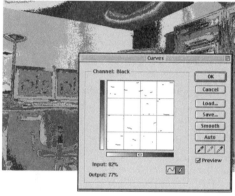

*Figure 7–30: Manipulating the curves can cause some pretty drastic results. The first of the three curves is the proper correction—the remaining two are great special effects.*

The Magnetic Lasso tool, added in version 5 as a way to save time when making selections, will discriminate between colors and find the edge, creating a fairly accurate selection. You can make the Magnetic Lasso tool more or less sensitive and accurate by manipulating the controls in the Options dialog box (Figure 7–31).

◆ **Lasso Width** will establish how sensitive the tool is to color differences in your image. The higher the number, the more sensitive and discriminatory the tool will be in its selection, so even shades of the same color will be separated.

◆ **Frequency** will set the number of points, or anchors, to be placed as your cursor changes direction while you move it around your image. These can help you in the event of a mistake, or an accidental wrong turn—simply retrace your steps to a previous point and click on it. You'll be able to resume making your selection in the proper direction.

◆ **Edge Contrast** will determine how drastically different surrounding and adjoining colors have to be in order for the Magnetic Lasso to include them. Use a high percentage if you have very stark color transitions.

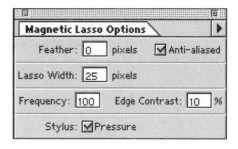

*Figure 7–31: The picture of my friend, Michali, lacks vibrancy of color. Her face is selected by using the Magnetic Lasso tool. The dialog box offers setting adjustments to make the tool more or less sensitive to color.*

Once the selection has been made, soften the edges by choosing Select -> Feather. Since my image is low-res, I'll choose a radius setting of 1 (I'd have chosen a higher number for a higher-res image). By doing this, I reduce the chance that my color correction will have a very hard edge and look unnatural.

**You may wonder why I would do it this way rather than just set the Feather Radius within the Magnetic Lasso's Options palette. Although this is a perfectly acceptable alternative, if you feather your selection separately, you can undo it without losing your selection, should you decide that your feather radius was too large or too small.**

To give Michali her color back there are a couple of steps that I can take:

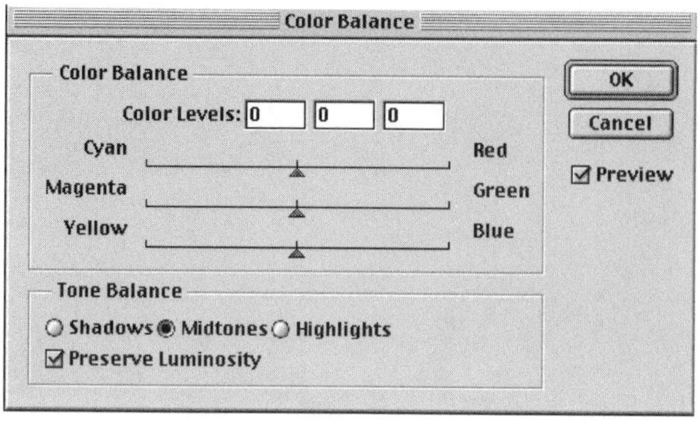

*Figure 7–32: The Color Balance dialog box.*

◆ Choose Image -> Adjust -> Color Balance to access the dialog box shown in Figure 7–32. There are three adjustment sliders that I can control, each allowing me to add colors to and simultaneously subtract colors from my image. With the radio buttons, I can do this for any of three tonal ranges: shadows, midtones, and highlights.

To make her more tan, I'm going to want to add both red and yellow by moving the sliders in those directions. As I do this, I will also be subtracting cyan and blue, respectively. I'll do this for all tonal ranges and experiment with the amounts of colors that I want to add until I achieve a color that I am happy with. (I also increased the shadows in the level adjustment.) Color Figure 23 shows the result.

◆ Another way that I can give her some color is by using the modes in the Layers palette. In my Color Picker, I've chosen a color that I think would be great for her tan or even a little darker than I would like. I'm going to add a new layer and, with my selection still active around her face, I'll fill the selection with my chosen color. In the Mode pull-down menu on the front of the Layers palette, I choose Overlay, which combines my chosen color with the underlying photograph and increases the color intensity in her skin, while not losing the defining features in her face.

## Adjusting Color With Hue/Saturation

Although there are many ways to use the Hue/Saturation adjustment mechanism in your work, I'll demonstrate this instead on buttons that you might create for your Web site. (See Chapter 6 for more about creating buttons.)

Figure 7–33 shows a few quick buttons that I made. They are a rich blue. Oftentimes when I create a site, I will make all of the buttons one color except for the one for the page that the user is on, which will be an obviously different color. For example, if the user is on the Products page of a certain Web site, all of the buttons might be blue except for the Products button, which would stand out as red. By standing apart from the others, your Web user will know immediately which page he or she is on.

*Figure 7–33: Simple blue buttons I created for a Web site.*

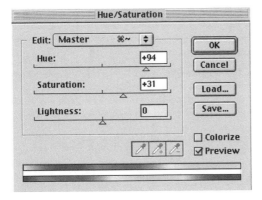

*Figure 7–34: The Hue/Saturation dialog box.*

Instead of recreating all of the buttons, I'm going to choose Image -> Adjust -> Hue/Saturation to bring up the dialog box shown in Figure 7–34. An improvement over the older controls found in Photoshop 4, the dialog box lets you change the color as well as its saturation and light/darkness. Use the top slider (Hue) to change the color completely, the center slider (Saturation) to add or subtract richness from the color, and the bottom slider (Lightness) to add highlights or shadows.

# COOL AND USEFUL EFFECTS FOR INLINE IMAGES

Whether or not you decide to use actual photography in your Web site construction, Photoshop offers unlimited potential to design and create cool effects. This section will offer recipes for creating and manipulating elements for photographic collages, picture frames and borders, as well as some Photoshop-original work, such as various techniques for creating lightning and clouds and using both native and third-party filters.

Figure 7–35 offers a glance at how some of the techniques you will see in this section have been used to enhance Web site design. Even though the subjects of many of the sites I have worked on (and shown here) are more corporate in nature and often do not leave room for elaborate design, there are ways you can manipulate and harness your imagination to make room for creativity.

Keep in mind as well that the techniques in this chapter (and throughout this book, for that matter) are not necessarily confined to the examples shown here—it is the underlying technique that is important, not the framework for the example. Take the lessons from this chapter, practice them, change some of the variables here and there, and apply them in different ways. Once you learn the basic framework, your possibilities will be endless.

## Cool Lightning Effects

There are a number of different ways to make lightning. I'll demonstrate two of them, as they can each have a very different effect.

### *Lightning Effect: Technique One*

1. Open a new file, 360 by 360 pixels, with a black background.
2. Create two new layers immediately, and make sure Layer 2 is your active layer.
3. Use white as your foreground color and make your Paintbrush the active tool.
4. From the Brushes palette, choose a brush that is 4 pixels in diameter with a soft edge. Begin drawing a jagged line from the top of your canvas toward the bottom, creating the main current in what will be an electrical storm. Use a smaller brush, 2 pixels in diameter, to create the "arms" of your current. Allow them to wander in crazy directions, as they might in a real storm.

**Not all of the brushes you'll need are provided in the default Brush palette. To create a new brush, choose New Brush from the palette menu, or click once on the empty part of the palette. To resize an existing brush, choose Brush Options from the palette menu, or double-click on your desired brush.**

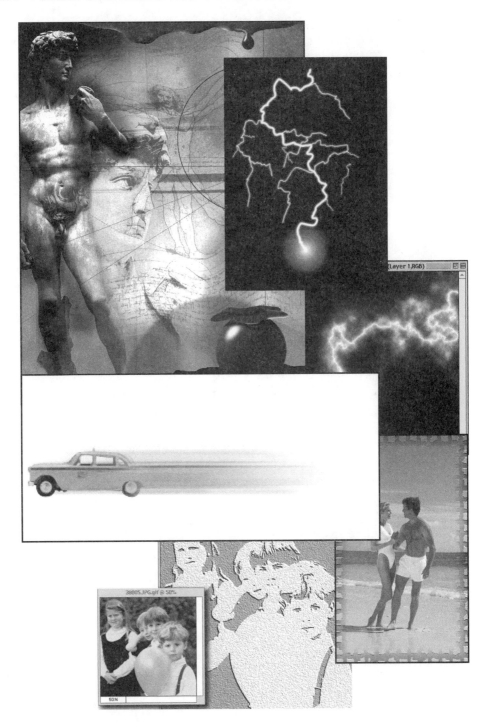

*Figure 7–35: Cool effects used in Web design.*

5. Change brushes once more. Choose one with a diameter of 1. These will be the faintest currents, which have either died out or are striking farther away. Figure 7–36 illustrates Steps 1 through 5.

6. Once you have your lightning bolts where you want them, make Layer 1 your active layer. Hold the Command button (Ctrl in Windows) while clicking Layer 2 in the Layers palette to select your lightning.

7. Choose Select -> Modify -> Expand and expand all the pixels by 1.

8. Choose Select -> Feather, and set your Feather radius to 1 to make the edges softer.

9. Fill your selection with a bright yellow to give your lightning a glow. Lower the layer opacity to 50%. Filling your selection with purple instead of white can create a nice effect, too.

10. As a final touch, we'll put a light flash where the lightning may have struck. In the Layers palette, choose New Layer (instead of clicking the New Layer icon at the bottom of the palette). You will see the dialog box shown in Figure 7–37.

11. Under the Mode pull-down menu, choose Screen and deselect the box Fill with screen neutral black. The black that exists there will be invisible to you, yet it will exist to make working with certain filters possible.

12. With the Circle marquee tool, make a circle around the bottom of your main current and feather it with a radius of 4.

13. Choose Filter -> Render -> Lens Flare to access the dialog box shown in Figure 7–38. Set the Flare to 155, directly centered, and click OK.

14. Use the Move tool to move your flare around if necessary. Figure 7–39 provides an example of a completed piece.

## *Lightning Effect: Technique Two*

Figure 7–40 shows my agency's old logo, which used this lightning technique as the main graphic feature. This particular technique is best designed over a black background, and creates a significantly more realistic lightning bolt than in the previous technique. The downside, however, is that the lightning here is more random, and not as easily manipulated.

1. Open a new file 360 by 360 pixels.

2. Make sure that your background and foreground colors are set to black and white, respectively.

3. Create a gradient from the top left corner to the bottom right.

4. Choose Filter -> Render -> Difference Clouds to fill your canvas with a cloud texture. The first time you do this you may not get a particularly great effect, so press Command and Z (Ctrl + Z in Windows) and then Command and F (Ctrl + F in Windows) to redo the filter until you get clouds with high contrasts, such as in Figure 7–41.

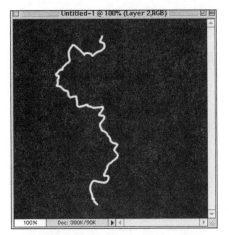

Create the main arm of your lightning in white on a black or dark blue background.

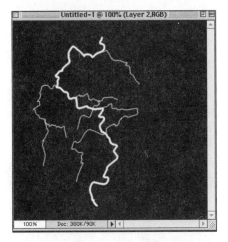

Use a smaller brush to create the "arms" of the lightning.

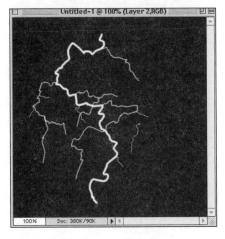

Your final, smaller brush will create the faintest arms, those that are in the background or have already faded.

*Figure 7–36: Creating lightning.*

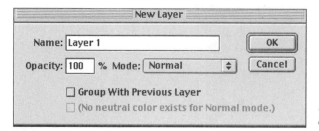

*Figure 7–37: The New Layer dialog box.*

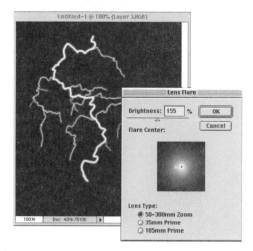

*Figure 7–38: The Lens Flare filter dialog box will provide a spark of light in your selection.*

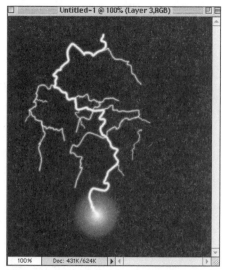

*Figure 7–39: The final image with the lens flare.*

*Figure 7–40: My agency's old logo uses the lightning effect as its main design feature.*

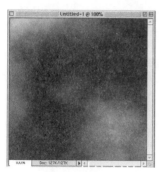

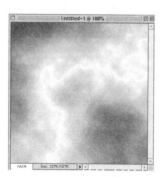

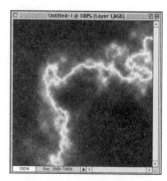

*Figure 7–41: The canvas filled with clouds from the Difference Clouds filter.*

*Figure 7–42: Inverting the clouds clearly shows where the lightning will be created.*

*Figure 7–43: The final image, after adjusting the Levels.*

*Figure 7–44: PFS web site with lightning effect.*

**5.** Press Command and I (Ctrl + I in Windows) to invert the colors. You will start to see where the lightning is on the canvas, as in Figure 7–42.

**6.** Open the Levels dialog box, and pull the Shadow arrow over to the right. Continue to pull it until the background gets darker and the lightning becomes the focal point of your canvas.

**7.** On a new layer, fill the canvas with a dark blue. Set the Color mode to Soft Light. The final outcome is shown in Figure 7–43.

Figure 7–44 (Color Figure 27) shows the home page of the PFS Web site (www.pfsnewmedia.com) which features the logo prominently. The lightning takes center stage and establishes the tone for the rest of the site.

## Creating Cool Collage Effects

Remember back in fourth grade, sitting at your desk with a smock on, carefully cutting and pasting magazine pictures to a piece of construction paper, vaguely wondering why you were bothering? Well, thanks to a few forward-thinking teachers, you are now well-prepared to move on from construction paper to today's high-tech collages.

But to safeguard against creating the electronic equivalent of a fourth grader's collage, there are few things you should be aware of and take into consideration before you create your collage, especially for the Web:

♦   Make sure your images relate to each other. Throwing together a random conglomeration of images most likely will not produce the effect you desire. Try to collect images that will somehow have the same theme, or at least the same medium. Sometimes combining photography with illustrations can work, but more often than not they will tend to look like a scattered mess.

♦   Map out your collage on paper first. Even though Photoshop's layers will allow you to move images easily from one place to another, knowing in advance where each should go will save you time and energy in the long run.

♦   Collages work best when there is a central image. If there is not a main subject to focus on, the collage will look jumbled, and the eye will not have any clear route to follow.

♦   Blended edges work better with other blended edges. Similarly, hard edges work well with other hard edges. Rarely, however, do they combine well.

♦   When creating a collage for the Web, remember that you have limited space in which to place the completed image. Because of this, you'll often be better off not creating collages with too much detail. Fine detail will often be lost on the viewer when seen on a monitor as opposed to a printed page.

♦   As you'll undoubtedly see throughout this book, quality of an image is often the trade-off in achieving a lower file size. Collages are likely to have a number of transitions throughout them, which will use a large number of colors. These colors may dither poorly when you reduce the file into a GIF for color reduction. Try to either create your images without multiple blends or use the browser-safe Web palette from the beginning. See Chapter 2 for more information on the Web palette.

Of course, none of the above rules is set in stone, nor do I mean to imply that they hold true in every case. But these and other tips that you'll discover as you practice are a solid set of guidelines that could prove to be the difference between your collage looking like a professional project and a fourth-grade homework assignment.

Figure 7–45 (also Color Figure 16) shows a collage that I did for one of my agency's brochure sell sheets. This collage, used in part of our Web site as well, combines both soft, blending collage effects with stark, hard-edged contrasts. The photo of

*Figure 7–45: A collage created for one of my agency's brochures.*

Michelangelo's David appears on the side of the image area, while a ghostly blow-up of his face from the same picture fades off near it. A wavy page of one of Da Vinci's most famous works, a depiction of the human form, provides a subtle, detailed background. A liquid blob of my own creation is melting in the foreground, as liquid from the top of the image drips and splashes on it.

1. Open two photographs to make your collage. Make sure that one of them has an obvious subject or object—like a family member or some other main feature. For this example, I will be using the two photographs shown in Figure 7–46, called Picture One and Picture Two. My pictures are currently 200 ppi—too large for the Web, but necessary for some of the effects I will use. We can reduce the size later for use on the Web.

2. With the Marquee tool, make a selection around a portion of the main subject in Picture One. Press Command and C (Ctrl + C in Windows) to copy the selection to your pasteboard.

3. Press Command and D (Ctrl + D in Windows) to deselect your selection.

*Figure 7–46: The two photos that will be used to create my collage.*

4. Press Command and V (Ctrl + V in Windows) to paste the image from your clipboard back into Picture One. Notice that it pastes into its own layer, named Layer 1 by default.

5. Choose Edit -> Free Transform and manipulate the size by dragging one of the corner handles outward. Hold the Shift button while dragging to constrain the proportions. Drag it out until the image is nearly three times its original size. Press Return (Enter in Windows) to activate the transformation.

6. Drag the Opacity slider on the Layers palette down to 40% for a more ghostly effect. Figure 7–47 shows the progress to this point.

7. Remove some of the color from the image on Layer 1 by pressing Command and L (Ctrl + L in Windows) to access the Levels dialog box. Manipulate Input Highlights by dragging the slider on the right out to the left, until you begin to lose tone and detail in the image. Do the same with the Output Highlights slider. Click OK when through. Figure 7–48 shows the effect of this.

8. Make the background layer active by clicking on it. By doing this, any new layer that you create will appear between your background and Layer 1.

9. We're now going to add Picture Two to the collage. You don't need to copy and paste to do this—instead simply choose the Move tool, and drag the entire image in Picture Two onto the canvas in Picture One. You'll notice that it appears on its own layer, Layer 2.

10. Create a mask of your image on Layer 2 (which should now be the active layer). Do this by dragging Layer 2 down to the Create Mask icon at the bottom of the Layers palette (the first icon on the left). Doing this has caused a number of things to happen:

*Figure 7–47: The image on Layer 2, enlarged and only 40% opaque.*

*Figure 7–48: The same image, made more ghostly by manipulating the input and output levels.*

◆ A new icon has appeared to the right of the Image icon on Layer 2 in the Layers palette. This icon shows the mask as white (image area) surrounded by black (transparent area).

◆ There is a chain link in between the Image icon and the Mask icon. When the link is present, you can move the image and the mask at the same time anywhere on your canvas. Turn the link off by clicking on it, and the mask remains permanent. Your image will be limited to moving only within the mask.

◆ Your Brush icon in the Layers palette, which used to indicate that the layer was both active and ready for manipulation, has changed to the Mask icon. Brushes and other tools won't work the same when in this mode, as we'll soon illustrate. You can return to Standard mode by clicking on the icon of your image on Layer 2 in the Layers palette. Figure 7–49 illustrates the changes in the Layers palette.

◆ Foreground and background colors in your toolbar have changed to black and white while in Mask mode to represent transparency and the solid area, respectively. Your original colors will return as soon as your image is returned to Standard mode.

11. While still in Mask mode, activate the Linear Gradient tool. Create a gradient from black to white, left to right over the entire image in Layer 2. Hold the Shift key down to ensure that your gradient stays straight and is not made at an angle. You'll see that instead of coloring your image in black and white as you may expect, the portion of your image that was covered in black has disappeared gradually as the gradient became more intense. Figure 7–50 illustrates this.

12. Reduce the Layer 2 opacity to 15% so that your image is more subtle.

13. Erase portions of your image on all layers as necessary so that your image looks complete without hard edges. Use the Transform function also, if your image needs some perspective.

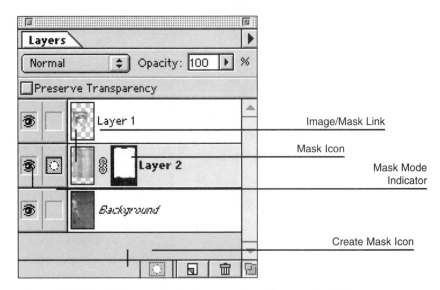

*Figure 7–49: The differences in the Layers palette after turning the image on Layer 2 into a mask.*

*Figure 7–50: The Gradient tool while in Mask mode
causes the areas in black to become transparent.*

14. For the final touch, choose Image -> Image Size and change your resolution from
    200 to 72 ppi (more suited for the Web). Click OK. The completed image is shown
    in Figure 7–51 (it is basically a recreation of the sales sheet shown in Figure 7–46,
    but without the melting sphere in the foreground).

Depending on the subject matter, you may benefit from keeping your collage faint
in the background and offsetting stark images in the foreground. Figure 7–52 shows
a situation where I did just that for a client's Web site to add "pop" to a few of their
products.

## Other Collage Tips: Defringing and Removing Mattes

In certain cases, you may be cutting and pasting images from one canvas onto another
without feathering the selections first. Oftentimes there will be a faint halo around your
image, where your selection picked up the background. If you experience this haloing,
choose Layer -> Matting -> Defringe and choose a width that will be wide enough to
remove the halo. If your halo came from a white or a black background, choose
Remove White Matte or Remove Black Matte, respectively.

*Figure 7–51: My final collage, after a little tweaking.*

*Figure 7–52: This collage, created for Automatic Switch Company (www.asco.com), uses stark images against a faded collage background.*

## Water Droplets

This one uses a number of filters in addition to some Layer effects to add realism.

1. Create a new canvas, 360 x 360 pixels, 72 ppi, RGB color.
2. With the background layer active (I know, I've preached against using the background layer to work on, but in this case we can make an exception), choose Filter -> Noise -> Add Noise to access the dialog box shown in Figure 7–53.

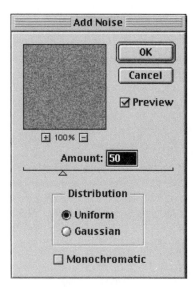

*Figure 7–53: The Add Noise dialog box.*

3. Set the Noise amount to 550, with both Uniform and Monochromatic selected. Click OK.

4. Choose Filter -> Blur -> Gaussian Blur. Set Radius to 2.6 pixels. Click OK. Figure 7–54 shows your canvas at this point.

5. Press Command and L to access the Levels dialog box. Set Input Levels to 128, .78, and 145. Click OK. Figure 7–55 shows your canvas at this point.

*Figure 7–54: The Add Noise filter makes your canvas look like a TV without reception.*

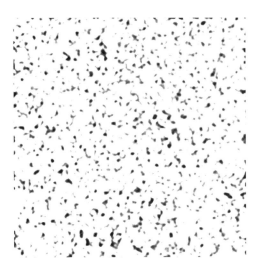

*Figure 7–55: By manipulating Levels on my noise-filled canvas, I've created shapes that resemble water droplets.*

Increasing the Shadow levels will make each drop bigger and create more drops. Increasing Highlights will create fewer, smaller drops. Manipulating Midtones will affect the thickness and visibility of your drops.

6.  Use the Magic Wand tool to select all the white on your canvas. Set Tolerance to 1 in the Magic Wand Options palette.

7.  Inverse the selection by choosing Select -> Inverse.

8.  Create a new layer by clicking the New Layer icon at the bottom of the Layers palette.

9.  Fill your selection with a light blue, or whatever color you feel best represents water droplets.

10. Choose Layer -> Effects -> Bevel and Emboss. Set the Style to Inner Bevel, with a Depth of 7. Click OK. Figure 7–56 shows a sample, and Figure 7–57 shows how this example can be used to make an object look wet.

I changed the Blend mode on the droplet layer to Overlay to give the impression that the drops were really lying on top of the object. I also used the Smudge tool to make the drops seem to streak down the glass, and added a slight drop shadow.

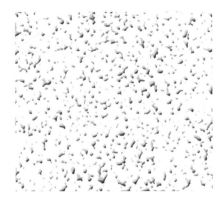

*Figure 7–56: The beveled edges give the water droplets some thickness.*

*Figure 7–57: The water droplets, when used with the proper blend mode, make my glass and lime appear to be wet.*

## Turning a 2D Image Into a 3D Image

Although it's kind of hidden and lost in the crowd of all the other filters, the 3D Transform function is probably the most fun tools in Photoshop 5. You can use this filter to take any flat surface and turn it into a 3D cube, cylinder, or sphere. Once you learn the basics of this new feature, your Web graphics will take on a whole new dimension.

1. Open or create a 2D image, similar to that shown in Figure 7–58. The Compuburger Instant Meal in the figure was developed by Jurges Cortina, one of the designers at my agency, using a combination of Infini-D 3D modeling software and Photoshop. Make sure that you have plenty of blank canvas around your image (you'll need it to get a good 3D effect without the edges getting cut off).

2. Choose Filter -> Render -> 3D Transform to access the dialog box shown in Figure 7–59.

3. The second set of tools in the 3D Transform toolbar makes up the shapes and methods to turn your flat image into a 2D object. Choose the first of these tools— the cube.

4. In the preview window, drag from the top left corner to the bottom right corner of your image. A 3D wireframe cube will appear, as shown in Figure 7–60.

5. You'll want the right face of the wire cube to fit snugly over your image. Use the Direct Selection tool (the white arrow in the upper right of the toolbar) and drag the lower right handle on the wireframe to the bottom right corner of your image. Drag the lower center handle to the bottom left corner of your image. The rest of the wireframe will be adjusting as well. Continue manipulating the wireframe until it looks similar to Figure 7–61.

*Figure 7–58: The original image created in Photoshop.*

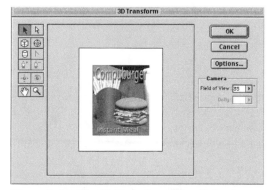

*Figure 7–59: The 3D Transform filter dialog box.*

*Figure 7–60: Wireframe around the image.*

*Figure 7–61: Wireframe molded around the image.*

6. The third set of tools in the 3D Transform box toolbar allows you to move your selection. Click on the Trackball tool (the circular one on the right), and drag your selection to the right and downward, enough so that your image displays three sides, creating the illusion of 3D.

7. Click OK to render your image, and it will look similar to Figure 7–62.

8. The annoying part of this filter is that instead of simply rendering the image, it makes a copy of it, so that the 3D image is directly above the original 2D image. Unfortunately, it's still on the same layer, so you'll have to use a selection technique to grab the 3D box (try the Polygon lasso, clicking on all corners of your 3D image). Cut and paste, then dispose of the layer containing the original image. The final result will be similar to Figure 7–63.

**You can remove the background from the piece while still in the 3D Transform filter by pushing the Option button and turning off the Display Background command. But beware: Turning this command off will turn your background black—probably not the effect you are seeking.**

## Creating the Illusion of Speed

A fairly easy trick, this effect will give the impression of a car (or anything else) moving quickly.

1. Open a picture of a car (or anything else that would look natural if it were moving fast). I chose the picture of the car (just something from a Photo CD that I had in my image library). Make sure that the subject of your image is on its own layer—not the background layer.

*Figure 7–62: After the image is rotated, click OK to accept the changes.*

*Figure 7–63: The final image after the background is removed.*

2. Move your main subject to one of the sides of your canvas to give yourself enough room to play, as shown in Figure 7–64.

3. Copy your image and paste it so that your copy appears on a new, higher layer. Make sure that your copy is lined up horizontally with the original image.

4. Lower the opacity of the layer containing the original image to around 50%.

5. Choose Filter -> Blur -> Motion Blur. This is the filter that will give us the moving effect. In the Motion Blur dialog box (shown in Figure 7–65) set the angle to 0°. With the preview box checked, move the distance slider to the right until you get the motion distance that you like. Click OK.

6. Your final image will look similar to the one in Figure 7–66. If necessary, take an eraser to the back end of the solid image on the topmost layer, as well as to the motion tail, to fade it out more if necessary, and your image will have the illusion of speed.

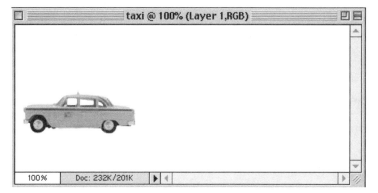

*Figure 7–64: The car image I'm using to demonstrate the speed effect. Move the object to one side to leave room for the motion trail.*

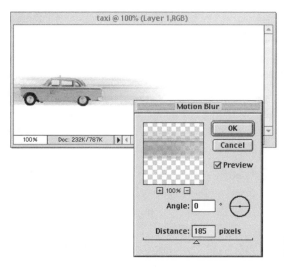

*Figure 7–65: The Motion Blur dialog box.*

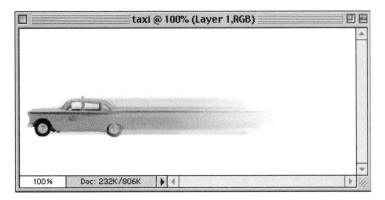

*Figure 7–66: The final image makes the car look like it's moving quickly.*

This type of effect practically begs to be turned into an animated GIF. Whether your subject is a car driving, a person running, or an airplane flying, you can easily create this effect in a number of different frames and create a small but eye-catching animation with it. See Chapter 8 for more information on creating animations.

# METHODS FOR FRAMING IMAGES

The next few examples illustrate and briefly explain a number of techniques that you can use to create cool framing effects for pictures. Most of the following take advantage of Photoshop's native filters, both alone and in combination with each other. Other effects will use third-party filters, which you have to buy separately from Photoshop. Some of these third-party filters are described in the next section.

## Drop Shadows

1. Press Command and A (Ctrl + A in Windows) to select all of your image.
2. Copy and paste the image so that it's on a new layer.
3. If necessary, increase the size of the canvas, keeping your image in the upper left.
4. Choose Layers -> Effects -> Drop Shadow and play with the settings. It will preview in real time, so you will know whether you need to continue changing the setting. Figure 7–67 shows the final result.

*Figure 7–67: Drop shadow.*

# Curved Corners

With the new Shape tools in Photoshop 6, making a frame or a selection with curved corners is easy.

1. Create a shape with rounded corners on its own layer (not the background layer). The shape will fill in with the foreground color.
2. Hold down the Command button (Ctrl in Windows) and click the layer with the shape in it to create a marquee selection of the shape.
3. Create a new layer and stroke the selection by choosing Edit -> Stroke and set Stroke Width and Location to the desired settings. Click OK when your variables have been set. The border will be created with your foreground color.
4. Hide or remove the original layer that held your shape. Paste the image you want to frame into the stroked selection.

Unfortunately, making frames with rounded corners isn't as easy as in version 5.5. Although this book is not a joint 5.5/6 book, it's worth a couple of lines to teach the 5.5 users how to make rounded corner frames:

1. In the Channels palette, create a new channel, Alpha 1, by clicking the New Channel icon at the bottom of the palette.
2. Create a selection near the center using the Rectangular marquee tool.
3. Feather your selection by choosing Select -> Feather and set Radius to 5.

4. Deselect your selection and open the Levels dialog box. Adjust the Highlights slider to 40, and Midtones to 1. Click OK.

5. Choose Select -> Load Selection and choose Alpha 1 from the Channel pull-down menu. Click OK. Click on the RGB channel.

6. With any of the selection tools, place your marquee where you would like to place it in the image.

7. Choose Edit -> Stroke and set Stroke Width to 3 pixels, and the Location to Inside.

8. Invert your selection by pressing Command, Shift and I (Ctrl + Shift + I in Windows) and press Delete to remove the excess background. Figure 7–68 illustrates this process.

You can also try using this process to create cool buttons with rounded edges, perhaps a combination of the rectangular and pill-shaped buttons that you'll find in Chapter 6, "Navigation, Buttons, and Bullets."

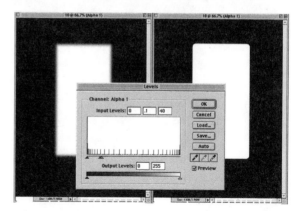

*Figure 7–68: Create a selection with corners by feathering a Rectangular marquee in the Channels palette, and using the Levels dialog box. Switch to RGB mode and erase the excess image.*

# Using Filters to Create Picture Borders

Following are some of the results of using various filters on the edges of photographs. These are merely representational border designs—experiment with other filters and combinations of filters using the simple recipes that follow.

## *Mosaic Tile Border*

1. Press Command and A to select all of your image.
2. Choose Select -> Modify -> Border and set the border width to 20.
3. Select Filter -> Texture -> Mosaic Tile. Figure 7–69 illustrates.

## *Cloud Border*

1. Press Command and A to select all of your image.
2. Choose Select -> Modify -> Border and set the border width to 20.
3. Select Filter -> Render -> Clouds. Figure 7–70 illustrates.

*Figure 7–69: Mosaic tile border.*

### *Polka Dot Border*

1. Hit Command and A to select all of your image.
2. Choose Select -> Modify -> Border and set the border width to 20.
3. Select Filter -> Pixelate -> Color Halftone. Figure 7–71 illustrates.

### *Brick Border*

1. Press Command and A to select all of your image
2. Choose Select -> Modify -> Border and set the border width to 20
3. Select Filter -> Texturizer and choose Brick texture. Figure 7–72 illustrates.

# "Spirograph" Frame

The Spirograph frame, as I call it, is just one of an infinite number of cool geometric designs you can create by starting with a standard shape as your base.

1. On a layer directly over the image you want to frame, choose a regular Square marquee selection.
2. Stroke the selection to create a border.

*Figure 7–70: Cloud border.*

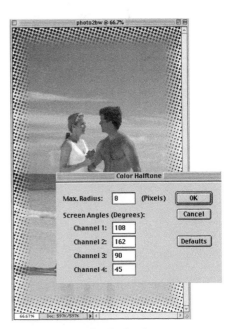

*Figure 7–71: Polka dot border.*

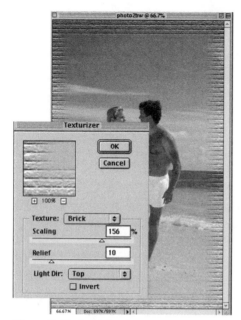

*Figure 7–72: Brick border.*

3. Create a new layer above the one on which you are working.

4. Create a smaller Square marquee selection, inside the original one.

5. Make sure that everything is deselected, and choose Filter -> Blur -> Radial Blur to access the dialog box. Set the amount to 15, and Click OK.

6. Open the Levels dialog box, and increase the shadows.

7. Complete steps 5 and 6 for both borders. Although I like my frame the way it is, by keeping the smaller square on its own layer, you give yourself the option of rotating it by 45° for a more circular frame design, for the final frame, as shown in Figure 7–73 (also Color Figure 17).

## The Tie-Dye Ring

If only I knew Photoshop when I was still in my hippie days of college, this would have been useful …

1. On a new layer above the image that you want to frame, create a Marquee circle selection, then inverse the selection by choosing Select -> Inverse.

2. With the Radial Gradient tool, set a gradient from white to black (use the rulers to find the center point of the circle selection).

3. Choose Filter -> Pixelate -> Color Halftone and leave the default settings.

*Figure 7–73: The Spirograph frame.*

4. Choose Filter -> Distort -> Twirl and set the Angle value to 999°.

5. Create one more circle selection outside where the color was affected by the Twirl filter, inverse the selection, and delete the contents.

6. Create a drop shadow using Layer Attributes to add some depth, as shown in Figure 7–74 (also Color Figure 17).

# USING THIRD-PARTY FILTERS FOR IMAGE EFFECTS

Photoshop's filters are arguably the features of the program that make it so much fun. But while its native filters offer so much in terms of enhancements and effects, some of the most exciting filters are made by outside companies. These are referred to as third-party filters, and can be purchased separately for various prices depending on the manufacturer.

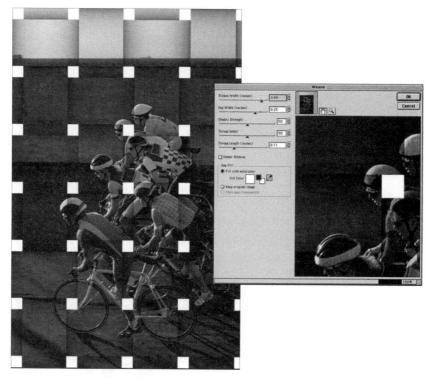

*Figure 7–73: The Weave filter.*

**To install third-party filters, simply place them into your Plug-ins folder in your Photoshop 6 folder.**

While there are a number of third-party filters on the market, my favorite filters are easily the new Alien Skin 4000 series, found at www.alienskin.com. These really give you a lot of flexibility, cool effects, and are by far the best filters on the market. Figures 7–75 to 7–78 are screen shots of a few of my favorites from this series.

# SUMMARY

By now your brain should be racing with ideas, your pen busily scribbling the new filters you want for next Christmas, and your ability to retouch artwork and create graphics from scratch should be expertly honed. The new Photoshop version 6, along with the already amazing features from previous versions and your own expertise, should combine to help you create advanced Web sites that are bound to attract and keep 'em coming back!

*Figure 7–74: The Tie-Dye ring.*

*Figure 7–75: The Melt filter.*

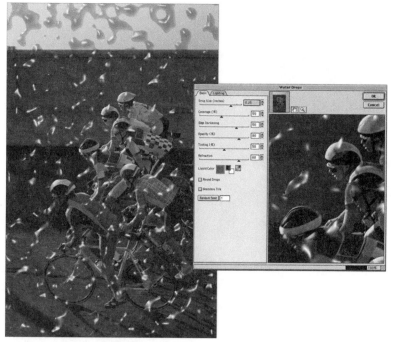

*Figure 7–76: The Water Drops filter.*

*Figure 7–77: The Squint filter.*

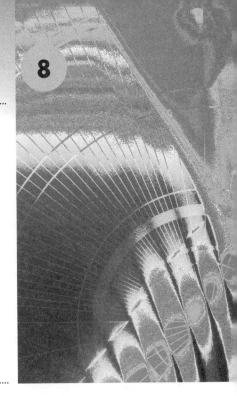

# IMAGEREADY: SPRINGBOARD TO THE WEB

The best new feature of Photoshop 5.5 was not a feature at all. It was the inclusion of an entire program—ImageReady. Once sold as a standalone program strictly for the web, ImageReady has been upgraded, improved, and is sold only with Photoshop now. The program picks up where Photoshop leaves off—it handles the exciting aspects of web development that can really kick your site into high gear.

ImageReady gives you the ability to quickly and easily create animation, Java rollovers, and sliced graphics. But before we get too deep into these individual aspects, let me provide a quick overview of the ImageReady basics.

## IMAGEREADY AND PHOTOSHOP: HOW THEY DIFFER, HOW THEY WORK TOGETHER

One of the nicest things about most of the Adobe products (I haven't seen them all, so I'll protect myself with use of the word) is that they all utilize a standard interface and production layout. This allows you, the designer, to find your way quickly around a variety of programs, so that even if you don't know the details, you're already at home with the generalities. Even Illustrator 9, which works with vector images as opposed to Photoshop's bitmap pictures, looks remarkably similar to Photoshop, even though their methods of creating and manipulating graphics are technically quite different.

The same holds true for Photoshop and ImageReady. In fact, the interface between the two programs looks so much alike that I sometimes find myself having to look at the icon at the top of the Tool palette just to see which program I'm currently in. Unlike Illustrator, however, which is purely a stand-alone program, ImageReady has been engineered to be more of an extension of Photoshop. Many of the tools are the same, as are the ways in which you may go about applying color corrections, working with layers, and so forth.

But for there to be a need for each program to exist independently from each other, they each have to do things that the other doesn't. In general, you'll be working most efficiently if you do the majority of your creating, manipulating, selecting, correcting, and retouching in Photoshop, and leave minor touch-up work to ImageReady. ImageReady's main function will be the special web effects that Photoshop can't come close to accomplishing: creating slices, animations, and rollovers for your web site.

Before we get into the details of how those effects are created, though, let's look at some of the ways that Photoshop and ImageReady can work together, and a few of the more general differences between the two programs.

## Quantum Leap: Jumping Between Programs

Adobe has made this very simple. Instead of the annoyance one might expect of having to save an image in one program and reopen it in another, Adobe has added a simple feature to the bottom of the Tool palette of each program. Shown in Figure 8–1, the Jump To button gives you easy access to either program, with virtually no hassles. To use the button, simply press it (or choose File -> Jump To -> ImageReady).

**You can make the Jump To button access other programs besides ImageReady and Photoshop. To make the Jump To button quickly access another program, such as Illustrator:**

1. **Make an alias (Macintosh) or a Shortcut (Windows) of the application that you want Jump To to access.**

2. **Put the alias or shortcut in the Jump To Graphics Editor folder, located in the Helpers folder inside the main Photoshop 6 folder.**

3. **If you want to jump to this new application from Photoshop, place curly brackets ({}) around the program name. If you want to jump to the new application from ImageReady, use straight brackets ([ ]).**

When you jump to ImageReady from Photoshop (and back again), the image you are working in will open in the other program. If you have made changes since your last jump, you will be notified and asked if you want to update it before making the jump.

*Figure 8–1: The Jump To button appears at the bottom of the Tool palette in both programs.*

You can avoid having to save an image manually or respond to a warning dialog box by setting both programs to auto-update your images every time you jump between programs. To auto-update in Photoshop, simply choose File -> Preferences -> General to access the dialog box. Check the box marked Auto-Update Open Documents. To auto-update in ImageReady, choose Window -> Show Optimize to open the Optimize palette. From the palette menu, choose Auto-Regenerate. A checkmark will indicate that it is turned on.

# Interface Differences

As you learned earlier, the Save for Web function in Photoshop 6 allows you to view your image as you tweak the settings in one of four ways: the original image, the image as optimized by the program, 2-Up (which shows you the original next to one image that you can optimize), or 4-Up (which shows you the original plus three preview window you can optimize individually).

In ImageReady you don't need to choose Save for Web for these options. The interface is built with these same tabs at the top of your canvas, so that you can see four versions of your image as you're working. This is helpful, since, as we'll see later in this chapter, the optimization settings happen in a palette, applicable while you work, rather than in a Save for Web dialog box.

**If you're working in the 2-Up or 4-Up tab, you will only be able to apply manipulations, such as brush strokes or color adjustments, to the original preview window. Most tools will become inactive in other preview windows.**

## *The Perils of Working in 2-Up or 4-Up*

There is a negative aspect to doing all your work in the 2-Up or 4-Up tab. By default, each time you make a change to your image, whether it is an airbrush stroke, a color balance adjustment, a format switch in the Optimize palette, and so forth, you'll have to wait for the each preview window to regenerate its optimization. Even on an extremely fast computer, this is likely to get pretty annoying.

You can turn off the auto-regeneration in the Optimize palette by selecting Auto-Regenerate from the Optimize palette's pull-down menu. Since it's turned on by default, selecting it now will turn it off. As Figure 8–2 shows, a small warning appears at the bottom of the preview windows now to remind you that you are not viewing these previews in their optimized state.

You can manually regenerate a preview window one of two ways:

◆   Click the Warning icon of the window you wish to regenerate.
◆   Choose Regenerate from the Optimize palette menu.

Beyond that, there really aren't too many differences. A few different tools in the Tool palette, some different options in the upper menu bar, but nothing so radical that you won't feel right at home in this program.

*Figure 8–2: The Warning icon indicates that the Auto-Regenerate feature has been turned off.*

# Layers and Layer Options

Since version 3, layers have been one of the most important and useful aspects of Photoshop. They are no less important in ImageReady. As we'll see, the Layers palette in ImageReady is where much of the work takes place for creating rollovers and animations.

The Layers palette is just as important in each though and, for the most part, looks the same. The Layers palette in Photoshop 6, in fact, took some of the better features that used to appear on earlier versions of ImageReady.

> Regardless of the differences, it is important to remember that by and large, what appears in the Layers palette in Photoshop will appear in the Layers palette in ImageReady. All independent layers, adjustment layers, and layer masks are preserved. And, although you can view the results of an Adjustment Layer in ImageReady, you can only create and edit them in Photoshop.

A few small changes are quickly apparent between the Photoshop and ImageReady Layers palettes. The first is the addition of the Fast Forward and Rewind buttons at the bottom left of the palette in ImageReady. As will be discussed later in this chapter, you can use these buttons to move through frames of an animation. The second—and most noticeable—change is how the palette and programs deal with Layer effects.

## Layer Effects

Layer effects were introduced in Photoshop 5 (and explained in detail in Chapter 1) as a way to create quickly the shadows, bevels, and glows that have become so predominant on the web. With the release of version 6, new Layer Attributes have been added—including the Color Fill effect, which does little more than fill the layer elements with your desired color.

The main difference between the programs is how the effects get applied. Instead of using a bulky dialog box, all of the Layer effects in ImageReady have their own palettes, as shown in Figure 8–3. The same variables can be set in these palettes that can be set in the corresponding Photoshop dialog boxes, but the palette makes it a bit more compact.

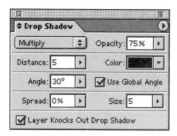

*Figure 8–3: Layer Effects are controlled through palettes in ImageReady.*

# Creating Styles (ImageReady)

Did you ever create a series of Layer effects for an image in Photoshop that you really liked a lot, and used over and over again? This typically involved either redoing the effects manually every time you wanted to place them, or having to invent an action to do create them for you.

ImageReady solves that problem by letting you set and save Styles. Styles are like small package that retain all the effects that you create. For example, if you create a really cool set of effects that include a 50% opaque drop shadow and a pillow emboss with a 12 pixel blur, you can bundle that into one established Style. That Style can then be used on any layer, in any document, at any time.

To create a Style:

1. In your Layers palette (in ImageReady—Styles are not available in Photoshop), create a Layer effect or series of effects.

2. Select one of the effects by clicking on it, or select all of the effects in a group by clicking the Style icon, shown in Figure 8–4.

3. Open the Styles palette by choosing Window -> Show Styles. The Styles palette is shown in Figure 8–5.

4. Drag the effect or set of effects to the Styles palette. It will appear and be saved for you to apply at any time.

You can name the Style if you'd like by selecting the style and choosing Style Options for the palette menu. The Styles palette is full of some really cool preset Styles, which include textures. Try some of these by dragging the desired Style to a layer in the Layers palette.

Styles can also retain rollover states that allow the image to change should a mouse roll over them in browser. Creating rollover states is discussed later in this chapter.

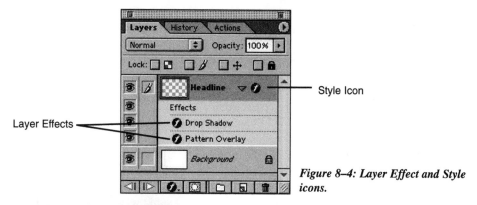

*Figure 8–4: Layer Effect and Style icons.*

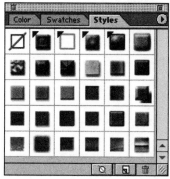

*Figure 8–5: The Styles palette.*

# Making Selections

Depending on what you need to do with your selections, either program can provide an advantage. Photoshop holds the edge, as some of the more advanced selection methods don't exist in ImageReady. These include using Quick Masks, creating paths and selections from paths, and Photoshop's new Extract function and Background eraser tool (introduced in Photoshop 5.5).

However, in the "this is so obviously needed that it should have been included in Photoshop too" category, ImageReady provides a different marquee selection tool. The Rounded Rectangular marquee tool lets you make rectangular selections with curved corners (you can control the extent of the curve in the Options palette). The same can be done in Photoshop by using the Shape tool; however, this tool definitely streamlines that process.

# The History Palette

While the History palette exists is both Photoshop and ImageReady, the latter of the two doesn't use it for much more than to provide a visible list of the commands you have made. Neither the History brush nor the Art History brush is available in ImageReady, so any type of History palette special effect (such as the one discussed in Chapter 1), is pretty much impossible in ImageReady.

# OPTIMIZING IMAGES

Optimizing images is a key to creating web graphics. This is obvious simply by how much emphasis Adobe has put on it with the changes it has made to both Photoshop and ImageReady. In Chapter 2 we took a long look at how the new Save for Web feature lets you optimize an image by manipulating variables. These variables were contained in one convenient location in the Save for Web dialog box.

The options provided in that dialog box are also found in ImageReady. The primary difference here is that the optimization settings are found in a separate palette (Figure 8–6) and optimization can be set while you are working on an image—not just when you are ready to save it.

To view the palette, choose Windows -> Show Optimize. The palette can be expanded by choosing More Options from the palette menu. Since the options that you will manipulate are the same as we've already reviewed in Chapter 2, I won't bore you with gory details again in this chapter.

# CREATING ANIMATIONS

When I wrote my first book, *Web Photoshop 5 To Go*, I spent a large number of pages discussing how to create an animation using a separate program, outside the Adobe family. In Macintosh, the predominant program was GIF Builder, while Windows users chose from a number of popular free and shareware programs, including GIF Movie Builder. With each of these programs, you needed to save each frame as a separate GIF file, then load each, frame by frame, into the animation program, which was kind of a pain.

With ImageReady, animations are done in a very convenient Animation palette, shown in Figure 8–7. What's better, you don't even need to save each frame as a separate file—you create frames as different layers, either in Photoshop or in ImageReady.

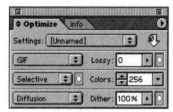

*Figure 8–6: The Optimize palette.*

*Figure 8–7: The Animation palette.*

For the sake of simplicity, I'll illustrate by creating an animation in ImageReady using a basic "bouncing ball" example, in which a simple ball starts at the bottom of the screen, bounces upward, back down again, and so forth. That way you'll have a clear frame of reference when comparing methods.

Just so that we're all on the same page, create a simple multilayered image using the following guidelines:

1. In Photoshop, create a new file, 72 x 216 pixels and immediately create two new layers. We'll begin working on Layer 2, at the top of the Layers palette.

2. With your Circular Shape tool, hold the Shift key for constraint and make a circle toward the bottom of your canvas. Make sure that your foreground color is whatever color you want your bouncing ball to be (I'm using red).

3. Create a new layer and change your foreground color to black. Within the circular selection, use your airbrush to put a shadow on the bottom and a small highlight on the top. You may need to adjust the layer opacity to get the proper shadow/highlight depth. Figure 8–8 gives an example of what your picture should look like.

4. From the Layers palette, choose Merge down to combine the shadow/highlight with the red circle. Rename the layer "Ball 1."

5. On Layer 1, use your Elliptical Marquee tool to make an oval beneath your red ball. Choose Select -> Feather with a feather radius of 5 to soften the edges. Click OK.

6. Fill the selection with black to create a shadow similar to that shown in Figure 8–8. Rename the layer "Shadow."

7. Reactivate the "Ball 1" layer, and choose Duplicate Layer from the palette pull-down menu. Name the new, duplicated layer "Ball 2" and click OK. Do this three times for a total of four separate balls. Name each successive layer "Ball 2," Ball 3," and so forth.

8. On each duplicated layer, move the ball upward with the Move tool. Hold down Shift key while moving, for constraint. When you're through, the canvas, with all the layers visible, will look like the canvas shown in Figure 8–9.

*Figure 8–8: The original red circle with a shadow cast below.*

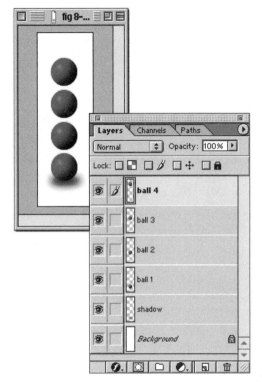

*Figure 8–9: The animation on its canvas, and the corresponding Layers palette.*

To make the ball actually "bounce," you'd create the animation sequence in ImageReady. In this particular bouncing ball example, as simple as it'll probably seem, we're actually doing it the hard way. But showing how to create this type of animation using multiple layers is the best way to illustrate how animation in ImageReady actually gets created. Simpler ways will be described later, in the section "Tweening Frames."

For this example, do the following:

1. Create the frames as individual layers in Photoshop, as you did in the previous example. This is convenient because you never have to save your original file as anything other than a .psd file. Figure 8–9 showed the original canvas and the corresponding Layers palette, with all layers visible, as it appears in Photoshop. I only used the ball in four states, so that this example won't go on forever. Later, when we discuss tweening animation, you'll see how you could also create this same bouncing ball effect with only two frames, but have a lot more fluidity of motion.

**Although you can always add new layers and do a lot of work in ImageReady, I would recommend doing the bulk of the work in Photoshop. Photoshop is just a better program for large scale changes. You can then make relatively minor changes and revisions while in ImageReady, as you are building your animation.**

2. Once you have prepared your graphic, and all the layers are built, open your canvas in ImageReady by clicking the Jump To button on the bottom of the Tools palette (see "Quantum Leap: Jumping Between Programs," earlier in this chapter).

3. In ImageReady, open the Animation palette by choosing Window -> Show Animation.

4. At this point, the Animation palette has only one frame, the first, as indicated by the frame number in the top left of the Frame icon. Notice that the preview shown looks exactly like your main canvas—since all the layers are visible, they all appear in the first frame of your animation, as shown in Figure 8–10. Pretty easy so far, right?

5. We're going to want the animation to start with the first frame showing the ball on the ground and a dark shadow underneath it. Turn off Ball 2, 3, and 4 layers by clicking the Eye icon at the far left of each of those layers. You'll see that the icon for Frame 1 in the Animation palette has changed as well.

 **At the bottom of the Layers palette and toward the left in ImageReady, you'll see an area that says Frame 1. This tells you in which frame of your animation you are currently working. As you create new frames, this Frame Indicator at the bottom of the Layers palette will change to reflect the frame in which you are currently working.**

6. Create a new animation frame either by clicking on the New Frame icon at the bottom of the Animation palette or by choosing New Frame from the Animation palette menu. You'll see a new frame window appear in the Animation palette, with the number 2 in the top left, indicating that it's the second frame. A black outline around the new window shows that this is the active frame—the one you will be adjusting. You'll also notice that upon creation, this frame looks identical to Frame 1. Did you see the change at the bottom of the Layers palette? The Frame Indicator now says Frame 2.

7. We're going to want two distinct changes to occur in this frame: First, we want the ball to move up a bit. Second, we want the underlying shadow to become a bit lighter, or more transparent. Hide the Frame 1 layer. You'll see that the ball disappears in your canvas and in the icon for Frame 2 in the Animation palette. However, nothing has changed in the icon for Frame 1.

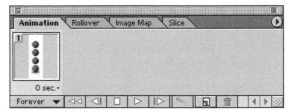

*Figure 8–10: When you open the Animation palette for the first time, only one frame exists, with the icon showing everything that is visible in the layer.*

8. Make the Ball 2 layer visible by clicking the empty box on the far left of the layer in the Layers palette. Also, make the Shadow layer active by clicking on it (you'll see that it's active once it is highlighted). Change Opacity to 66% in the Layers palette. Note the changes in the icon for Frame 2 in the Animation palette.

9. To see how these changes are affecting only the active animation frame, make Frame 1 active by clicking on it. A black border will appear to indicate that it is now active. You'll see in the Layers palette that the visible layers (and opacity for the Shadow layer) have changed to represent the animation state that was saved in Frame 1. Click back to Frame 2 to see the changes in the Layers palette again.

10. Make sure that Frame 2 is active, and then create a new frame in the Animation palette by clicking the New Frame icon. Frame 3 appears, looking identical to Frame 2.

11. Hide the Ball 2 layer and make the Ball 3 layer visible. Also, with the Shadow layer active, reduce the shadow opacity to 33%.

12. Create a new frame by clicking the New Frame Icon. Frame 4 appears, looking identical to Frame 3.

13. Hide Ball 3 and make Ball 4 visible. Also, reduce the opacity of the Shadow layer to 1%.

14. Now that the ball is as high as it can go, do the whole thing in reverse. Leave out the upper most and lower most states on the way down. The Animation palette will look similar to Figure 8–11.

**A quicker way to do this would be to click on Frame 2, then press Shift and click on Frame 3 (this will highlight both frames). Choose Copy Frames from the Animation palette menu. Make Frame 4 active by clicking on it. Create a new frame, Frame 5, and make it active. Make all the visible layers invisible, except for the background layer. Choose Paste Layers from the Animation palette menu. Highlight both of the newly pasted frames and choose Reverse Frames from the palette menu. Believe me, it only *sounds* confusing.**

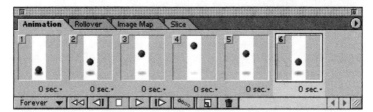

*Figure 8–11: The Animation palette after all of the frames have been created to make the ball bounce up and then back down.*

## Miscellaneous Animation Points

I briefly want to review some of the other things you should keep in mind about animation and frames that weren't covered in either the preceding or following sections:

◆ Although you created the layers in the previous example in Photoshop, you didn't necessarily have to. You can also create layers in ImageReady to use in your animation.

◆ If you alter a layer that only appears in one frame, say, Layer 4 in the preceding example, that change will only take place and be seen in the corresponding frame. However, if a change is made, either moving an element, painting, and so forth, to a layer seen in multiple frames, such as Layer 1 in the preceding example, that change is seen in every frame of the animation that uses those layers.

◆ If you use a Layer mask on an image that appears in multiple frames, the mask will be apparent in every frame. However, you can move the mask to different locations for each frame, even though the mask resides in just one layer.

◆ If you would like to save an individual file for each frame, you can still do so pretty easily. Choose Flatten Frames into Layers from the Animation palette menu. This will create one composite layer for each frame of your animation, and store each in your Layers palette. From there it's just a simple, but tedious, process of saving each frame as its own file.

## Playing and Stopping Your Animation

After that long series of instructions, I thought you could use a break, so here's a short recipe for playing and stopping.

1. Push the Play button (the triangle), at the bottom of the Animation palette to play the animation. Your animation will automatically loop forever, and the animation will play in your canvas.

2. To stop your animation from playing, push the Stop button (the square) at the bottom of the Animation palette (only available while the animation is playing).

You can change the number of times that your animation loops by choosing another option from the Loop pull-down menu. For a more realistic rendition of what your animation will look like, you can preview it in any browser that you have loaded onto your system. Choose File -> Preview In -> (your desired browser).

## Changing the Speed of Your Animation

By default, each frame will appear for 0 seconds, meaning that your animation will move very quickly (no delay between frames). In many cases, that may be exactly the way you want it. But, sometimes, slower can be better.

1. To change the speed of an individual frame, activate the frame by clicking on it.

2. At the bottom of the frame, click on the small arrow where it reads "0 sec."

3. Choose the speed from the presets given in the pop-up menu, or set your own time by choosing Other.

4. To change all the frames (or many frames in a row), click on the first frame you would like to change.

5. Hold the Shift key and click on the last frame you want to change. All of the frames in between will be highlighted as well.

6. Choose your desired time from the pop-up menu of any of the highlighted frames. Notice that the delay time changes for all frames.

7. To change the delay times for multiple, noncontiguous frames, activate a frame you would like to change, and press Command/Ctrl and click all other desired frames. The frames in between will not be highlighted.

8. Choose your desired delay time from the pop-up menu of any highlighted frame.

## Changing Frame Order and Deleting Frames

Similar to the way you work in layers, you can move a frame simply by clicking on the frame you want to move, and holding the mouse button down.

1. Drag with your mouse to move the frame in question to the position you desire.

2. Delete a frame either by dragging it to the Trash icon in the Animation palette, or choosing Delete Frame from the palette menu.

**If multiple frames are selected, all of those frames will be deleted or moved, not just the one that is active.**

## Tweening Frames

"Tweening" is essentially an easy way to create a number of frames in between (*between*—that's where the word *tweening* comes from) two existing frames for smooth animation. For instance, in our bouncing ball example, we wanted the ball to reach the top of the canvas while the underlying shadow faded to almost nothing, which we accomplished. But we could also accomplish it using just two frames, one for the ball and one for the shadow.

1. Create the same basic image that we created before, but this time use only three layers—keep the background layer empty, have the next layer contain your shadow, and the third layer contain the ball.

2. Open the Animation palette in ImageReady. The first and only frame will show both the ball and the shadow, just like your canvas.

3. Create a new frame by clicking on the New Frame icon.

4. Activate the Move tool. Make sure that the active layer is the one that contains the ball and, holding Shift for constraint, drag the ball to the top of the canvas. You'll see that in Frame 2 of the Animation palette, the ball is at the top of the canvas, while in Frame 1 it's at the bottom, even though the ball is in the same layer. Click on Frame 1, and you'll see that the ball moves inside the canvas itself. ImageReady will remember various states for different frames without creating additional layers.

This is an incredibly convenient way of working that'll save you the time of making multiple layers, but there is one drawback. When you move the contents of a layer to accommodate multiple frames of an animation, any changes that you make to that layer (color, paint strokes, etc.) will be seen in every frame of your animation. There is always a price for convenience.

5. With Frame 2 in the Animation palette active again, activate the layer that contains the shadow within the Layer palette. Reduce the opacity of the shadow to 1%, and you'll see the effect happen within Frame 2 in the Animation palette, while Frame 1 still shows the shadow at full opacity.

6. With Frame 2 still active, click the Tween button at the bottom of the Animation palette. Figure 8–12 shows the palette to this point, with the Tween button pointed out.

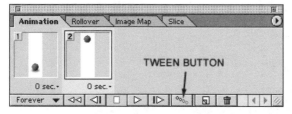

*Figure 8–12: The Animation palette displaying the two existing frames. The Tween button is the one that resembles a small comet.*

7. Pushing the Tween button will reveal the dialog box shown in Figure 8–13. It's a fairly straightforward dialog box with just a few options. The first option lets you choose which layers you will tween. Choosing All Layers means that the frames you create will use the elements from all the visible layers, while choosing Selected Layer means that the tween will only affect the layer that is currently active. In this case, you'll want to select All Layers, since you're trying to create an animation using both the ball and the shadow, which both reside on different layers.

The next set of options is called Parameters. Here you can select one or more of the available choices, which in this case would be Position (for the ball) and Opacity (for the shadow). We'll leave the Effects option unchecked, since it's used more for Layer effects types of animations, which we haven't involved in this example.

The third choice you'll have to make is labeled Tween With, and the options that appear within the pull-down menu will change depending on which and how many frames you have active.

◆   If you have just Frame 2 active, then the only choices that will be available will be Previous Frame, meaning that the tween will occur between the active frame and the frame directly before the active frame (Frame 1 in this case), or First Frame, which would create the tween *after* the active frame and before the first frame.

**If you had more than two frames existing in your animation, and had one of the center frames active when you pushed the Tween button, the First Frame option would be replaced with a Next Frame option. The First Frame option only appears in our example because the next frame after Frame 2 is the first frame.**

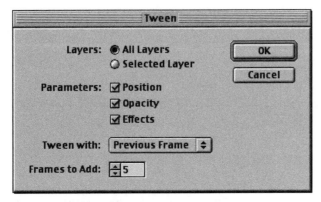

*Figure 8–13: The Tween dialog box.*

◆ If you have the first frame of your animation active, your choices would be Next Frame or Last Frame, which in this case are the same frame (Frame 2). The difference would be in where the tweened frames are placed, either after the first frame or after the last frame.

◆ If you have two contiguous frames selected, your only option will be Selection.

**You cannot tween noncontiguous frames.**

In this particular case, you'll want to choose Previous Frame.

Lastly, you'll have the option to select how many frames you want to add. The more frames you add, the more fluid your animation will look, but the larger the file size will be. For this example, I'm choosing to add four frames. Click OK when you've made your selections.

**8.** You'll see your new frames instantly added in your Animation palette, between Frames 1 and 2. Play the animation, and you'll see that you now have a smooth transition from the first position to the last, which likely creates a smoother animation than the original way we created the bouncing ball earlier in this chapter. Figure 8–14 shows the Animation palette with the tweened frames placed between the original frames.

**It's kind of a neat thing, but let's say you have your original Frames 1 and 2 again, and Frame 1 is active. If you create a new frame by pushing the New Frame button at the bottom of the Animation palette, the new frame appears as a duplicate of Frame 1, and is lodged in the middle. If you select all three frames at once, and then push the Tween button, you will not get the Tween dialog box at all. Instead, the middle frame will just automatically be repositioned and reworked to create a smoother transition between the first and last frames.**

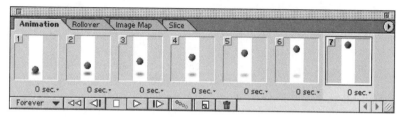

*Figure 8–14: The Animation palette with the Tween effect.*

# TRANSPARENCY AND ANIMATION

Mixing animation and transparency can produce some very ugly results.

The problem with having transparent files is that if you are creating an animation in which your image moves from one area to another, you will see right through the transparency in each frame, and into the frame preceding it. This will essentially destroy the desired moving effect, and you will end up with an animation that looks messy.

In ImageReady, you can keep one frame from showing through the transparent portion of the following frame(s) by "disposing" of a frame. Disposing of a frame means that you will discard, or hide, a frame before the next frame appears. This way, there is no threat of seeing that frame through the next frame.

To set a frame disposal:

1. Make the frame(s) that you want to dispose of, or hide, active.

2. Press Command/Ctrl and click (right-mouse click in Windows) on the icon for one of the selected frames. A pop-up menu will appear.

3. Choose Restore to Background to make the selected frames hide before the next frame appears. Choose Do Not Dispose to allow the selected frames to remain visible as the next frame plays (causing them to be seen through any transparent areas. Choose Automatic, the default selection, to allow ImageReady to determine for itself when a frame should or shouldn't be discarded.

## Optimizing an ImageReady Animation

By selecting a frame in your animation, you can use the Optimize palette to set the optimization variables. All frames will assume the same settings. Images that will retain animations must be saved in the GIF file format. If you optimize your GIF to have a Selective, Perceptual, or Adaptive palette, ImageReady will create a Color palette that takes into consideration each frame individually. In addition, it will reduce odd color shifts or "flickering" by applying unique dithering to each frame. This special attention also includes optimized treatment only to the areas of each frame that change, to help keep file size down for faster downloads.

Because animations have different properties than ordinary images (in that it may have different elements that move, shift, or otherwise change over the course of frames), the optimization settings can be a bit more involved. Beyond the variables provided in the Optimize palette, you can choose Optimize Animation from the Animation palette menu.

◆ Check the box for Optimize by Bounding Box to have ImageReady crop each frame of your animation to only retain the area that has been altered from the proceeding frame. This will ultimately help reduce the file size, and is checked on by default.

◆ Check the box for Redundant Pixel Removal to turn all unchanged pixels (between frames) into transparent pixels. This will also help reduce file size, and is also checked on by default.

As described earlier in this section, transparencies can be tricky when it comes to animation. Set the disposal method to Automatic when using the Redundant Pixel Removal option for ImageReady to determine whether or not transparency is appropriate.

## Saving and Opening an Animation

To save the image with all of its elements, including layers, as a Photoshop file, choose File -> Save or Save As. This will allow you to work on your image at a later point, with all layers retained, in either Photoshop or ImageReady.

If you reopen the image in Photoshop, whichever frame of your animation was selected when you last saved it in ImageReady will be visible in Photoshop. If you add a layer in Photoshop and manipulate it (by placing text, imagery, paint, etc., on it), and then jump back to ImageReady, the new layer will appear, and the manipulations will show up in the selected frame. If you make alterations to a layer in Photoshop that appear in multiple frames of your animation, those changes will show up in each respective frame.

Choose File -> Save Optimized or Save Optimized As to save your animation as a GIF, with all of the optimization settings. The dialog box will allow you to choose whether or not you want ImageReady to generate HTML text for you.

# SLICING IMAGES

Slicing images is a practice that has become relatively commonplace for graphics on the Internet. By "slicing," I'm referring to literally cutting up an image into smaller pieces, then having them reassembled in an HTML table within your browser.

There are a number of reasons why you would want to slice your images into smaller pieces just to put them back together again later. Not only does slicing your image into smaller pieces help make it load faster, but it is also the mechanism with which you can create JavaScript rollovers in ImageReady. Rollovers are discussed later in this chapter.

Slicing an image in Photoshop version 5 or lower was a complete drag. It took forever, and there were inevitably mistakes that made you have to go back and do the whole thing over again in many cases. With the inclusion of ImageReady in version 5.5, slicing images became much easier. ImageReady's Slice tool made the job quick and painless. Now, with 6, the Slice tool has found its way to Photoshop, so you don't necessarily need to do your slicing in ImageReady—you can do it in Photoshop, instead.

So why, then, is this the first time that you're really hearing about it?

Well, even though it's offered in Photoshop, it doesn't make sense to write about it twice, since it basically does the same thing in both programs. You can create slices in either, and they will transfer between programs just like layers do. But personally, I like creating slices in ImageReady better that I like creating them in Photoshop for a few reasons:

◆ You can optimize slices individually in both programs, but in Photoshop you need to go out of the way to open the Save for Web dialog box from the File menu to do so, while ImageReady uses the much more convenient Optimize palette.

◆ Setting a URL address, Target Frame, Message Text, and so forth is more convenient in ImageReady, where a floating palette allows you to set these parameters easily. You can set them in Photoshop as well, but you have to double-click on each frame to access the dialog box.

Creating slices in ImageReady merely comes down to mastering one tool—the Slice tool, shown in Figure 8–15. If you know how to use the Rectangular marquee tool, then you know how to use the Slice tool. There are, however, a lot of options and nuances that you need to learn to take full advantage of the slice function so, without further babbling …

To create slices in your image:

1. In the toolbar, make the Slice tool active by clicking on it. You'll see a slight change in your image, as a yellow outline with symbols in the upper left corner suddenly appear. Photoshop places this there automatically, to indicate that the original slice is the image itself.

2. With the Slice tool, drag with your cursor to select the area where you want to make your first slice. This will feel much like using the Rectangular marquee tool, and much of the controls are exactly the same. For example, dragging while holding the Shift key will constrain the proportions, holding the Option key (Alt in Windows) will allow you to drag from the middle instead of the corner, and so forth.

3. For the sake of this example, let's suppose that you create your first slice from the upper left corner of your image. The result would look similar to Figure 8–16. Notice, however, that two other slices suddenly accompany the slice you just created. Not only that, but the area outside the slice you just created appears to have a slight film over it, diminishing the colors in your image.

 *Figure 8–15: The Tool palette, with the*
*Slice and Slice Select tools pointed out.*

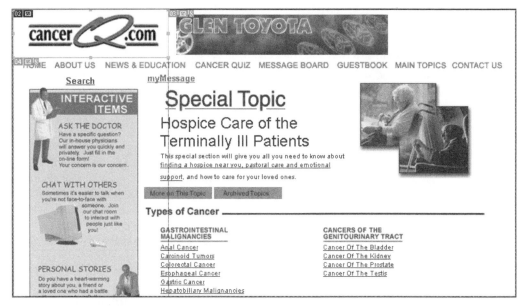

*Figure 8–16: Slicing up an image.*

4. If you are familiar with how HTML tables are created, then you will easily understand that the other slices are necessary in order to assemble your image properly in HTML. These slices, generated by ImageReady, are called auto-slices. Auto-slices differ in quality from the slice you created, otherwise known as a user-slice. User-slices, as we will see, have more functionality to them and are displayed with the full color of your image, as opposed to the slightly washed out look seen in the auto-slices.

5. Continue using the Slice tool to make further slices to your image. As you create more user-slices, more auto-slices are also created, until you have filled your image with auto-slices.

6. As you create slices, you will notice that each individual slice is numbered. Slices are numbered from left to right, with slice number one residing in the upper left portion of your image.

If you are more comfortable creating slices from guides you have set, you can do this as well. Simply place the guides in such a way that they break up your image as desired. Then choose Slice -> Create Slice from Guides. All slices created will be user-slices, and they will be created in place of any slices that already exist.

## Selecting a Slice

1. To select either a user-slice or an auto-slice, choose the Slice Select tool.
2. Click on the slice of your choice. That slice becomes active, as indicated by the bright yellow bounding box. If you have selected an auto-slice, that portion of your image will display in its normal color for the duration of time that it is selected.
3. Hold the Shift key and click on another slice to select more than one at a time.
4. If you select an auto-slice, you can click in the slice and drag a selection to include multiple slices. Clicking and dragging when starting from a user-slice will move that slice elsewhere in your image. You can select all slices or deselect all slices by choosing Select -> All Slice or Select -> Deselect All, respectively.

## Turning an Auto-Slice Into a User-Slice

1. Select on auto-slice.
2. Choose Slice -> Promote to User Slice. The new user-slice will be indicated by a change in color quality of that image portion and the inclusion of handlebars around the bounding box.

Other choices or actions you will make, such as making certain selections in the Slice palette (discussed later in this section), will also force an auto-slice to become a user-slice. ImageReady really does prefer slices to be user-slices, and it is my prediction (you heard it here first) that future versions of ImageReady will simply do away with auto-slices altogether.

### *Why You Would Want to Promote an Auto-Slice*

Promoting auto-slices to user-slices gives you the freedom to manipulate them more freely. This includes the ability to customize optimization settings for each slice, as well as to link them together and distribute optimization settings. Some settings you may make in the Slice palette (discussed later this chapter) will automatically promote an auto-slice to a user-slice.

## Optimizing Slices

In case you haven't noticed, optimization has been the word of the day in this chapter. Many of the improvements in this upgrade either directly or indirectly have something to do with optimizing your files. To optimize a slice, simply use the Slice Select tool and click on the slice you want to optimize. Then follow the directions for optimization that were explained earlier in this chapter..

**If you have a lot of slices and want to apply the same optimization setting to some or all of them, but don't want to do it for each one individually, you can link slices together. Optimizing linked slices will distribute the same optimization settings across each slice in the linked "chain." All auto-slices are linked together in a group as they are created.**

To link slices, simply select the slices you would like to link with the Select Slice tool, and choose Slice -> Link Slices. If the first slice you select is an auto-slice, then all slices that you are linking together (even user-slices), will become part of the auto-slice group. If the first slice selected is a user-slice, then any auto-slice that is selected will automatically be upgraded to a user-slice. Different groups of slices will be delineated by the different colors of information in the upper left of the slices.

## Resizing and/or Moving a Slice

1. Make the Slice Select tool active by clicking on it.

2. Click on the slice that you want to resize. If it is a user-slice, resize the slice by manipulating the handlebars on the bounding box. If you have selected an auto-slice, you will need to promote it to a user-slice if you want to resize or move your slice.

3. If you move your slice in such a way that it overlaps another slice, ImageReady will divide the slice underneath. This division will include separate slices for the visible areas outside the overlapped area, as well as a slice for the area of the intersection. These slices will become apparent when you save the optimized image and the HTML table is generated. In the meantime, however, while you are working, the underlying slice is preserved for you to move, enhance, or otherwise manipulate.

## Dividing a Slice

This is actually pretty cool, and it can save you a lot of time if you follow these steps:

1. Select a slice by clicking on it with the Slice Select tool.

2. From the Slice palette menu, choose Divide Slice to access the dialog box shown in Figure 8–17.

3. Check the Preview checkbox to see the divisions as they are being created.

4. In the dialog box, choose, by clicking on the respective checkbox, whether to divide your slice horizontally, vertically, or both.

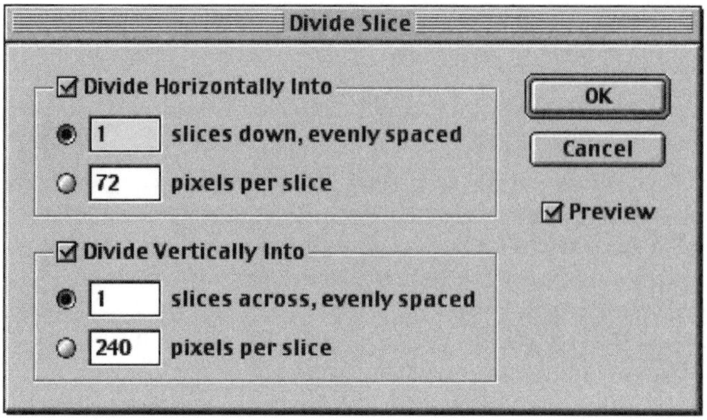

*Figure 8–17: The Divide Slice dialog box.*

5. Within each area, you can decide whether you want to divide your slice into equal parts (simply fill in the desired value), or by a certain number of pixels for each division. If you choose the latter, and do not enter a value that will divide your slice equally, ImageReady will make as many divisions as possible, and then make one last slice from whatever is left over. So, for example, if your slice is 70 pixels, and you divide into slices of 30 pixels each, you will get two slices at 30 pixels, and one slice at 10 pixels.

# Combining Slices

You can easily combine two or more slices into one slice, should you decide that you either have too many slices to manage easily, or that, from a time management/optimization point of view, there is no value to having separate slices for one portion of your image.

1. With the Slice Select tool, select the slices you want to combine (hold the Shift key to make multiple selections). Bear in mind that you do not need to select only user-slices to make a combination. Auto-slices can be used as well. In addition, slices that you choose can be noncontiguous.

2. Choose Slice -> Combine Slices. A new user-slice is created (it is always a user-slice, even if two auto-slices were selected as the candidates to combine), taking its dimensions from the rectangle that can be created from the outside edge of the selected slices. If the selected slices are not contiguous, the new slice will either replace all underlying slices, or will overlap the underlying slices. Overlapping slices are discussed earlier in this chapter.

**Combined slices will retain the optimization of the first slice that was selected before you chose to combine them.**

## Aligning Slices With One Another

Much like aligning elements that reside in layers, you can align slices, too. You can align slices either horizontally (by top, center, or bottom), or vertically (by top, center, or bottom).

1. With the Slice Select tool, select the slices you want to combine (hold the Shift key to make multiple selections). For alignment of slices, you must choose two or more user-slices—auto-slices can't be aligned. Promoting your auto-slice to a user-slice is discussed earlier in this chapter.

2. Choose Slices -> Align ->[your preference of alignment]. If any areas overlap as a result of the alignment, the overlap area will become its own user-slice.

## When Looking at Slices Gets Annoying

Just push the button to hide slices on the toolbar. It's located directly under the foreground and background color swatches, on the right.

## Where it Gets Interesting: Using the Slice Palette

As with almost anything else in Photoshop or ImageReady, the real magic starts when you are in one of the palettes. The Slice palette, shown in Figure 8–18 and accessible by choosing Window -> Show Slice, really gives you the flexibility to put the slices to good use. Precise movements of individual slices, adding hyperlink information for image mapping, and writing ALT tags are just some of the things you can accomplish in this palette.

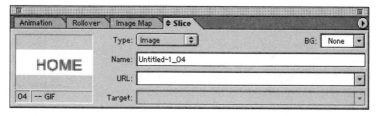

*Figure 8–18: The Slice palette.*

To use the palette, you first have to select a slice with the Slice Select tool . The Slice palette will retain different information for each slice in your image, although you will have fewer options available for auto-slices, which is one of the reasons that you will want to promote auto-slices to user-slices. In fact, many of the options that you make in this palette will change your auto-slices into user-slices automatically.

To use the Slice palette:

1. Select the type from the Type pull-down menu. Choose Image to continue working with the slice as an image. This is the default. Choose No Image to drop out the image from the slice area. The slice palette will change a bit, revealing a text area. Use this area to fill in the missing space with browser-generated text, if you would like, or leave it blank to drop out the image without adding text.

**NOTE: If you choose No Image for your Type, the preview window in the palette and your canvas will still show the image. And if you fill in the area with HTML text in the palette, it won't appear in the canvas, either. To see the results of these options, you have to select File -> Preview In -> [your desired browser].**

2. Select your background color from the BG pull-down menu. The background color you pick will fill in the transparent areas of your slice if you have chosen Image as your Type. If you choose No Image as your Type, the background color will fill in the entire area of your slice.

3. If a particular slice is one solid color, use the Color Picker to determine its hexadecimal code. Then set the slice to No Image and, in the BG pull-down menu, access the Color Picker and fill in the hexadecimal value. (See next section for more information on the BG pull-down menu). This will help eliminate colors from the image, and decrease download time.

You can select from a number of options in the BG pull-down menu. The color swatches at the bottom are the colors from the web-safe Color palette. You may also choose None, which leaves the background as transparent (unless you are saving as a JPEG, in which case the background color will default to the Matte option in the Optimize palette. The Matte option in the BG pull-down area will also cause the color to be placed in the Optimize palette. Foreground and Background will fill in your transparent or empty area with either your foreground or background color, respectively. Choose Other to access the Color Picker.

1. In the Name area, you can change the file name that ImageReady had chosen for the slice in question. Typically, these are pretty straightforward names that incorporate the slice number—I would advise thinking twice before changing the name.

2. If the slice is part of an image map, and you would like the user to access another HTML page when he or she clicks on this particular slice, provide the appropriate web page address in the URL text area.

3. If you use frames in your web site (which divide your browser window into various segments) use the Target text area to specify in which frame you wish the corresponding URL to open. The name that you enter here must match the name you have given to the frame in your HTML text. The Target area will be grayed out until you have entered an address in the URL area. If you are working in a frames site, but do not want the URL you have specified to open in one of the frames you have named in your HTML text, you can select one of the options provided in the Target pull-down menu.

   ◆ _blank: This will open the page in its own browser window, which will appear in front of the original one.

   ◆ _self: This will cause the new frame to open in the same frame that held the link.

   ◆ _parent: Loads the image in the framset that contains the file clicked on.

   ◆ _top: This will load your new page into the entire browser, overriding all of the frames.

4. Expand the Slice palette to include more options by choosing Show Options from the palette menu. Figure 8–19 shows what the palette, including the extended options, will look like.

5. The Precision area on the bottom left of the palette allows you to control the size and position of the selected slice. Manipulating it in any way will change either the dimensions or location of your slice, or both. Be prepared that this could cause an overlapping of slices and could change the HTML table that ImageReady will create. An explanation of overlapping slices is provided earlier in this chapter.

6. Click the Constrain Proportions checkbox to maintain the original proportions of the selected slice.

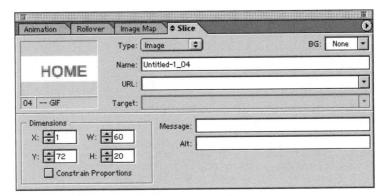

*Figure 8–19: The Slice palette with the options visible.*

7. Enter a phrase, direction, or statement in the Message area that you wish to appear in the browser status area (typically the bottom left portion of the browser frame). This usually displays the URL that the user will link to should he or she click on a particular part of your image. This is fine, and no one will complain about it, but what looks nicer from a marketing or an aesthetic standpoint: "http://www.your-sitename.com/products.html" or "Click here to find out more about our wide product variety"? Remember, it's all in the marketing, baby.

## Saving Image Slices

Typically, you would save any image by choosing either File -> Save (to save your image using the same name and file type), or File -> Save As (to save your image using a different name or file type). Doing so after placing slices in your image will simply preserve your slices, so that next time you open your image, the slices that you made will still be there.

A different result can be achieved by choosing File -> Save Optimized As. Choosing this will bring up the dialog box shown in Figure 8–20. Notice that the file name has an .html extension, and not the .jpg or .gif extension that you might expect. That's because once you push the OK button, ImageReady will not only save each slice as its own separate file (and contain all of these files in its own folder), but it will write the HTML code for you for the <TABLE> assembly. Just cut and paste this into your own HTML text.

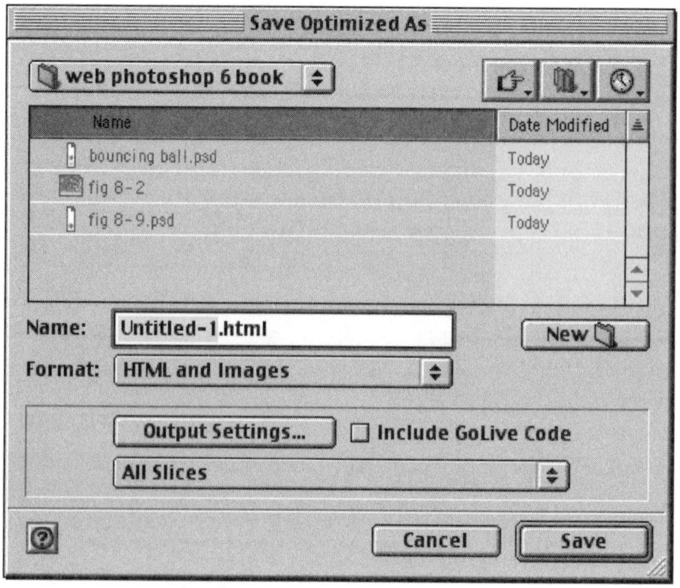

*Figure 8–20: The Save Optimized As dialog box.*

**Check out the HTML Options button for more in-depth control when ImageReady writes your HTML files. You can, for example, instruct ImageReady to write all of your HTML tags in uppercase, which I personally prefer.**

If you copy the ImageReady text into your own HTML text, and then make changes to the slice configuration in ImageReady, you don't need to copy and paste again. Simply save your changes by choosing File -> Save Optimized As. Then select File -> Update HTML, and locate the HTML text page that you wish to update.

**Although it doesn't seem to make sense, after numerous trials and errors, it would appear that not only does ImageReady update the table in your HTML text, it also pretty much wipes out anything else you had in there—other images, lines of copy, and so forth. Be careful and experiment with this feature before you use it—you don't want to lose anything that you worked hard to write.**

# CREATING JAVASCRIPT ROLLOVERS

Creating a JavaScript rollover is easy. Take a quarter stick of butter, and a teaspoon of flour ... Java ... rollover ... that's a joke, son, don't you get it?

Sorry—in the interest of bringing important information to my readers as quickly as possible, I am still up typing at 3:16 a.m., and Foghorn J. Leghorn is the only thing keeping me company.

Anyway, JavaScript rollovers are pretty easy in ImageReady. But before I get into how to make them, let me provide a quick explanation of what they are. Have you ever been to a website, where when you move your mouse over a button or an image, the button changes color, or shape, or makes something appear elsewhere in the browser? That's a rollover. These are usually done with JavaScript, much like the one shown at the end of Chapter 6 from the original book, *Web Photoshop 5 To Go*. Typically these can be formidable to write (although the savvy non-Java programming language designer will usually just borrow a script from another site), but they are spreading on the web. It won't be long before rollovers are as common on the web as animated GIFs, and any semblance of class on the Internet will be gone, replaced by the New Jersey diner standard of web design.

Fortunately, ImageReady allows you to create rollovers without having to write one line of code. The palette setup makes JavaScript rollovers as easy to create as animation (examined earlier in this chapter) and, similar to the ImageReady animation process, the tie-in to the Layers palette makes rollovers that much more familiar.

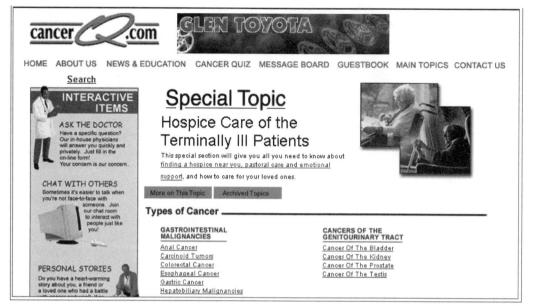

*Figure 8–21: We'll make the buttons on this navigation bar have rollover effects.*

For the purposes of this example, I'll be using the simple navigation bar shown in Figure 8–21, which is part of a larger page layout.

The entire page was created and laid out in Photoshop. The idea for this example is that as the user rolls his or her cursor over the Home button, it will add a drop shadow. As the cursor moves over the About Us button, a line of text will appear elsewhere on the site. And finally, when the user's cursor moves over the Products button, an animation will start elsewhere on the page. Granted, this mish-mosh of effects would create a pretty ugly web site, but for the sake of this chapter it'll create a pretty useful example.

To achieve each of these effects, the entire page will need to be sliced into smaller parts. Slicing an image was discussed earlier in this chapter. The slices that I have created for this example are shown in Figure 8–22.

# Adding a Drop Shadow to the Home Button

Probably the most common type of rollover, this simple effect will change the very portion of the image that the user rolls his or her cursor over. In this instance, we will make a drop shadow appear behind the Home button. More commonly the change would be a shift in color, but considering that this is a black and white book, I've made the change more visible.

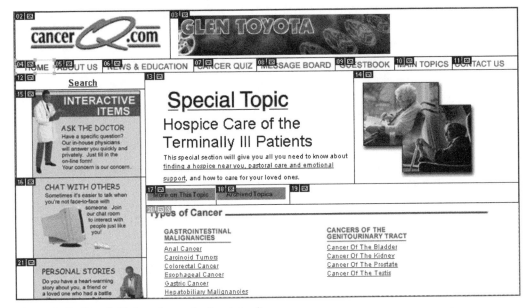

*Figure 8–22: I've divided up the navigation into slices.*

1. Make the Slice Selection tool active by clicking on it.

2. Make sure that the slices in your image are visible by choosing Window -> Show Slices.

3. Make the slice containing the word *Home* active by clicking on it. You'll see that the slice lights up in a bright yellow color.

4. Open the Rollover palette by choosing Window -> Show Rollover. The palette appears in Figure 8–23. Notice that the first frame, or state, is named Normal to indicate that this is how the image appears when the cursor is not being rolled over it.

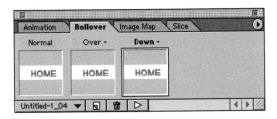

*Figure 8–23: The Rollover palette.*

5.  Create a new rollover state by clicking the New State button on the bottom of the Rollover palette (you can also do this by choosing New State from the Rollover palette menu. This new state will, by default, be labeled Over, to indicate that it is what will happen when the cursor is moved over the image.

6.  Notice that the preview window in the Over state looks identical to the image in the Normal preview window. This will change in just a moment.

7.  With the slice for the word *Home* still active, choose Select -> Create Selection from Slice to make an active marquee selection in the slice area.

8.  When I created the text buttons, I placed all of the words at once, so they all appear on the same layer. For the rollover to work, we're going to need the word *Home* to appear on a separate layer (remember that we're going to add rollover effects through the use of different layers, much like we did when creating animations). Choose Layer -> New -> Layer Via Copy. The word *Home* will appear in its own unique layer, as well as still existing in its original layer. In the original layer, the text is still editable, so you can change the copy, font, size, and so forth at any time. Once you copy all or part of the text onto a new layer, the copy that appears in that new layer will not be editable—it will just be a graphic representation of the word *Home*.

9.  Because you were in the Over state when you created your new layer, that layer is only visible when the Over state is active. Just for testing purposes, make the Normal state active by clicking on it. You can see that even though your new layer exists while in this state, it become invisible. Make the Over state active again by clicking on it which, in turn, will make your new layer visible again.

10. Make the new layer, the one with only the word *Home* in it, active by clicking on it in the Layers palette.

11. Add a drop shadow to the word *Home* by using the Layer effects. Layer effects, described in greater detail in Chapter 5, can still be accessed in ImageReady through the Layer -> Layer Effects menu. An easier way, however, is by pushing the small black circle with "f" inside it at the bottom of the Layers palette. A pop-up menu featuring the Layers effects options appears. Choose Drop Shadow for the current example.

12. Unlike Photoshop, which gives you a full dialog box for the creation of Layer effects, ImageReady lets you adjust each effect by supplying a unique palette for it (the Layer Options palette changes names and variables, depending on which Layer effect you choose). The palette for Drop Shadow is shown earlier in this chapter. Use the palette to create a drop shadow for the word *Home*.

13. To see your rollover at work, you'll need to open your image in a browser. Choose File -> Preview In -> (desired browser). Provided you have enough RAM, the browser that you selected will open and display your image. Roll over the word *Home* to see the drop shadow work.

# A Few Other Things You Should Know

The following points are a few extra things that you should know about creating rollovers. These were not covered in the preceding section because they were not needed for the last example. Although Over states are the most common, the process does not have to end there. You can continue adding states by clicking the New State button. Each new state will appear with a different function, in the following order:

◆ Down: The change will occur when the user clicks on the image. It will last for as long as the user keeps his or her mouse button down.

◆ Click: This will change the appearance of your rollover after the user has clicked on it. The effect will last until the user either clicks on another rollover element or navigates to another page.

◆ Out: This changes the image when the user moves his or her cursor out of the rollover area. This is pretty much a waste of time, as the Normal state is typically fine for this.

◆ Up: This will change the image after the user has clicked off the image but still has his or her cursor over it. Again, this is fairly useless, as the Over state is fine for this. Do you get the feeling that the programming guys at Adobe went a little state-happy?

◆ None: This state doesn't appear in the browser no matter what you do with your cursor—it just saves the image as it currently exists, so you can use it later.

The preceding list described each state, and listed them in the order that they appear. You can change the function of any state, however, if you want them to occur in a different order. Just click on the small arrow next to the name of each state and select your desired function from the pull-down menu. You cannot change the function of the first state, which is marked Normal.

The pull-down menu will also offer an option named Custom. Choose this to create your own function. To make this work, though, you will need to write or supply your own JavaScript code for your HTML text.

# Creating a Change Elsewhere in Your Image

This is really not so radically different from the example that we just examined. In fact, it's pretty much exactly the same, with one small thing to note. The reason that I have listed it separately is that for some reason, this tends to be a common question that people have asked me since they got the new version.

For this example, the effect we're looking for is that as the cursor moves over the words About Us, the line "We are an advertising, communications, and production company" will appear at the bottom of the image. This is so similar to the last example of the

Home button that I won't bother to list the directions numerically. This time, you will use the Slice Selection tool to select the About Us button. Follow the steps in the preceding example from there. When you are working in the Over state, simply add the line of text anyplace on the image that you would like it. Because it is text, it will automatically be placed in its own layer. This layer will be invisible in the Normal state, and visible in the Over state.

The trick here is to realize that the preview window in your active state will only show the slice you have selected—in this case, the About Us button. It will not preview the text you have placed, since it exists elsewhere on the page. The only way to check that it is working is either to see which layers are visible as you activate various states, or to preview your image and test it in your browser.

## Triggering an Animation as a State

As I mentioned in the introduction to the rollover section, we will try now to make an animation begin elsewhere on the page when the user rolls his or her cursor over the Products button. Once again, this is super simple. Once you have the slice containing the word *Product* selected, and are working in the Over state (or any other state), start building your animation as described earlier in this chapter. The entire animation will be created in the Over state and will only activate when the user's cursor moves over the word *Products*.

# SUMMARY

As the Web becomes more a part of our everyday lives, audiences will come to expect more dynamic elements in the Web pages they view. Static images alone will not be sufficient to retain viewers and ensure return visitors. While animation alone is not enough to turn an ineffective Web site into an effective one, the movement and interest it can generate can play an important part in taking advantage of this expanding technology.

# chapter 9

# REAL-LIFE EXAMPLE:

# A COMPLETE

# WALKTHROUGH

Well, if you read this same chapter of my last book, *Web Photoshop 5 To Go*, you might be surprised at how different the content is this time around. As I outlined the detail that I'd was going to write about in this chapter, even I was surprised at how much the web really has changed. Years ago, I wrote about using the rulers and guides to aid you in the carving of an image, then how to write the HTML code to reassemble. Now, I don't even need to touch HTML—in fact, it's actually been quite awhile since I've even seen an HTML text.

This chapter will walk you through the creation of a web site that my agency developed for one of our clients, including the marketing and some of the research that went into it, and the graphic design and layout. I'll stop short, though, of giving detail about DreamWeaver (the program that was used to assemble and write the basic code for the site), or giving detail about the database development and shopping cart for the e-commerce portion.

# THE CLIENT

Based on their name, you might expect that Union County Flower Supply is a small local business. But in actuality, UCFS is the largest wholesale floral and gift supplier on the east coast. With a warehouse of over 25,000 products on the shelves at any given time, they had built a traditional brick-and-mortar distribution company that spanned three decades. Now, they were ready to bring their business to the web, and they looked to us to build an e-commerce web site for them.

At the point that they contacted us, they had no real database for their products, no brand identity that we needed to adhere to—basically, we had an open canvas to play with. The end result of our efforts is shown in Figure 9–1 (also Color Figure 18).

# THE MARKET

Our first step, before we even started thinking about the site itself, was to understand the market. Different audiences, or demographics, will respond to different types of layouts and different types of design. We conducted our research through a combination of surveys, interviews, focus panels, and talking to our client about

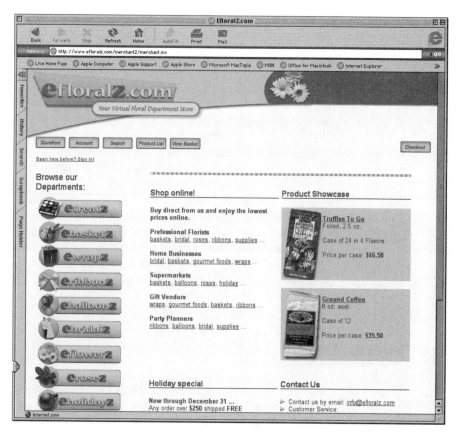

*Figure 9–1: The site my company built for Union County Floral Supply.*

their customers. What we learned was that their target audience of small gift and floral gift retailers were, among other facts and figures, business people. But at the same time they tended to be artistic in nature, creative people who were more familiar with local happenings than the latest close on Wall Street. They tended to be in their mid-forties and older, with the buying decision makers pretty evenly divided between men and women.

At the same time, Union County wanted to reach beyond their traditional audience of retailers, and introduce the end user into their customer mix for the first time. This was to be a secondary target, by far, but still a consideration.

# THE BRAND

Besides trying to bring a slightly new audience into the mix, the site and the marketing that would support it would try to reach a new geographic area as well. But in order to reach outside their existing markets, we wouldn't be able to brand the site using the Union County name. Instead, using the letters "e" (a bit overused, but what the heck), and the letter "z" to work with it, we named the site Efloralz.com, and created a series of sub-brands for various categories of products, like EBasketz, EBalloonz, and so forth.

We developed the logo that appears in Figure 9–2 not only to remain consistent throughout the site, but also to appear on all marketing and paperwork for Union County. That included business cards, truck sides, requisition orders, and any other place that we could plaster marketing material. It took advantage of a serif font for a slight corporate appeal, but with a little flare in recognition of the audience's tastes.

The tag was simple—no fluff needed to explain to a busy audience exactly where they were and what they could expect. After a couple of renditions, "Your Virtual Floral Department Store" was what we decided on, incorporating that message with the logo design.

*Figure 9–2: The logo we developed.*

We decided that the colors should be pastels, which seemed to make the most sense given the information we had compiled on the likely audience for the site. Otherwise, we went into the project with the idea that we would keep the site relatively clean, and not overburden it with too much frivolous information.

# Variable Constraints

A small snag occurred early in the game that kept us from developing the design quite the way we wanted it. Our client had already chosen a specific host for his site, and was pretty sold on them. If you do not host the sites that you build, host and server issues are bound to come up. It's not entirely necessary that you host sites that you create—my agency never has, and we've never had any problems using certain, pre-determined hosts. But once in awhile, when you need to work with hosts other than the ones you're used to, you can run into headaches.

Our particular headache, without getting into details, was that this particular host would only support a specific shopping cart program by a manufacturer with which we weren't familiar. Our first choice was to create our own shopping cart site using ASP programming, but apparently that wasn't an option.

So we set out to learn the language of this e-commerce program (easy enough for me—I just write the contract, anyway!). But the hard part came when we realized that we'd have to create our graphics in a certain way to accommodate the program.

Constraints like this diminish the fun that you can have in developing the site in the first place. What we ended up doing was a combination of giving in to the program on some fronts, and tricking it to give in to us on others.

# Intent of Use

This was not going to be a site for a lot of "window shopping." We needed to make users comfortable with the site at first glance, but make sure that they could find what they were looking for easily, place items in their cart, and make their purchases with as little hassle as possible. The customers were mostly owners of small stores or chains, and likely didn't have time to look for products. If the products were too hard to find, they'd just give up, and likely never come back.

# War on Design

An internal war was brewing between the design department and the marketing department of my agency. A friendly war, of course, but a war all the same. The design and production guys wanted to do something really elaborate—something that would artistically break boundaries. But the marketing guys wanted simple—easy navigation, soft design, fast download time.

After a number of highly productive brainstorming meetings, the marketing department finally won. Truthfully, the marketing department always wins. Hundreds of sites on the web boast amazing graphics, or extremely complex interactivity that goes far beyond the norm—but in most cases, it goes far beyond the audience, too. The basic design and structure, especially if the site is being built to generate money, should always put the market over art. Art for the sake of art has no place in corporate web design—these aren't museum pieces, they're corporate tools.

**If you are doing the creative design for a web site, I highly recommend that you "brainstorm" as much as possible before you get started. If you are working on a project alone, get a friend or relative to bounce ideas off. The more perspectives that you get on an idea, the better the idea will be in the end, and the greater chance you'll have to reach a larger audience.**

I only make such a strict point of it because I know the temptation will always be there to create beyond-amazing Internet artwork. And there is a place for it on the web, but you have to be reaching a certain audience interested in that type of design, or it's a wasted effort. It's a trap that many web developers fall victim to, and they bring their sites down with them.

So, with that debate behind us, we went to work on the site.

## Navigational Hierarchy

We're still not at Photoshop yet. Before we even opened the program, we created a schematic on paper (digitized and illustrated in Figure 9–3). The hierarchy acts as a map for us to follow when programming the infrastructure of the site, and ensures that the navigation will be easy to follow. Although it doesn't show where the buttons will be or how the page will lay out, it does show which pages will provide links to which other pages.

The Home page, at the top of what looks like a pyramid, is the page where people enter the site. From that page, they are able to go directly to any number of other pages, including the sub-branded pages for balloons, baskets, weddings, and other categorized products. Entering one of the sub-brands, or second-tier pages, gives you access to certain other third-tier pages. It's really almost as if the second-tier pages are their own distinct web sites, in a sense, and each needs to contain easy access to the other pages that are associated with it.

As we'll see in the upcoming sections, this schematic is really used as a blueprint for site development. Along with knowing your audience, quality navigation ranks up there as one of the most important necessities for success.

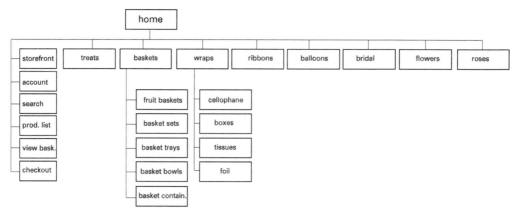

*Figure 9–3: The schematic displays the navigation for the site.*

# The Layout

Layout sketches of the site were first drawn by hand, very roughly, as interpreted from sketches made during brainstorming sessions. As you can see from the sketches shown in Figure 9–4 (and the final result shown back in Figure 9–1), the layout kept pretty much in line with what we were trying to accomplish. It was simple and to the point, focusing largely on navigation with a few visual elements to add character.

To keep users from scrolling too far down to find all of the buttons, we broke the primary navigation up into two areas: the buttons that appear in a horizontal row toward the top are the "shopping" or "function" buttons. They give you access to the more technical, tool-oriented parts of the site, such as accessing your account, searching for a specific product, seeing what's in your shopping cart, or checking out. The buttons that cascade vertically along the left side are the "product" buttons—the ones that give the user access to various product categories for them to read about and eventually purchase.

 **We placed these buttons toward the top and left of the page purposely, since these are the areas of any browser where the largest amount of information can be seen without scrolling. There are very few circumstances under which you will want to force your user to scroll very far in order to find a button.**

The titlebar remains consistent throughout the site, providing the Efloralz.com logo prominently at the top left (see previous Note), and a few flowers off to the right. At one point we played with the idea of changing this icon, depending on which sub-brand the user was in (a basket image if they were in the Ebasketz.com area), but in the end decided that leaving the floral image there throughout the site would be a better way of promoting the core brand element.

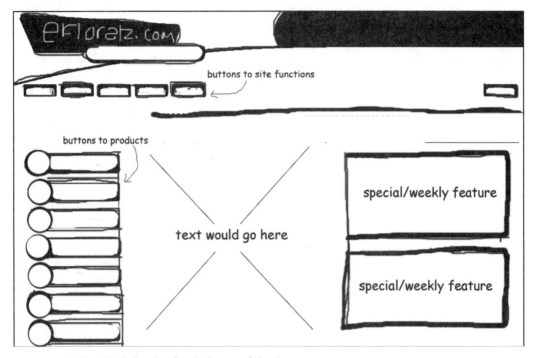

*Figure 9–4: The initial sketches for the layout of the site.*

Both the logo and the flower icons would be placed in an upper band of color to separate them from the rest of the site. The band would have a slight arch to it, again for personality, but this element would end up causing a few problems later on in the development of the site (as we'll see later).

The center area of the site would be saved for the content. In the first version of this site, we used this area on the Home page to advertise items on sale, as well as to promote a contest to help increase return visits.

 **Online games, contests, and sweepstakes are popular and very effective ways of drawing new clients and retaining existing clients.**

As you can see by the more recent screen shot shown in Figure 9–1 (back on page 248), this has changed over time and, at the time of this writing, provides a graphically designed Product Showcase and an easy-link area for certain professionals to access desired areas of the site. Internal pages of the site are used to present images and descriptions of various products.

# THE LOGO—WE FINALLY GET TO DESIGN SOMETHING!

Although many logo possibilities were submitted, the one shown earlier and shown again in Figure 9–5 was the one they accepted. Simple but stylish, it makes use of rounded corners and angled outlines to be a little hip, but concentrates on bold fonts to display the name of the site with extreme clarity—necessary in these early days of brand development. The tag line was worked into the overall logo for one cohesive billboard.

To create the logos, the designers did the following:

1.  Opened a canvas 288 x 144 pixels, RGB, 300ppi. They immediately created a new layer, Layer 1 to work on, and saved the file as "logo.psd."

**Note** ➤ **Wait a second—back in Chapter 2, we said that web graphics should be created at 72ppi. And that's the same resolution that was used in almost every example in this book. So why are we suddenly using print resolutions for a web graphic? The answer is that because this is a logo, we're obviously going to need to use it on print material eventually. So, we created it at high resolution to begin with. That way we make sure that the logos will be exactly the same on the site and in print, without having to recreate anything. Remember—it's fine to create something big and make it smaller. But it's never good to create something small and then enlarge it.**

2.  On Layer 1, the main billboard was made. Because it has rounded edges, it automatically falls into the category "pain in the neck to create." The new Shape tool was considered (the one that is a square with rounded corners), but it's still a box, so it wouldn't work. So we tried to use it anyway, and then use the Free Transform command on it, but that just looked awkward.

*Figure 9–5: The Efloralz.com logo, again.*

3. Finally, with the Polygonal Lasso tool activated, a selection was made in the general shape desired, as displayed in Figure 9–6. With the selection made, the designer opened the Channels palette and pushed the New Channel icon at the bottom of the palette. Notice that the foreground and background have changed to white and black, if they weren't already.

4. The selection was feathered (Select -> Feather) by 10 pixels, causing the corners to look rounded. The selection was then filled with white. As shown in Figure 9–7, the edges are soft because of the feathering.

5. The image was deselected.

6. Accessing the Levels dialog box (Image -> Adjust -> Levels), the two extreme markers, controlling the shadows and highlights, were brought to the center, until they overlapped with the midtones marker, The result was a hardening of the selection edge, but with rounded corners, as shown in Figure 9–8.

7. A selection was made of the white area by pressing Command (Ctrl in Windows) and clicking on the active channel, and then it was loaded back into the main composite by activating the RGB channel.

8. The Gradient tool was used to transition the color in the selection from light green at the top to a darker shade at the bottom.

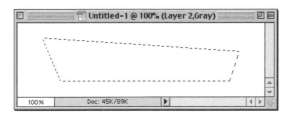

*Figure 9–6: The selection was created with the Polygonal lasso tool. It has the shape we want, but lacks the round corners.*

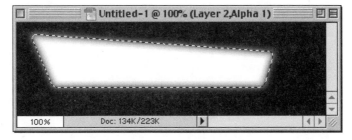

*Fig 9–7: The selection in the Channels palette, feathered and filled with white.*

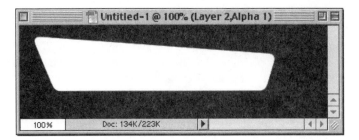

*Figure 9–8: The selection has rounded corners after the Levels adjustments are applied.*

9.  The Drop Shadow Layer attribute dialog box was accessed from the bottom of the Layers palette. A slight drop shadow with a significant blur was applied below and to the right of the image.

10. The Type tool was activated, and the designer clicked on the far left of the banner. A new Text layer was automatically created, and the "Efloralz.com" lettering was placed. The size and color of the text was manipulated using the Options palette and Character palette as the copy was being placed. The Enter button was pushed to accept the text.

11. We wanted a little more depth than just a drop shadow, so a new layer was created and placed below the text layer. With this new layer active, a selection was made of the text by pressing Command and clicking on the type layer (Ctrl and click in Windows.)

12. One of the selection tools was activated and, using the arrow keys, the selection was nudged two pixels to the right and two pixels down. It was then filled with black.

13. For more depth, a very light drop shadow was created with layer attributes, similar to the one made earlier for the main image. Figure 9–9 shows the logo at this point.

14. To make the long pill-shaped area for the tag line, a new layer was created and placed above the text layer. The rounded-corner Shape tool was used with a light color in the foreground.

*Figure 9–9: The logo after the drop shade has been added.*

**15.** The Stroke Layer attribute was used to place a dark outline around the shape, and the drop shadow that was originally placed was copied (the drop shadow sublayer was activated, and the Layer -> Attribute -> Copy Attribute was selected) and pasted onto the pill-shape layer (by activating the pill-shape layer and selecting Layer -> Attributes -> Paste Attribute).

**16.** Finally, the tag line "Your Virtual Floral Department Store" was place in the pill shape. The final logo is shown in Figure 9–10.

Before we moved on to another design aspect, all of the layers except the background were linked together (a non-background layer was active, and the box immediately to the left of each Layer Preview icon was clicked to show the chain link icon) and merged into one layer (Layer palette drop-down menu -> Merge Layers). The end result was to have two layers—the one with the logo on it and the background layer.

# THE TITLEBAR/BACKGROUND

Remember a few pages back I mentioned that the curve of the titlebar caused a few problems? Well, the problem was that out initial idea (when we presented it to our client) was to create this site in frames, with the top frame being the upper titlebar, and the lower frame housing everything else. This would have been fine, especially considering that the top titlebar never had to change at all, and the extra frame would keep the site name in view at all times, even if the page had to scroll.

What we didn't realize until later, though, was that the shopping cart program wasn't too fond of frames. So suddenly, what was supposed to be a relatively simple titlebar, became just another hurdle.

If you read the part of Chapter 4 that discussed how to make an upper border, you'll see the first method we thought to use. Great idea if this were a straight, horizontal titlebar. But the curve in the lower portion of the bar makes that method impossible.

*Figure 9–10: The final logo all assembled.*

To get around this, we took a fairly unorthodox method and made a really huge background, 1,200 pixels wide by 5,000 pixels high (it needed to be very high, since we could never really be sure how long the list of products would be after any given search.

1. With a new canvas, 1,200 x 5,000 pixels, a new layer was created directly over the background layer.

2. The curvature of the upper titlebar was made by combining the Ellipse marquee tool and the Rectangular marquee tool. First the canvas was changed to be in Full View mode by pushing the F key once (this causes the canvas to be housed with a gray workspace around the edges, rather than encased in a window). Then, because the designer needed room to create very large selections, he zoomed out by pushing Command (Ctrl in Windows) and minus (the minus sign) until whole canvas was displayed at a very low percentage of its actual size.

3. Using the Ellipse marquee tool, an oval selection was created toward the top left of the canvas, so that the left downward slope of the oval was running off the canvas and into the gray work area. This is displayed in the left image of Figure 9–11.

4. With the rulers open, a horizontal guide was created at the very top of the oval, as shown in the center image of Figure 9–11. With the selection still active, the tool was changed to the Rectangular marquee. With the Shift key held down (to add to the selection), a rectangular selection was created, with the top left corner of the rectangle made at the point where the ruler meets the top of the oval. This rectangular selection was extended to the far right edge of the canvas, as illustrated in the right image of Figure 9–11.

 **Let me address the flood of e-mails that this example will evoke from more experienced designers: Yes, I know that the Pen tool would have been a better choice for creating this curve, but there really wasn't a good place in this book to cover the Pen tool in depth, and this seemed like a lousy place to start. The Pen tool is covered, though, in *Photoshop 6 Primer*.**

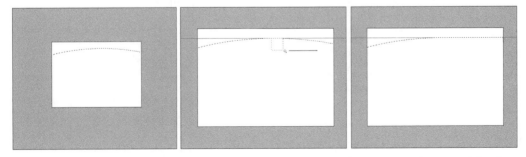

*Figure 9–11: The three steps used to make the upper curve. Because the curve turns into a straight edge, a combination of marquee tools was used.*

5. The selection was inverted (Select -> Inverse). This is shown in Figure 9–12.

6. The selection was filled with the lavender shade we chose to create the basics for the upper margin.

7. With the upper margin still selected, the Elliptical marquee tool was reactivated. While pressing the Option, Alt and the Shift key (for intersections), a large circle was created to encompass about 40% of the upper margin, starting from the right side. The remaining selection was the intersection between the selection that existed and the large circle that I just made. Figure 9–13 illustrates.

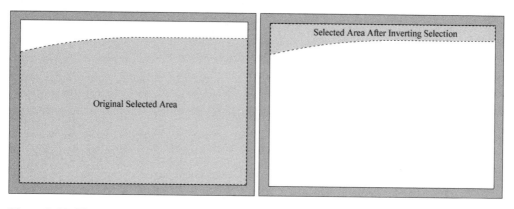

*Figure 9–12: The upper bar selection started taking shape by inverting the selection and then deselecting the lower selection.*

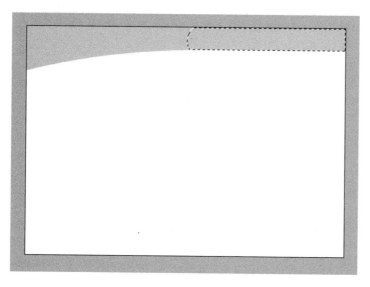

*Figure 9–13: Intersection was used to grab the right side of the upper bar.*

8. A darker purple was used to fill the current selection, and a Drop Shadow Layer attribute was applied to create a very slight drop shadow below the whole upper bar.

9. For a bit more color, we found a flower picture in our stock image photo library. In order to make a selection of the flower, which was on a plain white background, the Magic Wand tool was used to create a selection of the white, and then the selection was inverted, creating the final selection around the flower image. It was then dragged with the Move tool onto the upper bar of the background canvas, and positioned into place.

10. The logo canvas was reactivated and, with the logo layer active, the Move tool was used to drag the logo onto the background canvas we just created. The logo was automatically placed in its own layer and positioned into place on the titlebar. Figure 9–14 shows the final background with the logo in position.

We already determined that we would use a soft, canary yellow color for the background. But since the background was so large, we'd obviously need to make the body of the background transparent and fill the background color by using a hexadecimal value for the yellow we wanted.

That would have been as easy as making the current white background transparent and then saving the image using the Save for Web feature, except for one hitch: the drop shadows under the upper bar and the logo. With GIFs, pixels are either transparent or they're not. There's no partial transparency. So making the white pixels in the background layer transparent would make the area under the drop shadows look very awkward.

To fix this, we first had to activate the background layer, then fill it with the yellow color we decided on. Once the background layer was filled with color, the layers were flattened (Layer palette drop-down menu -> Flatten Layers). The Magic Eraser tool was used to make the body of the background transparent, although the yellow still remained underneath the drop shadow, which was our goal.

*Figure 9–14: The final upper bar with the logo in place.*

**I don't always specify it, but it's always a good idea to save a copy of the file as a .psd before you flatten anything. It never hurts to have a copy of your image with its original layers lying around in the event there are future changes.**

The image was saved using the Save for Web dialog box and by choosing GIF as the desired format. Figure 9–15 shows the Save for Web dialog box with the settings that were used.

## The Buttons, Step 1: Creating the Design

None of the buttons were particularly hard to create, and because the buttons that run horizontally are kind of boring, we'll skip the details about how those were created, and move on right to the vertical buttons on the left. Although, as we'll see, these weren't that difficult to create, either, they're at least a little more interesting (plus they had rollover states in the early version of the site).

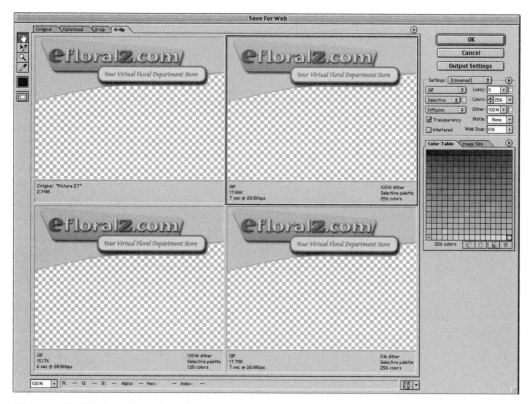

*Figure 9–15: The Save for Web dialog box showing the settings used for my background.*

Although some of us voted to create the buttons in the same shape as the logo, the group that wanted more standard pill-shaped buttons eventually won out. The buttons themselves, then, were pretty easy to create. In an entirely new document, the Shape tool (the one with the rounded corners) was used to create the initial button on its own layer. It was then selected (by pressing Command or Ctrl in Windows and clicking on the layer), and a gradient of light green to darker green was applied with the Gradient tool (the Shift key was held as the gradient was applied from the top to the bottom of the shape). A purple stroke was created around the edge by choosing Edit -> Stroke.

With the basic shape of the button created, it was duplicated eight times to create a vertical column of buttons. To do this, the Move tool was activated, and the Option (Alt in Windows) key was held to cause the cursor to change into two small, black and white arrows. With the Shift key also held (for constraint), the button was dragged downward. And then again, and again. With each new drag, the button duplicated itself, until we had all the buttons we needed. Figure 9–16 shows the process.

**We established how many buttons were needed in the initial schematic that we worked with earlier.**

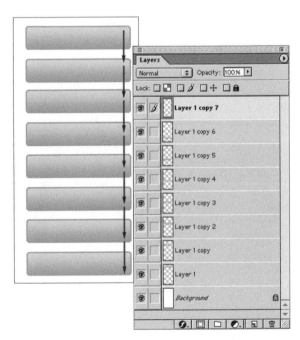

*Figure 9–16: The buttons along the left side were created by duplicating one shape.*

It's likely that each time the button was duplicated, each duplication appeared on its own layer. If this happened, it's a good thing—we'll need the various layers when we create our rollover effect in ImageReady later. If they didn't appear on their own layer as you created them (I don't know, sometimes they do, sometimes they don't—I can't figure out why it happens and then sometimes doesn't), you'll need to select each individually and choose Layer -> New -> Layer Via Cut.

With the column of buttons in place, the Type tool was used to place the text on each button, similar to the text we used when we created the logo. The name of each button was created on its own layer, directly above its respective button, and then it was merged with that button by pressing Command (Ctrl in Windows) and E (the keyboard shortcut for merging a layer with the one directly below it).

Remember, once a Text layer is merged with another layer, you can no longer edit it. In other words, check for spelling errors before you merge them.

The images that represent each button were placed in the same way that the flower image was placed on the upper bar earlier. These were also merged with their respective buttons.

The file was saved as a Photoshop document to preserve the layers. Figure 9–17 shows the final button column.

# THE BUTTONS, STEP 2: SLICING AND LINKING

With the bulk of our Photoshop work done, the designers launched ImageReady by clicking the link button at the very bottom of the toolbar (thankfully we had the necessary billion megs of RAM to keep both programs open at the same time).

Inside ImageReady is where we made each button link to a different page as well as have a rollover effect associated with it. But first, the button bar needed to be carved up with the Slice tool.

In the olden days, slicing an image was done by using the guides in Photoshop to mark off where you wanted to divide an image. Then, using the Rectangular marquee tool, a selection was made of each area as marked by the guides, cut, and pasted into a new canvas. That portion of the image was then saved either as a GIF or JPEG (if it was a GIF then it had to first be indexed, which was another pain). Once all of the

*Figure 9–17: The final button column.*

pieces were saved individually, they had to be reassembled in an HTML table, which more than likely was coded manually.

If you were off by even one pixel when you initially carved the image, the entire reassembled table would look like a mess in your browser. Ultimately, you were almost always off by at least one pixel the first time you cut up an image. It was a thrilling process.

I tell you this not simply to recount history, but so that newer designers can understand the hassles we went through and appreciate the ease with which we'll divide the upcoming image. As you read, keep in mind that this portion of this same chapter in my original book, *Photoshop 5 To Go*, used almost eight pages, including full HTML code for the table, to explain how this process is done.

To carve up the button bar, we took the following steps:

1. The Slice tool was activated.

2. A rectangular selection was made around the top button, just as if the Rectangular marquee tool was being used to create a regular selection. A bright yellow outline showed where the slice was made, and the rest of the image became a bit dull relative to the top button. Figure 9–18 shows the sliced button at this point.

3. The same process was used to create slices around each of the other buttons; the final result is shown in Figure 9–19.

*Figure 9–18: The button bar with its first slice. The outline (yellow on your monitor) shows the slice that was just created (the yellow means that slice is active), and the rest of the image becomes a bit more dull, as though a screen were placed over it.*

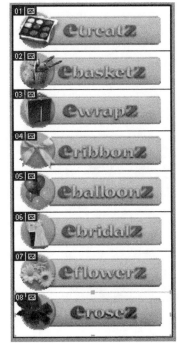

*Figure 9–19: The button bar with each button sliced up.*

And, well, that's about it. Obviously, with more complex images, slicing can be…oh, who am I kidding? Slicing is about the easiest thing you'll do in either program, regardless of the image. Just drag to create. Pretty easy.

With the slices made, we were able to do a lot more with the buttons. Before we did anything else, though, we used the Magic Eraser to make the white background transparent, so the background could show through. This was done by activating the background layer, selecting the Magic Eraser tool, and just clicking on the white background. It instantly became transparent.

**A quicker way to make the white transparent would have been simply to hide the background layer by clicking on the Eyeball icon in the Layers palette. But if we had done that, I'd have missed a good opportunity to show you once again how the Magic Eraser tool could be used.**

With the background out of the way, our first real priority was to link each button to go to a different page of the site. To do this, we opened the Slices palette. With the Slice Select tool now activated, the first slice we created (the top button, labeled "slice 01" in the canvas) was selected by clicking on it. The image inside that particular slice was previewed as an icon inside the Slice palette, as shown in Figure 9–20.

Within the Slice palette, the area for the URL was filled in with the path that would lead to that portion of the site. This same process was done for each slice. Because this particular site was not created with frames, there wasn't any real need to set the Target, so that area was left blank. The BG was left as None, since we wanted to preserve the transparency we had made earlier.

In the name area, we created our own name for the button, since it's just easier for us to reference later using our own naming convention than by using the default names that ImageReady supplies. This same process was done for each slice in the button bar.

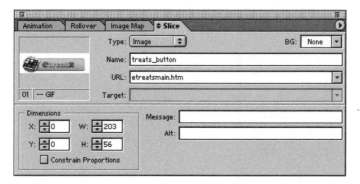

*Figure 9–20: The Slice palette after the first slice is selected.*

# THE BUTTONS, STEP 3: ROLLOVER STATES

To make the site a little more interactive, we wanted to create a rollover state for each button that would allow it to change when the user moved his or her cursor over it. For these buttons, we thought that a slight bevel and drop shadow would be fine for providing the interaction we were seeking.

To create the rollover states, we did the following:

1. With the Slice Select tool activated, "slice 01" was selected by clicking on it.

2. We added a layer-based slice by choosing Layer -> Layer Based Slice. Later in this example it'll be clear why we did that.

3. The Rollover palette, shown in Figure 9–21, was opened. The icon in the first state, named Normal, was the image that appeared in the active slice. This icon shows what the image in the slice will look like when the user's cursor is not over it.

4. In the Layers palette, the layer that contained the first button was made active.

5. A new rollover state was created by pushing the New State button at the bottom of the Rollover palette. The new state, called Over, shows what will happen when a user's cursor is over the image in that slice. For now, the Over state looks identical to the Normal state.

6. With the Over state active (there is a black outline around it), we opened the Drop Shadow Layer Attribute dialog box from the Layers palette and created a subtle but noticeable drop shadow.

7. We created a new rollover state. The next one is called Down by default, and it affects the image when the mouse is clicked on it in the browser.

8. With the Down state active, we opened the Bevel and Emboss dialog box from the Layers palette. This time, we created an Inner Bevel effect that was also subtle but still noticeable.

9. Figure 9–22 shows the differences in the Layers palette, depending on which Rollover state is active. As you can see, when the Normal state is active, the Layers palette looks exactly as it did before we started. But when the Over state is

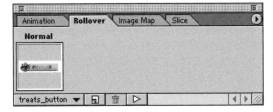

*Figure 9–21: The Rollover palette.*

active, the Drop Shadow sublayer appears. When we activate the Down state, the Bevel and Emboss sublayer appears, too. The Rollover palette remembers changes that you make to the canvas depending on which state you're in.

10. Now we needed to do the same for the other buttons. But instead of going through the process over again, we first saved the attributes that we created in the Styles palette. To do this, we opened the Styles palette, shown in Figure 9–23. The Styles palette lets us save various style configurations, like the ones we just created for the button, so that we only have to create them once. It's an easy way to use the same one over and over again. As you can see, there are a number of styles preset for you in the palette.

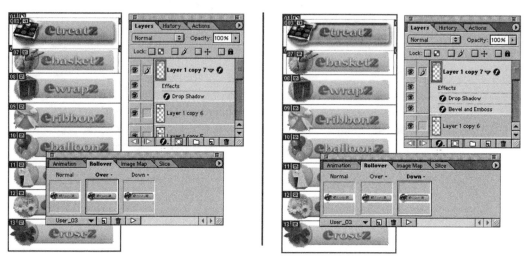

*Figure 9–22: The Layers palette changes based on which rollover state is active.*

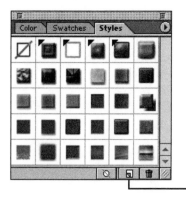

———— New Style

*Figure 9–23: The Styles palette.*

11. To save our style, we clicked on the Create New Style button at the bottom of the Styles palette (it's basically the same icon that lets you create a new layer in the Layers palette). The dialog box that appears in Figure 9–24 appears. We made sure all three choices were marked with an X, and clicked OK.

> **Remember earlier when we created a layer-based slice, and said that we would understand why later in this example? Well, it's later. By creating a layer-based slice, we were able to activate the last option in that dialog box, which allowed us to save the rollover states as well as the attributes.**

12. The Styles Palette showed the new style we saved as a gray box (indicating that the color never changes) along with the attributes we created. The small triangle in the top corner of the style indicates that the rollover states were saved as well.

13. We created the same rollover states for all the rest of the buttons, but this time much more quickly. Using the Slice Select tool, we selected each button individually, and clicked on the style that we created in the Styles palette. The styles, along with the rollover states, were instantly applied.

14. To save the buttons, we first chose File -> Save As and saved the file the way it was, just in case we needed to make changes later. Then, we opened the Optimize palette. From the palette submenu, we selected Show Options, which opened the palette further. We chose GIF as the format of choice, and made sure that the Transparency box was checked. We then chose File -> Save Optimized As. Inside the dialog box, shown in Figure 9–25, we named the file and clicked OK.

> **Notice that the file extension is .html. ImageReady will write the code for you, and save the slices in a directory called Images.**

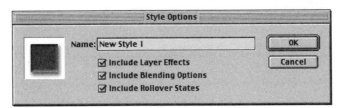

*Figure 9–24: The New Style dialog box.*

# PUTTING THE REST OF THE SITE TOGETHER

The information that exists in the middle of the site was volatile information meant to change often, so it wasn't made up of much more than text, links, and photographs set up in a table format. The site was ultimately put together in DreamWeaver, using portions of the rollover code that ImageReady had written for us.

# SUMMARY

Well, that's it. If you've been doing this for awhile, you already know that this is far easier than it ever used to be. Changes in popular design have combined with vast improvements in technology to make sites easy to create to add on interactive features to. Although you'll want to do more of your assembly either manually or in DreamWeaver, ImageReady, and Photoshop can combine to be a powerful creative force in design and interaction.

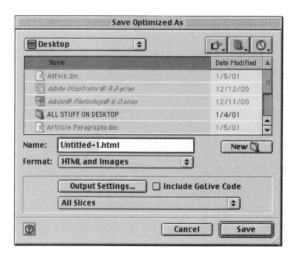

*Figure 9–25: The Save Optimized As dialog box.*

# chapter 10

# TIPS, TRICKS,

# AND SUGGESTIONS

The interesting part of creating Web sites is the unique combination of art and science—on the one hand, nothing but your imagination will confine you creatively, while on the other hand, current technology limits you to using certain colors, image sizes, and formats. Most of what I've tried to demonstrate in this book has fallen on the technical side—sure, I used creative examples as illustrations, but those were to demonstrate certain techniques that hopefully you will apply to your own work.

While technique, talent, and knowledge are 95% of the tools you'll need (besides equipment, of course!), sage wisdom from experienced sources never hurts. Certain pitfalls exist in creating sites that can cause frustration in those of us with little patience for problems. However, in almost all cases, there are work-arounds to keep problems to a minimum, and to help ensure a more streamlined Web creation experience.

So let me put on my high-pointed cap, brush my beard, and take a perch at the top of a snow-capped mountain (I'm going to be the sage, wise and experienced), while you get ready to downshift out of creative mode and learn some of the tricks of the trade. Take or leave any of the following bits of advice in this chapter—I find them useful ideas that may or may not apply to your specific style of working. Some of these suggestions don't have anything to do with Photoshop, but may be helpful in the grand scheme of Web design (if you feel guilty accepting free advice, please feel free to send me a check directly, and consider this chapter "shareware").

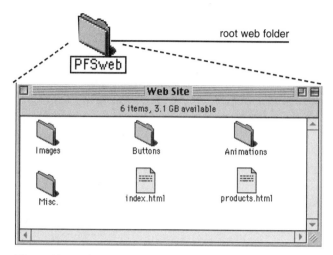

*Figure 10–1: The organization of my web folder.*

# KEEP YOUR FILES ORGANIZED

As shown in Figure 10–1, I find it helpful to set up four separate folders before starting any Web job:

◆   Images
◆   Buttons
◆   Animations
◆   Misc

While my main directory houses all of my code files, I distribute all other media into their respective folders. This not only helps me find certain files later, but it is also very useful when it comes time to FTP my files to the server.

# OPTIMIZING PERFORMANCE

Just because you are working with smaller file sizes for Web sites doesn't mean that you won't have just reason to heighten Photoshop's performance. Photoshop 6 takes up more RAM than ever before, with users reporting to need nearly 90 megs located to the program just to keep it open and functional for period of time. And that's without even opening ImageReady.

The following are a few ways you can optimize Photoshop's performance both in general and for the Web.

## Setting Up Scratch Disks

Even with low-res files, Photoshop can eat up RAM rather quickly. Possibly nothing is more annoying than really getting into a design, knowing in your head what you want to happen, choosing a filter and, just as the effect is about to happen, getting that ugly message from Photoshop saying that it cannot complete the demand due to a of lack of RAM.

Since Photoshop 5, you can create up to four separate scratch disk sources, combining for up to 200 GB of scratch space. You can set the sources for the extra space by choosing File -> Preferences -> Plug-Ins and Scratch Disks. Figure 10–2 shows the dialog box that appears. Since scratch space involves using empty storage memory in place of RAM when RAM runs out, you can use any source available. This includes your hard drive, any networked computers that are available, external hard drives, even Jaz, Zip, SyQuest, or other storage devices (although these sources are usually frowned on as scratch sources and will cause the program to run more slowly).

Any changes that you make to the Scratch Disk preferences will not be available until the next time that you open Photoshop, so restart Photoshop after making your choices.

## Other Solutions to Memory Problems

Because everyone's computer and hardware accessibility is different, not everyone will have access to multiple scratch sources. If you fall into this category, and do not have access to additional RAM, there are still a few things you can do:

◆ The History palette is a terrific feature. But it's a veritable monster when it comes to eating RAM. In the History palette pull-down menu, choose History Options to

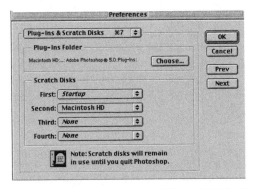

*Figure 10–2: The Plug-Ins and Scratch Disks dialog box.*

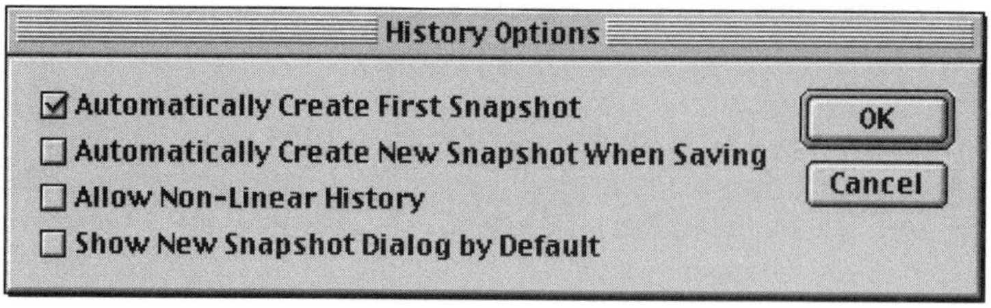

*Figure 10–3: The History Options in the History palette pull-down menu will help you optimize Photoshop's performance.*

access the dialog box shown in Figure 10–3. Make sure that the checkbox marked Allow Non-Linear History is left unchecked. Also, make sure that Maximum History States is lowered to the lowest number of undos you will need by adjusting the value in the Edit -> Preferences -> General dialog box. The lower the number, the less memory will be used.

♦   When you do run out of RAM, choose Edit -> Purge and select either Undo, Clipboard, Pattern, Histories or All. Choosing All will free up the most amount of actual RAM, but remember—you cannot undo a purge, so make sure you really want this before you do it.

# Extensions Made Easy

Every image that you create and save for the Web has to have a file extension at the end of the name. Depending on the type of image, the extension will usually be either .jpg for JPEGs, .gif for GIFs, or .png for PNGs. Users of newer Mac systems will have the extension created for them, but if you type over it when naming or renaming your file, it won't be added at all, unless you add it manually. The opposite is true in Windows. Newer operating systems will thankfully create the extensions in lowercase, but will also add the extension to the name whether you type over it or not.

> **If you don't see the file extension after your file name on a Windows system, don't type it in yourself. The file name is still there, you just can't see it. Adding the extension yourself will just create a mess, and you'll have trouble opening your file. To see what extension the file has, right-click on the icon and choose Properties.**

In either case, you'll want to make sure that the extension exists, and that it is lowercase. Although it's not as much of a problem as it used to be, many servers are still case-sensitive, especially when it comes to reading file extensions.

**Preferences**

Saving Files

| | |
|---|---|
| **Image Previews:** | Always Save |

☑ Icon ☐ Full Size
☑ Macintosh Thumbnail
☑ Windows Thumbnail

**Append File Extension:** Always

☑ Use Lower Case

─ File Compatibility ─
☑ Maximize backwards compatibility in Photoshop format
☐ Enable advanced TIFF save options

Recent file list contains: 4 files

OK
Cancel
Prev
Next

*Figure 10–4: The Saving Files dialog box.*

Macintosh users can adjust this to happen automatically by choosing Edit -> Preferences -> Saving Files to access the dialog box shown in Figure 10–4 (you'll be referring to this file a few times when trying to optimize Photoshop). A pull-down menu for Append File Extension gives you three choices: Never (default), Always, and Ask When Saving. Choosing Always will automatically add the extension to every file you save, in lowercase letters. If you choose Ask When Saving, you will notice an addition to the Save As dialog box, as shown in Figure 10–5. At the bottom, check the box marked Use Lower Case.

**Adding file extensions doesn't just apply to graphics. On the Web, practically everything you put online will need a file extension, including your HTML documents. You can apply either the three-letter extension of .htm or the four-letter extension of .html. Use the shorter extension whenever possible. Macintosh users who use the .htm ending will be able to grab files from the browser when necessary, and just double-click on them to open them in SimpleText. HTML documents marked .html will come off the browser as either a Netscape or IE file and you will first need to go into SimpleText and choose File -> Open and locate the file on your hard drive in order to open it.**

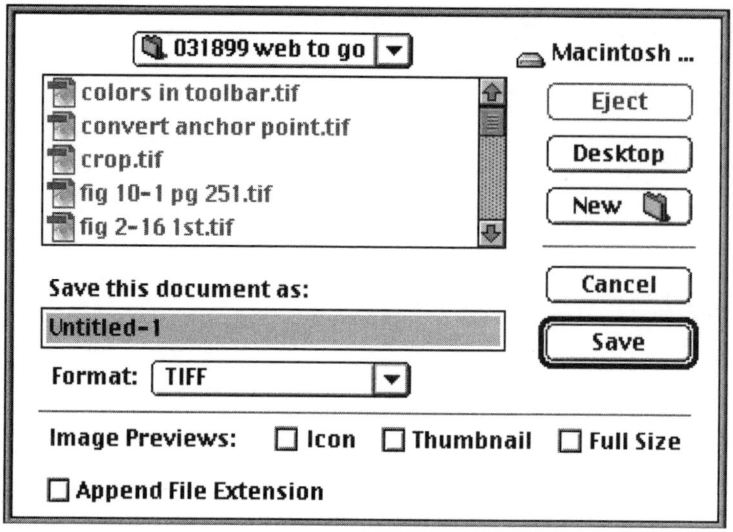

*Figure 10–5: After choosing Ask When Saving from the Preferences dialog box, a check box is added at the bottom to include the file extension.*

# SAVE MULTIPLE COPIES OF IMAGES

With hard disk space fairly easy to come by, few computers today are sold with less than 4 GB of hard disk space and for those that are, you can pick up an additional 4 GB external drive for relatively little money. Zip drives also provide an inexpensive solution for backing up and archiving files. Therefore, there is no excuse for not saving multiple copies of all images. It may seem frivolous at first, but anyone thinking ahead will realize that change is inevitable. You don't want to spend a lot of time creating a really cool graphic that needed 20 layers to perfect, just to find out six months later when you want to remove a portion that the only version you have left is a flattened GIF. Try to save the original Photoshop file and, if you're going to be using any transparencies, save your image again as a regular GIF, and then finally as a transparent GIF. Try opening a transparent GIF in Photoshop—it's not a pretty sight.

# IMPORTING VECTOR GRAPHICS

I want to make a prediction. Now, don't hold me to this, but if I were to bet money, I'd say that in the next few years, designers will be using one, mega-huge, ultra-complex Adobe program that will take about 400 megs just to open. It will be an amalgamation (isn't that a cool word?) of Photoshop, ImageReady, InDesign, and Illustrator. So enjoy design as you know it while you've got it—because it won't last.

Why do I make this prediction? Well, for a while now many of the Adobe programs have started to look alike, incorporating Photoshop's palette configuration. Then, the Layers palette (the star player in Photoshop) started to work interchangeably from one Adobe program to another. With Photoshop 6, though, we get what is probably the most telling clue of them all: Photoshop is no longer just a bitmap program.

Of course, Photoshop is still labeled a bitmap program, but for the first time, you can do more than just import vector images. You can create them as well, at least on a limited basis.

## Importing Vector Images

As we'll see in the next section, vector images can be created on a limited basis. But for now, designers are still likely to do much of their vector work in Illustrator and to import the files into Photoshop.

There are a number of ways that you can bring a vector image into Photoshop, all of which are pretty easy:

◆ Choose File -> Open and select the vector file you would like to rasterize. Doing so will bring up the dialog box shown in Figure 10–6. You can choose the size and resolution you would like your image to be before you turn it into a bitmap. If you're uncertain, you're best off using a high resolution, such as 300ppi, and resizing down later.

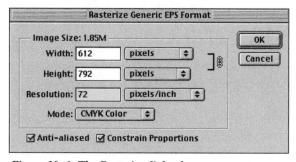

*Figure 10–6: The Rasterize dialog box.*

◆ If you are placing your vector graphic into an already-open file to become part of an existing image, choose File -> Place. Your vector graphic will open on its own layer, with the Free Transform handles around it. You can manipulate the image and make it the desired size before it rasterizes.

◆ Simply cut/copy from a vector-based program and paste into Photoshop. A dialog box will give you the option of pasting as pixels or paths.

◆ Drag directly from the canvas of a vector program to an open canvas in Photoshop. You will have no choices with this method—Photoshop rasterizes and determines the size of the image by itself.

## Creating Vector Images in Photoshop

The new Shape tool isn't really all that new. In fact, like a few other "new" features in Photoshop 6, the Shape tool already existed in earlier versions of ImageReady. When you use the Shape tool, you have three button options that appear on the far left of the Options palette. The first one allows you to create a Shape layer. Push this and drag to create a shape. You'll see that the shape is placed in its own layer and looks like a mask layer (which it is).

The shape that exists in that layer is a vector image. At any time, you can resize the shape by increasing the canvas size in the Image Size dialog box, or by using the Transform or Free Transform functions. As you increase or decrease the size, the shape will never lose its sharpness, since it's a vector image.

To turn the shape into a bitmap, choose Layer -> Rasterize -> Shape.

**Type in Photoshop is vector as well, which allows for the manipulations that were shown in Chapter 5.**

# PRESENT GRAPHICS AND TEXT FROM A MARKETING STANDPOINT

The whole idea of having a website is to present certain information to potential viewers. Whether you are trying to sell your new invention for a better mouse trap or you simply want to meet a person for a cyber relationship, you will want to present your information in a concise, logical order that will allow your user to gain the most from your site.

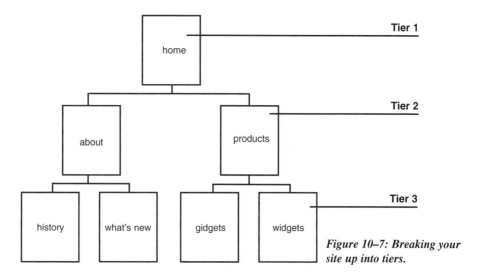

*Figure 10–7: Breaking your site up into tiers.*

To do this, try to follow the basic rule of "graphics first, copy later." Let's say that you have a three-tiered Web site, as shown in Figure 10–7. Your first tier is the Home page—the most crucial page on your site. Depending on how you set this page up, people will either continue to search through your site or hit the Back button and start over again at Yahoo!. Provide just enough copy to give a general sense of what your site is all about, but concentrate on a really outstanding layout and graphics to "grab" your audience and reel them in.

Once you've hooked your user, the second tier, which among other things could have a page for products, for example, should try to balance the graphics with the copy. Not too much of either, but just enough to remain interesting. The third tier, which could be an explanation of one of the products, should provide significantly more copy and ease up on the graphics—by the time your user's are this far into the site, they are genuinely interested—you no longer need to sell them on your site. Figure 10–8 shows a site that illustrates this.

# BUY A MOUSE TRAP

Mice are bad. They're great tools if you're using business applications, but will hinder your abilities in Photoshop. Buy yourself an electronic tablet. Personally, I like the WACOM Tablets, even though I sometimes find that their extension for my Mac will conflict with the extensions for other SCSI devices. The electronic tablets will give you greater design control, by allowing you to use your fingers for detailed painting and manipulating, as opposed to the mouse, which works more via your wrist.

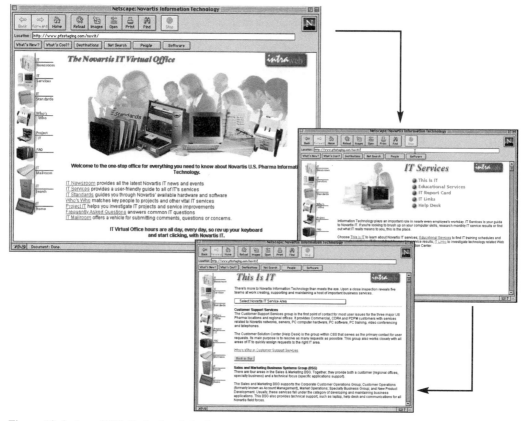

*Figure 10–8: A real Website broken into tiers.*

# PLAN AHEAD FOR LARGER PROJECTS

In my experience in designing Web sites for both my own agency and for corporate clients, I have learned the importance of preparing for larger projects in advance. Once a Web site is published, the customer will often want to print an accompanying brochure or catalog along with it, and advanced preparation on your part can only lead to increased payment.

Try to determine in advance the likelihood of that happening (even if clients are adamant against printing anything, oftentimes they change their minds) and prepare for it. Think about taking the following steps for future work:

◆ Scan in all photography at a high resolution and archive it someplace. Set up an action to automate a size reduction to 72ppi for Web graphics to save time. Your archive of hi-res files can be used for future print work.

◆ Write all text in a word processing program, such as MS Word, WordPerfect, or even layout programs such as PageMaker or QuarkXPress. It's a good thing to have on record and will help you to develop other marketing material later, saving you the agony of isolating text in your HTML files and then reformatting.

◆ Design the site to be somehow interactive with a printed piece. For example, a mass mail campaign could direct users to special pages to which they otherwise wouldn't have access. Explore other unique possibilities for combining print with the Web.

Don't miss opportunities to extend contracts and earn more for yourself or your company—they're usually no more than a proposal away. Clients will appreciate the well-roundedness that you show and your ability to keep designs consistent throughout all media pieces. Keeping organized and planning ahead for these opportunities will help ensure success in these ventures.

# MAKING HIGH QUALITY, SMALL FILE SIZE PDFS

PDFs are becoming all the rage on the Web, and the quicker you learn to make them, the more money you can charge when creating your Web sites. Clients will use PDFs for everything from financial records, annual reports, and catalog pages to medical forms and necessary human resources paperwork.

With PDF, you can put multiple pages in one file. These pages can retain their original page layout and allow a reader instantly to jump from one page to the next or even to find a topic through a concentrated keyword search. Really advanced PDFs can embed animations and video as well. But for most PDFs that just deal with static pages, the trick to creating PDFs is to make them as high in quality as possible, but to keep the file size down.

To do this, however, you'll need more than just Photoshop. You're also going to need another program developed by Adobe called Acrobat Distiller. Once you have these, and have installed them onto your system, you'll want to complete the following steps:

1. Scan in your page at around 300ppi (you'll need to scan it in at least at 200ppi to make this process work well). Because one of the main selling points of PDFs is that you can have multiple elements and retain their particular layout, scan a page that has a good amount of text on it for this example.

While you can scan directly into Photoshop, you don't have to—you can also scan directly into Acrobat. However, you won't be able to manipulate the scan to any significant extent in Acrobat.

Save yourself the agonizing experience of having to speak with an Acrobat tech support operator. You'll have trouble with further steps if you scan or save your PDF with more than 8-bit color.

2. Save your scan as a Photoshop PDF.

Before the next step, open a folder on the Acrobat Install CD-ROM named Drivers. Install the drivers in this folder. These will update your printer preferences. Your system printer folder now will have tons of printers in it—open the folder and delete the ones you don't need, except the one named Adobe Distiller PPD. Then choose PSPrinter as your designated output source.

3. Open Acrobat Exchange.

4. Choose File -> Open and open the PDF file that you saved in Photoshop.

5. You're going to want to change the text on the page into editable text, so it doesn't increase the file size. Choose Document -> Capture from the main pull-down menu. Make the necessary choices in the ensuing dialog box, and click OK. Acrobat will go through your document and pick out the portions of your image that it can recognize as text and turn it into editable copy.

6. Choose File -> Print. The Acrobat Virtual Printer should be the printer that appears in your print dialog box. Click OK.

7. Push the radio button for binary, and select All Fonts from the Font pull-down menu. Click OK. A PostScript file will be saved to your desired directory.

8. Open Acrobat Distiller. Choose File -> Open from the main pull-down menu and use the directory to locate the PostScript file that was saved in Step 7. Distiller will compress your file, significantly reducing the file size. When it's done, you'll have a new PDF file, ready for the Web!

Don't take either Acrobat or Distiller out of its main Acrobat folder —if you do, you may run into problems, since both programs rely on plug-ins found in a Plug-ins folder in the Acrobat directory.

# USE KEYBOARD COMMANDS

You'll always need to use a mouse or an electronic tablet for drawing, painting, shading, and most other artistic functions in Photoshop. But for everything else, you're better off learning the keyboard commands as much as possible, and staying away from all the menus. There are literally hundreds of keyboard commands in Photoshop—way too many to list here.

   Certain commands, like the single key shortcuts for each tool, can be found by moving your cursor over the tool and leaving it there for about two seconds (or check out Chapter 1). Many palettes can be accessed easily too by using the function keys—try each of the keys between F5–F9 to see which palette is accessed. Many other keyboard commands can be discovered by looking at the pull-down menus: Each separate function that has a keyboard command will list it. But the many others that are not listed in Photoshop can really prove to be helpful. The following is a brief list of the keyboard commands I have found most useful when working in Photoshop (commands in parentheses indicate Windows commands):

| | |
|---|---|
| Feather Selection: | Command (Ctrl) + Option (Alt) + D |
| Add to Selection: | Shift + drag/click with a selection tool |
| Subtract from Selection: | Option (Alt) + drag/click with a selection tool |
| Keep Selection Intersection: | Option (Alt) + Shift + drag/click with a selection tool |
| Move Marquee: | Arrows with selection tool active |
| Move Marquee 10 Pixels: | Shift + Arrow with selection tool active |
| Move Selection: | Arrows with Move tool active |
| Move Selection 10 Pixels: | Shift + Arrow with Move tool active |
| Move Up One Layer: | Option (Alt) + ] |
| Move Down One Layer: | Option (Alt) + [ |
| Send Layer Backward: | Command (Ctrl) + [ |
| Send Layer Forward: | Command (Ctrl) + ] |
| Send Layer to Back: | Command (Ctrl) + Shift + [ |
| Send Layer to Front: | Command (Ctrl) + Shift + ] |
| Hide All but One Layer: | Option (Alt) + click Eye icon of desired layer |
| Create New Layer: | Command (Ctrl) + Option (Alt) + Shift + N |
| Preserve Layer Transparency: | / while in active layer |
| Merge Linked: | Command (Ctrl) + E |

| | |
|---|---|
| Change Layer Opacity: | single number for increments of 10%, two number for increments of 1% while selection tool or Move tool is active |
| Desaturate: | Command (Ctrl) + Shift + U |
| Cycle through Brush Palette: | [ or ] while a paint tool is active |
| Temporarily Activate Hand Tool: | Spacebar |
| Temporarily Activate Move Tool: | Command (Ctrl) |
| Show/Hide Palettes and Toolbar: | Tab |
| Show/Hide just Palettes: | Shift + Tab |

There are plenty of other keyboard commands that can prove helpful. For a more complete list, please refer to my other book, *Photoshop 6 Primer.*

# SUMMARY

Through the pages of this chapter, as well as all of the chapters in this book, it has become clear that there are many facets of the Internet and Photoshop that you'll need to understand to master the art of Web design. Web designing can be a uniquely creative experience that will not only challenge your imagination but could possibly prepare you for a rapidly growing segment of the job market.

I hope that you close this book with confidence that you have learned something of value and have a stronger urge to continue practicing and learning Photoshop and Web site development. Despite any negative aspects that I tried to (honestly) warn you about, there is practically nothing more rewarding than building a Web page and knowing that millions of Web surfers are viewing your work, gathering information, perhaps even marveling at your incredible Photoshop skills. If they do, make sure you let them know where you learned it ….

Thanks for reading, good luck, and happy designing!

# INDEX